THE SMART SET: GEORGE JEAN NATHAN AND H.L. MENCKEN

THOMAS QUINN CURTISS

APPLAUSE
NEW YORK • LONDON

An Applause Original
THE SMART SET:
George Jean Nathan & H.L.Mencken
by Thomas Quinn Curtiss
Copyright © 1998 by Thomas Quinn Curtiss

Library of Congress Cataloging-in-Publication Data

Curtiss, Thomas Quinn
    The smart set : George Jean Nathan and H.L. Mencken / by Thomas
    Quinn Curtiss.
        p.   cm.
    Includes index.
    ISBN 1-55783-312-5
    1. Nathan, George Jean. 1882-1958--Friends and associates.
2. Mencken, H.L. (Henry Louis), 1880 - 1956- - Friends and associates
3. New York (New York)- -Intellectual life- -20th century
4. Criticism- -United States--History- -20th century. 5. Authors.
American- -20th century- -Biography. 6. Editors- -United States-
-Biography. 7.Critics- -United States- -Biography. 8. Dramatic
criticism- -United States. 9. Smart set (New York, N.Y.) I. Title.
PS3527 .A7276   1997
818' .5209
(B)- -DC21   97-28457
                                                              CIP

British Library Cataloging-in-Publication Data
A catalogue record of this book is available from the British Library.

APPLAUSE BOOKS   A&C BLACK

211 West 71st Street   Howard Road, Eaton Socon
New York, NY 10023   Huntington, Cambs PE19 3EZ
Phone (212) 496-7511   Phone 0171-242 0946
Fax: (212) 721-2856   Fax 0171-831 8478

Distributed in the U.K. and European Union by A&C Black

Table of Contents

H.L. Mencken & George Jean Nathan

PART ONE

Item in *The Fort Wayne Sentinel*, Feb. 14, 1882:

> Charles Nathan, the wholesale liquor dealer, is willing to open packages of his very oldest liquor in quantities unlimited. Last night he was made the proud father of a handsome baby boy with eyes as black as night and, in brief, 'a pocket edition of his papa'.

Future readers of the sophisticated critic George Jean Nathan were always astonished to learn that the prophet of the urban life was born not in an international metropolis but in a bustling, growing Indiana town. The popular poet, James Whitcomb Riley, with his verse about the frost on pumpkins; George Ade and Booth Tarkington, with their broad humor; the realistic novelist, Theodore Dreiser; and Paul Dresser, Dreiser's brother, who composed those lasting barbershop quartet favorites, "Just Tell Them That You Saw Me — And They Will Know the Rest", "My Gal Sal," and "Moonlight on the Wabash," which became the state's unoffical anthem — these are expected and appropriate products of post-Civil War Indiana. Their works recall the burly joys, simple virtues, and rough kindliness of a recently frontier society. But who would believe that George Jean Nathan, like them, had been a middle-class, midwestern boy?

Connoisseurs of contrast should be pleased, too, that the renowned scoffer and professional enemy of sentimentality made his entrance into the world as the clock struck midnight on Saint Valentine's Day.

Charles Naret Nathan, George Jean's father, had originally been named Charles Naret, but when his father died and his mother remarried he took his stepfather's surname. A wholesale liquor merchant, he had come to Fort Wayne in the mid-1870s after a life of roaming, where he had met and married Ella Nirdlinger, the daughter of pioneer parents, on November 15, 1880.

Charles purchased a gabled mansion on West Berry Street in which the newlyweds made their home. It was in this house that George Jean Nathan was born fourteen months later. He was the first of the couple's two children. A second son, Frederick—who quickly acquired the diminutive, Fritz—was born under the same roof in 1885.

Charles Naret Nathan was a European of remarkable erudition. He had been born in Alsace. His father, Jean-Jacques Naret, was a leading criminal lawyer of Paris, and his mother, Renée Callot, was born in Thionville, Lorraine.

Before coming to the United States, he had owned the Eugène Péret vineyards in France—hence, his liquor merchanting—and one of the largest coffee plantations near Bahia, Brazil. He had spent six years in Buenos Aires; eight in Brazil, at Bahia and Rio; two in India; and three in Beijing, China. Two of his brothers had settled in Chicago and he lived there before making an initial visit to Fort Wayne. His aptitude for languages was phenomenal. French and German were the twin tongues of his childhood. He had mastered English before he attended Heidelberg. During his roving he taught himself Italian, Spanish, and Portuguese. In the East he studied Chinese dialects and learned to speak Mandarin fluently.

George Jean's mother, Ella, had been born in Fort Wayne, the daughter of Frederick Nirdlinger and his wife, the former Hannah Myerson. Both of Hannah's parents came from Nirdlinger, Germany, the source of the family name. Nirdlinger and his wife were born and bred in Chambersburg, Pennsylvania, and they had come west to Fort Wayne by covered wagon, being among the first settlers.

Fort Wayne at that time was a frontier outpost. The inhabitants lived in tents and a lone wagon trail led to the isolated settlement. Nirdlinger was a cattleman possessing a contagious energy. His daughter Ella was born shortly after her parents came to Fort Wayne and she was to see the muddy, primitive settlement of tents grow into a thriving midwest trading post.

In her early teens she was enrolled at St. Mary's Academy in

South Bend, Indiana. St. Mary's, founded in 1844 under the guidance of the Sisters of the Holy Cross, a French order, later became St. Mary's College, one of the foremost Catholic women's universities in the country. St. Mary's accepted girls of all faiths and even in the 1870s was equal to the best finishing schools in the land.

Among Ella Nirdlinger's schoolmates was another Ella, Ella Quinlan, with whom she retained a lasting affection and of whom she frequently spoke to her children. Innately serious and fearful of the future, Ella Quinlan contemplated becoming a nun. The Mother Superior doubted that she was suited for the cloistered life, but the girl protested that she had seen a vision. As she knelt at the chapel altar, she said, the statue of the Blessed Virgin had smiled on her.

This, she believed, was a summoning call, but the Mother Superior, familiar with such manifestations of adolescent hysteria, was not to be persuaded. A kindly woman, she proposed a test. After graduation, Ella would promise to attend dances and parties with young men of her age and social station. If she then decided that the worldly life was not for her, it would be time enough to consider taking orders. Ella Quinlan, though convinced of her own commitment, solemnly promised.

During the Easter vacation that spring, Ella Quinlan's father took her to the theatre to see James O'Neill in *A Tale of Two Cities*. She was caught up in the drama of the French Revolution, in tears when O'Neill, as the self-sacrificing English nobleman, Sydney Carton, mounted the steps of the guillotine's scaffold to render the famous lines: "It is a far, far better thing I do now than I ever did before." After the performance her father, an old friend of O'Neill, took her to the star's dressing-room and introduced her to the matinée idol. The actor and the convent girl fell in love and two years later Ella Quinlan married James O'Neill. Their second son was Eugene O'Neill, who was to be one of George Jean Nathan's few intimate friends.

Although both of Nathan's parents were partially Jewish, neither of them seems to have been bound very closely to Judaism and they did not raise their sons in the Jewish faith. Charles Nathan, for many years a prominent man of affairs in the Middle West, was a Mason. He regarded Fort Wayne as his home — there he was married and there his children were born. In 1888 business took him to Cleveland, Ohio, and he moved there with his family. When he died in 1904 it was discovered that he had left instructions to be buried in the Jewish cemetery in Fort Wayne.

Nathan's mother — as was the case with both her sons — was converted to Catholicism, perhaps as a result of her convent schooling. Her youngest son, Frederick, became a convert when he married a Catholic girl. George Jean was baptized a Catholic during the last year of his life, though his conversion was not — as was generally supposed — a last-minute, death-bed decision.

Since the Nathan family moved to Cleveland when George Jean was only six, his memories of his childhood years in Fort Wayne were misty. His father's funeral forced his brief return to his birthplace in 1904, but it held no attraction or interest for him in later life. In 1925 Nathan told Dr. Goldberg, his first biographer, that for him a nation was its metropolis. "To that extent," he remarked, "as an American I am a New Yorker of New Yorkers. I don't like the country. I am a cockney. In the city, life reaches its fullest flower. The rural districts are for arrested imaginations and city men when they get sick. I have not been back to Fort Wayne in twenty years, and I'll probably never go back. Ditto Cleveland. My future is in New York — and London, Paris and Rome."

The move to Cleveland brought him to the theatre and metropolitan surroundings. He remembered that shortly after arriving there he was taken to the theatre for the first time by an old nurse. The play was *King Lear* with the harassed ancient being acted to the hilt by some now-forgotten but then very noisy barnstormer.

It was in Cleveland that he began his general education, and it was a far more extensive one than that of most American boys of his class at that time. His father, an admirer of the European system, arranged that he be tutored privately in addition to attending school. George Jean received individual instruction in English literature, history, French, and Spanish, his father having a special penchant for Spanish, which he spoke fluently. He was anxious for his son to follow his example. But the young Nathan, though a good linguist otherwise, found it a stumbling block — perhaps due to his father's insistence. Later, at Cornell, he pursued Spanish again but finally gave it up, though he learned to read it well enough.

The strenuous program of his official education did not dull the boy's intellectual curiosity. At an early age he was an omnivorous reader of history and plays. After devouring the works of such boyhood favorites as Horatio Alger and James Fenimore Cooper, he tackled Goethe's *Faust* at twelve. By fifteen he had read all of Shakespeare and, under his father's singular orders, six Restoration comedies. At eleven he began to write plays himself and these scribblings were acted by the neighborhood children in a theatre rigged up in the family stable.

At Cleveland High School he was submitted to the usual curriculum, making a good showing in everything except mathematics. Yet, though algebra and geometry bored him, he seems to have inherited an aptitude for business and figures.

The home life of the Nathans was in the comfortable bourgeois tradition of the late nineteenth century. Charles was proud of his handsome, intelligent older son and his wife's pride in her child lasted all her life. Yet there was no coddling of the boy. Charles was too strong and dominating a personality to allow silly indulgence and their moderate wealth did not lull George Jean's cultural sensibilities or stifle his development.

The Nathan household differed from those about it by its Europeanism and by its connections with the theatre. One of George Jean's uncles was S.F. Nixon, a theatrical producer in partnership with J. Zimmerman in Philadelphia. When George Jean was ten, Sarah Bernhardt, visiting Cleveland for an engagement under the Nixon-Zimmerman management, was a guest at the Nathan home. As a souvenir of her stay there she slipped an amethyst ring on the finger of the youngster. He wore it, perhaps as a symbol of his devotion to the theatre, until his death.

But his interest in the stage began before the Sarah Bernhardt visit. From seven on, he attended the theatre constantly, not only in Cleveland but whenever he was taken to New York or Philadelphia by his parents. His memories of his initial theatregoing, he confessed, were less than dignified.

In place of what was unquestionably a fine bit of acting by Tomasso Salvini in *La Morte Civile* (*circa* 1889), he seemed to remember the toboggan in the second act of Hoyt's *A Midnight Bell*. And in place of some probably admirable work by Booth and Barrett, it appeared that his acuter recollection was of the funny scene in *The County Fair* where Neil Burgess, dressed up like a woman, shocked the country folk when he leaned out of a barn window upon the lower half of which a bill poster had pasted the legs of a chorus girl in tights, and of an awfully cunning girl in Henry V. Donnelly's stock company named Sandol Milliken. The doubtless memorable performance of Richard Mansfield in *Don Juan* (which he saw at the Garden Theater on a New York visit at the age of nine) was dim, but his memory lit up at the mention of the unknown actor in a melodrama called *The Ensign* who, in the role of an unpolished American seaman facing the modish and contemptuous English villain on the deck of a United States man-o'-war boomed in the fellow's teeth: "We ain't got no manners, but we kin fight like hell!"

And, so too, did his memory quicken at the mention of Fritz Ebert, the tiny comedian of the troops known as "The Lilliputians," at the trick scenery of the Byrne Brothers' *Eight Bells* and Charles Yale's *Devil's Auction,* at Charley Bigelow and Lillian Russell in *The Princess Nicotine,* at Digby Bell in *The Tar and the Tartar,* at Cora Urquhart Potter's wonderful brown hair and Vashti Earl's blonde hair and Christine Blessing's big blue eyes and Thomas Q. Seabrooke in *The Isle of Champagne* and at his first sight of Dennan Thompson and the scene where E.S. Willard mixed up the name Lucy with the letter he was dictating in the first act of *The Professor's Love Story,* and Katherine Florence's makeup in *The Girl I Left Behind Me* and the exciting fire-station scene in *The Still Alarm* and a very bad play named *Gloriaba* (which he then admired) and Camille D'Arville in *Madeleine or the Magic Kiss* (they gave away pictures of Miss D'Arville on celluloid buttons) and Robert Downing's biceps and the minstrels Barlow and Wilson and

Virginia Earl as the lunch counter girl in Hoyt's *A Hole in the Ground*, and Della Fox rolling down De Wolf Hopper's extended leg in *Wang*.

His growing interest in the theatre was encouraged by his mother's brother, Charles Frederick Nirdlinger. Nirdlinger had served as dramatic critic for *The New York Herald*, *The Paris Herald*, *The Illustrated American*, and *The Criterion*, and was also the author of many plays, among them *The First Lady of the Land* (in which Elsie Ferguson starred as Dolly Madison).

When George Jean reached his teens his father arranged for him to spend alternate summers abroad. He had been in Europe with his father as early as 1890, and in 1898 — at sixteen — he was taken to study in Paris under the guidance of his French professor, M. Decrain. In the spring of 1900 Nathan graduated from Cleveland High School with honors and the following summer he spent in Italy, studying graphic arts in Bologna, Naples, Venice, and Rome.

Although Harvard would seem to have been an obvious choice for college — Nirdlinger, now his mentor, was a Harvard man — Nathan had other ideas.

"I never could bring myself to view Harvard as the right university for me," he remarked later. "I did not like what it stood for and its English imitativeness was offensive to me. I chose Cornell for the simple reason that it seemed to me, of all the Eastern American universities, to approach the German university most closely. I still believe that it does. Various eminent German scholars incidentally agree in this. In addition, it is a charming and beautiful place. Another reason that influenced my choice was its traditional hold on Cleveland and the fact that most of the young men I liked and respected, my best friends, either had gone or were planning to go there."

His parents being persuaded, George Jean Nathan entered Cornell.

There are few subjects on which George Jean Nathan did not express a forthright opinion and in the 1920s he summed up his view of higher learning in the United States.

The idea still persists in certain quarters that the larger American universities are educational institutes, that is, places to which young men go in search of knowledge. Curiously enough, the idea is true. But the truth is not quite that which the majority of persons believe it to be. The larger eastern American universities are educational institutions and they are, too, places to which young men go in search of knowledge, but the education that the average young man gets from them has infinitely less to do with Latin, Greek, epistemology, economics, the Purvanmimnasa system of Hindu philosophy and the Pali grammar of Kachayana than with Irving Berlin's latest fox-trot, the right kind of pleated trousers, the way to make drinkable synthetic gin, the technique of what Scott Fitzgerald calls necking, athletic diversions, and the trick of going to New York for a day without the faculty's catching on to it.

For one boy who is athirst for knowledge, who wishes to learn the difference between the theory of least squares and anthropogeography and what distinguishes the Battle of Echmulh from the Portuguese navigator Mascarenhas and the poetry of Swinburne, there are a dozen who care no more for knowledge of any shape, size or kind than a burnt-cork salesman cares for Dahomey. Ask twenty boys of these educational cabarets which they would rather know: the history of French literature or Ann Pennington's telephone number, and if nineteen do not answer the way I think they would, I am a very unobservant beagle.

Some boys go to college and eventually succeed in getting out. Others go and never succeed in getting out. The latter are called professors.

Whatever doubts Nathan may have had in the fall of 1900, he threw himself at once into both his studies and the social life of the campus.

Cornell is a lovely spot, a little town of towers reminiscent somehow of a Tyrol hamlet. "When the hours strike," he wrote Hendrik W. Van Loon who, fresh from Holland, attended the summer courses at Cornell at the time Nathan was an undergraduate, "there is carried to us the tinkly notes of that strange tune which becomes so much a part of the Cornellian's mind that he will suddenly hear it in Moscow or leave Pekin when the jingling of a falling spoon starts a corresponding reverberation in that deep cavern of his mind where lie buried his dearest recollections."

At Cornell, Nathan took the Arts course, specializing for four years in literature, drama, history, languages, and psychology to obtain his bachelor's degree.

The summer of 1902 Nathan spent abroad with his father on what proved to be their last journey to Europe together. They visited London, Berlin, and Heidelberg, where George Jean took classes, perfecting his German.

Following his father's example, George Jean began practicing fencing during his sophomore year at Cornell, won the Amsler Gold Medal at Cornell, and after graduation took part in matches in France, Germany, and Italy.

During his years at Cornell he kept a copious scrapbook: photographs of the college grounds; reports of track athletics on Percy field; accounts of the varsity crew; the meetings of Kappa Sigma Lodge (his fraternity); programs of the Regatta concerts; banquet menus; invitations to various social functions; articles from the New York papers on the Cornell football games and ticket stubs of the games he attended. He preserved letters, telegrams, and copies of *The Cornell Widow* (of which he became business manager and contributor in 1903), as well as a mousey moustache he wore to some comic ball and a pink garter with bronze clasp thrown from the stage by one of the girls in the Bowery Burlesquers Company which played *On the Yu-con* at the Star theatre in Ithaca.

Nathan was popular and something of a leader in the set of students preoccupied by the arts and literature. His own style of writing had developed very early. Even before graduating from high school he had written a characteristic essay, "Love, A Scientific Analysis," arguing that passion was a mad delusion and that "obviously, there was no such thing as love."

The theatre in all its forms — from dramatic literature to the Bon-Ton Burlesquers — exercised an increasing hold upon him. He began to read widely in the modern Europeans: Shaw and Hauptmann, Barrie, Maeterlinck and Pinero, Herview, Rostand

and Porto-Riche, Strindberg and Heijermans, D'Annunzio and von Hofmannsthal.

On holidays he often visited New York and Philadelphia where his uncle, S. F. Nixon, managed the Chestnut Street Theater. There—on passes—he saw *The Sultan of Sulu*, *A Chinese Honeymoon*, Henry Irving on his final American tour, and William Gillette in *Secret Service*. A typhoid scare closed Cornell in February 1903 and took Nathan to Manhattan to inspect all the new shows, including the revue at Weber and Fields' Music-Hall.

The new American literature which began to blossom at the turn of the century aroused his enthusiasm, especially the work of Stephen Crane, Ambrose Bierce, George Ade, and the critic, James Gibbons Huneker. He wrote a paper on the novels of Frank Norris and he wrote light verse about the charms of the girls on Philadelphia's Chestnut Street in *The Cornell Widow*.

He was elected to the Senior Honorary Society, Quill and Dagger, and became a member of the Savage Club, the Sunday Night Club, and the Masque. He composed the book and lyrics for "a *commedietta* in one *actlette* and one *scenelette*" titled *Stranded Stars* for the Kappa Sigma dramatic talents. He performed in several drama club productions, getting good reviews. He attended dances and kept a fat notebook crammed with the addresses and telephone numbers of the girls he danced with; he served on class cotillion committees and drank his share with what he called "bibbling vereins." There is no doubt he enjoyed himself immensely at college, but pleasure-taking did not interfere with his studies. He had already acquired the sense of balance that permitted him both to play hard and to work hard.

The climax of his collegiate years came the week before he received his diploma with his chairmanship of the Cornell Spring Day festivities, the annual jamboree of the university.

As a senior marshal he led a parade of his classmates disguised as cowboys, Indians, tramps, and famous stage beauties to the picnic grounds, which had been designed to resemble a county fair with its amusement tents and hot-dog and lemonade stands.

Nathan, carefully labelled with a tag reading "In Case of Emergency Return to Kappa Sigma Lodge," mounted a stand and gave a mocking retirement address, modelled after George Washington's farewell to his troops. Then he served as barker before the tent in which — for a quarter a head — the mysterious Mzupzi (publicized for the last month in the college papers and by widely distributed handbills) would be revealed. Mzupzi, dressed as an Indian princeling, turned out to be the two-year-old son of the black cook at the Cayuga Hotel, but those that entered were sworn not to reveal the secret and business was brisk.

Spring Day lasted from ten o'clock on Friday morning until the following Tuesday and landed no less than fifty participants in the Cornell infirmary.

"But there was a nurse there," Nathan recalled, "who was so beautiful that the boys would frequently and deliberately sprain ankles in order to be ministered to by her. I remember four sprained ankles of my own, to say nothing of three sprained wrists and a hypothetical terrible case of cramps."

The Spring Day festivities were topped off by the Masque Society's performance of *Dew Berry*, Nathan's parody of David Belasco's *Du Barry*, in which he played the part of the Duc de Raisehelli. *Dew Berry*, though only a college skit, is a hilarious spoofing of the Belasco grand manner and was inspired by Nathan's ardent study of the Weber and Fields extravaganzas.

Dew Berry is discovered in her boudoir, her night-table crowded with beer bottles and Illinois law books. Louis XV, possessing a rich Dutch comic accent, rushes about exclaiming "Gott! I got such jealousness!" When the envious monarch fires on a rival, and la Dew Berry shrieks out in alarm, "Are you shot?" the favored one retorts, "No, I'm only half shot." Nathan was later to incorporate this style of spoofing into his dramatic criticism; indeed, *Dew Berry* may be regarded as an early essay in Nathanism.

After graduating from Cornell, Nathan had planned to take his Master's degree at Oxford. His father's sudden death in August 1904 caused him to change his mind and after spending the remainder of the summer with his mother and brother in Cleveland, he decided to attend the University of Bologna for a year to complete his formal education.

That state institution of higher learning, founded in the eleventh century, is one of the oldest and most respected in Europe. In 1158, Frederick I Barbarossa granted immunities and privileges to his scholars that were eventually extended to all universities. There Nathan improved his Italian and studied Italian literature, drama, and the masterpieces of the city's art galleries. He joined the university's fencing team, tried his hand at writing romantic verse in Italian, and for holiday recreation went to Milan to visit the theatres.

Upon his return to the US, Nathan's uncle Fred Nirdlinger invited his nephew to spend a few days in New York and discuss plans for the future before going on to Cleveland for a reunion with his mother and brother. While studying in Bologna, Nathan had considered his career. His work on the Cornell publication had whet his appetite for journalism and he had already contributed features on the theatre to papers in Cleveland and Philadelphia. New York, he decided, was the place for him and if he could find a post on one of Manhattan journals he was sure that he could make his mark. Nirdlinger was well-connected, having had held the post of dramatic critic on *The New York Herald*. He had also represented that paper overseas as its continental correspondent and was a close friend of its owner, James Gordon Bennett. He also knew William C. Reick, the managing director of *The Herald*. Reick had worked his way up from the position of delivery boy on a grocery wagon in New Brunswick, New Jersey. When young and poor in Philadelphia another of Nathan's uncles, S. F. Nixon, had helped him find work, as had Nixon's partner, J. Fred Zimmerman, who had hired him as a press agent when he was between newspaper assignments.

The combined family influence, together with Nathan's clippings from *The Cornell Widow*, resulted in a position as a cub reporter on *The Herald* when he moved to New York in the autumn of 1905. His salary was to be $15 a week. Fortunately, that would be supplemented by money from home.

Nathan began at the very bottom of the newspaper ladder as a general reporter. After an apprenticeship in the police courts, he was assigned to cover a series of sensational murder trials, most of them out of town. One case proved to Nathan the value of the showy argument against sound logic, which he sometimes found useful in his later criticism.

A physician was on trial in a little town in New Jersey, charged with having killed his wife by giving her drugs whose action and effect were indistinguishable from those of ptomaine poisoning. Things looked pretty bad for the defendant. Among the four attorneys for the accused was a little, bewhiskered, taciturn yokel of some fifty years who hadn't so much as opened his mouth once since the beginning of the trial. None of the newspapermen present could solve the mystery of his presence: he seemed a sheer waste of good money on the part of the defendant.

The star witness for the prosecution had provided damaging testimony against the doctor. The defense badly needed to destroy this witness' credibility.

The witness had previously sworn that he, a stranger in the town, had arrived on the night of the alleged murder. It was the first time he had ever been in the little town. He had left the next morning and had not been back before being summoned as a witness by the prosecution. On the night in question, he testified, he had gotten off the train at the depot and had walked up the main street of the town and gone directly to the accused's house.

The cross-examination of the important star witness for the State proceeded — the usual questioning and requestioning. These all centered upon his presence in the little town on the night in question. The cross-examination had been going on for about five hours when suddenly the little bewhiskered lawyer hopped to his feet, brushed back the other attorneys for the defense, and approached the man in the witness box.

"You say that you got out at the depot and walked directly up the main thoroughfare of this city to the defendant's residence?" he inquired.

The witness nodded.

"Well, then," asked the little lawyer, "tell the gentlemen of the jury what you saw when you walked up the main thoroughfare."

The witness, somewhat perplexed, replied that he had seen nothing.

"What? nothing!" exclaimed the little lawyer. "You saw nothing?"

"Nothing," answered the witness.

"Do you mean to say that you can face the jury and deliberately say you saw nothing" — here the little lawyer paused dramatically — "nothing unusual?"

The witness, nonplussed, again made negative answer.

The little lawyer turned to the jury:

"You have heard the witness say, gentlemen of the jury, that he walked up the main street of our city and yet saw absolutely nothing in the least unusual. I ask you, gentlemen, can you therefore for one moment believe that this witness has told the truth and that he was actually in our city on the night he says he was? You certainly cannot. For if he had walked up the main thoroughfare he could not possibly — he could not conceivably — have missed seeing the fine three-story school-building which we recently erected."

The jury, composed of villagers who had paid their good taxes for the little school-building and were immensely proud of it smiled their agreement. Their eventual verdict — a unanimous one — was not guilty.

After his stint at covering out-of-town murder trials, Nathan was transferred to the sports field. Here the work was less taxing. Indeed, he reported one of the Vanderbilt cup races entirely from imagination.

The details had been supplied by the sports department and Nathan's contribution was to be a piece on the general atmosphere. He consulted the weather reports and a rainy day was predicted. Instead of travelling to Long Island in bad weather, he dined with a *Herald* colleague at the Hofbrauhaus and after a hearty dinner, accompanied by many a seidel of foaming beer, he wrote a three-column story of the races that earned special commendation and was tacked to the bulletin board of the editorial room as an example of vivid reporting.

As tribute to his gifts he was transferred to the Sunday department and his salary was raised to $30 a week. Here it was his duty to write two special stories of 3,500 words apiece each week. Again he found fancy preferable to fact. Meeting James J. Corbett — "Gentleman Jim" — at a horse show on the Jersey coast, he concocted a tale of the gallant pugilist's rescue of a fair lady from the ocean waves. Again a Nathan story went up on the city room's bulletin board and again there was not a word of truth in it, though Corbett, on reading it, was deeply affected.

Another imaginative Nathan feature was about a mysterious hermit living on Long Island. On its appearance, reporters from other newspapers were sent down, only to discover it a hoax. But, not to be outdone, they pushed the same fantasy along in their respective journals for weeks.

Meanwhile, Nathan, in addition to his other *Herald* duties, had slipped into dramatic criticism, acting as third stringer when one was needed. His first review was of a Lincoln J. Carter melodrama, *Bedford's Hope*, acted at the old Fourteenth Street Theater.

"A few lines will do," said Thomas Wise, the *Herald* drama editor, as he handed Nathan the tickets. But Nathan, finding the blood-and-thunder thriller a typical specimen of a vanishing form of theatre — the sort of loud and gaudy suspense story he had loved as a boy — was more generous and wrote an extended estimate of its qualities.

The New York that Nathan discovered during his early newspaper days delighted him and in later years he contended that the 1900s were far more festive than the Gay Nineties; for him, at least, they were. Uncle Fred had gotten him rooms in a small, quiet, and comfortable hotel, managed by a French couple, near Union Square. The hotel — demi-pension — with its continental ease and atmosphere, its Gallic cuisine, and its bohemian clientele was very much like the one described in Huneker's novel of the period, *Painted Veils*.

There was a civilized leisure and an engaging innocence to the

New York of the early century. One of the exciting night-sights of the town, for example, was a cow munching grass on the roof of Hammerstein's Victoria at Broadway and 42nd Street.

Summertime seemed to transform the city into a continental village. At the cool and breezy window-tables of Delmonico's and Sherry's string orchestras played softly. In the old beer-gardens one might sip a beer under the trees to the strains of *Rosen aus dem Suden*. On the terrace of the Hotel Knickerbocker Richard Harding Davis, Bob Collier, and John Fox, Jr. would gather over the juleps, and at the roof-garden of the Beaux Arts, with the stars above and Bryant Park below, George Ade, Booth Tarkington, Finley Peter Dunne, and S. S. McClure would sit listening to the violins sing Lehár.

There were sidewalk tables under the great striped awning at Bustanoby's in Columbus Circle and tables on the grass at the Casino in Central Park. One might lounge at ease on the high roof-gardens of the Waldorf, the Astor, and Majestic Hotels and the Hudson breezes gained fragrance from the countless frost-covered rickeys at the Claremont. Rigo played his fiddle at the Café Boulevard and at Scheffel Hall, in the Union Square district, one could spend the whole evening over a dollar-and-a-half bottle of Rhine wine, listening to Huneker, Vance Thompson, and Percy Pollard discussing Beethoven, Chopin, and Lillian Russell.

The favorite rendezvous of the newspaper fraternity in those days was the barroom in the cellar of Weber and Fields' music hall, where Joe Weber's brother, "Mock," presided as host. Nathan had first found it on trips from Cornell. Marie Dressler, starring in the show above, was queen of the revels here and would come down each evening to sit around with the assembled bibuli. Diamond Jim Brady, Herbert Bayard Swope — then also a reporter on *The Herald* — Nicolas Biddle, and Foxhall Keene were regular customers and their entrance would be greeted by a welcoming speech from "Mock" Weber, who looked like a miniature Ben Turpin or a caricature of Frank Harris.

Captain Churchill's restaurant at Broadway and 46th Street (Churchill, an ex-police captain, was on good terms with the newspaper coterie), Jack's (on Sixth Avenue, facing the newly constructed Hippodrome) which remained open twenty-four hours daily and drew rounders (people making the rounds) of all professions for breakfast after a night on the town, the Brevoort terrace on lower Fifth Avenue, and Pabst's spacious, high-windowed beer tavern in Columbus Circle were other meeting places. Nathan soon found himself with a host of new friends.

He was invited to join a fraternity of journalists, authors, and figures of the publishing world that met weekly in a private dining-room at Sherry's. S.S. McClure, John Fox, Jr., Bob Collier, and Owen Johnson were members and it was their custom to have peach Melba served as the first course. To demonstrate their distaste for this syrupy dish all members would hurl their portion against the walls and ceiling of the upstairs room. The origin of this ritual was unknown.

One evening Richard Harding Davis was a guest of the club, having been invited to meet some ladies of the theatre. During dinner he was captivated by the charms of one young actress and asked permission to see her home. Fox overheard his request, stole down, and, having bribed the driver, took the cabby's place on the box. Disguised in the cabby's cape and floppy oilskin hat he waited in the rain. When Davis and the actresses appeared in due course, Davis shouted an address — that of an apartment house on 96th Street — but Fox drove the cab to Coney Island and there abandoned his post, leaving the couple to fend for themselves amid thunder and lightning.

The Manhattan literati of that time seem to have had rather sophomoric tastes. One of the more daring diversions of the inseparable trio of Davis, George Ade, and Booth Tarkington was to hire a hack and drive up and down Eighth Avenue, stealing melons from the stands in front of grocery stores. One night Nathan encountered them in the King Cole Bar of the Knickerbocker burdened down with the loot of an evening's excursion.

Writing his mother from the Cornell Club, he proudly reported that he had made an indelible impression at his university. "I understand at Cornell they now remark: 'As George used to say' and 'As George used to do'." But in the theatrical whirl of Manhattan he had yet to find his place. Despite his gentlemanly pose, and despite his skill as a reporter, he still felt himself an outsider. He had made some firm friendships among his newspaper colleagues, but he was ill at ease at large social gatherings and disguised his nervousness by an aloof manner. He could not banter brightly with strangers. He was simply not a good mixer and he never really became one.

At one of his Uncle Fred's soirées he stood, as usual, isolated in a dark corner. A pretty blonde girl brought him a plate from the buffet table; more forward than he, she suggested that they sit together away from the gleeful hubbub. She, too, had only recently come to New York. She was a dancer and sometime illustrator's model. Her name was Mae Murray. They sat happily talking together until the early hours when the party broke up and everyone went off to breakfast at "Jack's" on Sixth Avenue.

The following season Mae Murray was featured in Ziegfeld's "Follies" and her exquisite figure and her inviting, pouting lips bewitched the town. Her face gazed out from the Hearst Sunday supplements. In the 1920s, when she had become a famous film star, they met again, and the critic thanked the actress for easing the strain of his self-consciousness at that long-ago supper party.

One Thanksgiving Day, Nathan was invited by his theatre-managing uncle, S. F. Nixon, to inspect the tryout of a new play at the Chestnut Street Theater in Philadelphia. Travelling back to New York the next day, Nathan found himself seated opposite a stunning girl in the dining car. She was Evelyn Nesbit and her debut as a chorus girl in *Florodora* had caused a traffic jam of broughams before the stage door of the Casino Theater on Thirty-ninth Street. The table in her dressing-room was overcrowded with pink roses in silver vases and gold-topped champagne bottles in perspiring buckets. There were expensive presents and proposals, both honorable and dishonorable. Her face had tempted many an artist's brush and her photograph had adorned the Sunday papers across the country.

Nathan knew George Lederer, the Casino's manager and producer of such beauty-studded musical comedies as *The Belle of New*

York, Havana The Whirl of the Town, In Gay New York, and *The Wild Rose,* and soon Miss Nesbit was explaining her dilemma as lunch was served. Lederer wanted her for his new show, but she was thinking of retiring from the stage. She had received a marriage proposal from the Pittsburgh steel millionaire, Harry K. Thaw.

Rumors of this were already public and there had been a flutter in the society columns at the prospect of the "socialite" Thaw taking a chorus girl as his bride. At the moment Thaw was abroad with his mother, who was trying to dissuade him from such a misalliance. Should she go with the theatre or marriage, Miss Nesbit inquired of Nathan. Nathan was noncommital. He never gave personal advice as he required it all, he said, for himself. He did add that he personally preferred the theatre to marriage.

Miss Nesbit, he knew, had another passionate admirer, the brilliant and erratic architect, Stanford White, who had retained front-row seats for all the performances of *Florodora* at the Casino — or so Lederer had told Nathan. The designs for some of New York's most magnificent buildings and monuments had come from White's worktable. He had designed the ornate Madison Square Garden; the marble arch at Washington Square; and the Metropolitan Club, a replica of an Italian Renaissance palace with its colonnaded courtyard. Sherry's restaurant, the Medici residence of William C. Whitney on Fifth Avenue, and the Venetian residence of Mrs. Stuyvesant Fish on Madison Avenue were products of his penchant for grandeur and display.

White was an exuberant, defiant bohemian whose art realized the megalomaniacal delusions of American millionaires whose fabulous fortunes permitted them to fancy themselves the monarchs of Renaissance Italy and France and of ancient Rome. White despised the middle-class morality of his time and the mere mention of the professional prude, Comstock, drove him into a mad fury.

Comstock, self-appointed guardian of public morals, had placed fig-leaves over the sex of all the nude statues in the Metropolitan Museum of Art. When he saw — in 1890 — Saint-Gaudens' Diana perched over Madison Square Garden, he was aghast. The sight of a naked pagan goddess — however chaste — flying over

New York was an offense against civic decency. He stirred his followers to action and protesting letters filled the newspapers. This cacophonous overture having fallen on deaf ears, he threatened legal prosecution if the naked Diana was not at once taken down.

But White was quicker than Comstock. In a towering rage he went to see J. P. Morgan, a partner in the Madison Square Garden enterprise. Morgan, though a contributor to Comstock's organization, soon muzzled the censor.

White worshipped adolescent beauty and made no secret of it. If his patrons saw themselves as Renaissance rulers, he saw himself as a Renaissance artist, "beyond the good and evil" of the Comstocks, and it was this delusion and his bold flaunting of it that cost him his life.

Almost nightly he could be seen dining with lovely young actresses and models at Rector's, and the speculation about his private life was by no means limited to the Broadway gossip of the lobster palaces. In the national mind he had implanted the image of himself as a sensual worshipper of beauty.

There were wide-spread whispers about a birthday banquet he had tendered Diamond Jim Brady in White's studio apartment in a tower of Madison Square Garden. The guest of honor and ten other men-about-town had joined White for supper in his skyscraper quarters. When the time for dessert came an immense Jack Horner pie was wheeled into the dining room by the waiters who laboriously lifted it onto the table. Red ribbons were handed to each guest and to Brady, the "birthday child," a white one. When the ribbons were pulled at White's command a beautiful girl emerged from beneath the crust of the pie with Brady's white ribbon as her only adornment. The other guests protested against such favoritism and White clapped his hands. The doors opened and other girls, as destitute of attire and inhibitions as the girl of the pie, pranced in to soothe jealous tempers.

But to return to Miss Nesbit, shortly after her meeting with Nathan on the Pennsylvania Railroad she did marry Thaw. One evening when White was at supper at Rector's, Thaw appeared and nervously scanned the main hall of the restaurant. His gaze fell on

White and he stared at him grimly for some minutes. Very pale and visibly agitated, the recent bridegroom appeared to be deliberating. He reached toward his bulging hip pocket, but — as though hesitating — let his hand fall to his side. Then he swung round and departed in great haste.

A few nights later there was a gala opening at the Madison Square roof-garden. For this rite of spring Edgar Allen Wolfe, a theatrical novice, had prepared a revue, *Mlle. Champagne*. Nathan was on hand to cover the premiere and very early in the evening it was apparent that Wolfe had made a botch of the occasion.

There were groans of boredom and displeasure. The show was stale and flat. Wolfe, near an exit door, suffered keenly the audible disapproval. This was his first show and he had invited his mother from her upstate home to attend his debut.

Suddenly pistol shots rang out and Wolfe's mother fainted in terror, certain that a discontented first-nighter had assassinated her son for providing such a tiresome entertainment.

There were frightened shrieks and a stampede threatened in the dark. The houselights went on and over a front table slumped the body of White. Thaw stood over him, a revolver in his hand.

At the sensational trial that followed, Thaw was acquitted of the first-degree murder charge and sent to a hospital for the criminally insane. However, he soon escaped and no effort was made to recapture him.

His lawyers pleaded temporary insanity at the trial and stressed the defense of the home. Several distinguished alienists gave opinions on the witness stand and questioned Thaw. His wife had confessed to him that she had been White's mistress and the righteous anger of a jealous husband was taken into consideration by the jury. In the verdict middle class morality labeled White a pagan libertine whose murder was justified. But Nathan saw the case in another light.

"The Thaw jury," he told a friend, "was influenced less by the learned findings of Dr. Allen McLand Hamilton than by Evelyn Nesbit's little white lace baby-collars."

Evelyn Nesbit and Thaw were subsequently divorced and she

revealed the loathsome details of her wedding night in her memoirs, which appeared perennially in the cheap Sunday supplements.

At college Nathan had been a happy extrovert, the instigator of innumerable undergraduate pranks, a leader of the brighter and more liberated spirits, very much the campus blade of fiction. In New York, as he tested the waters of the wider world, his manner was more guarded, but he adjusted himself slowly to the new scene and the new demands.

As a rising and inquisitive journalist and as a personable young man he found entrée into the varied circles of society. A handsome, cultivated bachelor, a good dancer, an amusing talker once the ice was broken, and the gallant escort of pretty girls, he was an ideal extra man at society teas, dinner parties, and balls, though he was, even then, selective in accepting invitations. Sometimes his fellow slaves at *The Herald* office would lure him on drinking bouts and slumming excursions to the Tenderloin and the Bowery, but he was always reluctant to sacrifice an evening at the theatre for either high or low company.

New York—the New York that O. Henry had called the Baghdad on the Hudson—was a glorious adventure and a challenge. Cautious by nature and analytical in temperament, Nathan remained an independent observer, but there is no doubt that he often joined in the fun.

He saw the arrogant plutocracy straining vainly to impose an aristocratic decorum to its palatial Fifth Avenue châteaux and its Renaissance castles on Madison Avenue, but the starched, high-collared dullness, a pathetic pretense for authority and dignity, was crumbling in grotesque decay. A silly, self-mocking stupidity was the new way of doing things. The Knickerbocker nobility was expiring not with a whine but with a foolish snigger at itself.

Ladies in society never dined in public restaurants. The old guard of the Four Hundred shook its collective head when it learned that Mrs. Stuyvesant Fish had entered Delmonico's one Sunday evening on the arm of Harry Lehr. Lehr, a calculating climber from Baltimore, had married a Philadelphia heiress. Coming to New York, he had replaced the late Ward McAllister as the arbiter of fashions and attitudes among the wealthy. With his high-pitched voice and girlish simpering, he was an appropriate jester at the Knickerbocker court. He had made his debut in Manhattan as Mrs. William Astor's chamberlain, but found her fastidious standards obsolete. "Dull people are always formal," he cackled derisively when given his congé.

It was time for society to laugh at itself, he decided. The hour to shock the gaping peasants, ever amazed by the caprices of the rich, had chimed when the bells of Grace Church tolled the funeral knell for Ward McAllister.

Lehr was the first to laugh at himself. When he travelled abroad he would sign the hotel register with a smirk and a flourish: "Harry Lehr, Esq., valet, dog, wife." At Newport he diverted the yawning dowagers with his female impersonations, some of them of other hostesses. He was well stocked in woman's ware: wide-brimmed "Merry Widow" hats, evening gowns with regal trains, artful wigs. At the keyboard he rendered Victor Herbert's honeyed melodies in a flutey falsetto and with moaning, heartfelt sighs, or banged out ragtime airs until the crystal chandeliers of the stately drawingrooms and the priceless Gobelins on their walls, catching the rhythm, swayed with him.

His impudent malice startled the staid, but it appealed to Mrs. Stuyvesant Fish, weary of the old formality and anxious to be the leader of the New Order. He arranged extravagant banquets and fancy-dress balls which she eagerly financed.

A circus show was given in her Madison Avenue ballroom starring a baby elephant in pink bows. The guests munched peanuts and Cracker Jacks, quaffed sodapop, and sniffed their perfumed handkerchiefs to dispel the odor of the sawdust ring.

Lehr supervised a doll dinner party at which everyone was supposed to converse in baby-talk, and a black magic fête at which white mice were let loose to set the ladies shrieking as they climbed in undignified fright on to the chairs and tables.

Once, accompanied by Mrs. Fish, Lehr boarded a horsecar on Sixth Avenue and bribed the driver to pass him the reins. Whipping up the horses and ringing the bell madly, he called out in the imperious tones of a conductor: "Next stop: Woodlawn Cemetery." The terrified passengers descended in haste, taking fancy leaps from the moving car.

His masterpiece was the Monkey Dinner, widely chronicled at the time. Guests were bidden to be presented to a foreign nobleman, "Prince del Drago," who turned out to be a chimpanzee in royal regalia. Other monkeys in dress suits accompanied the ladies to their places at the table. One elderly and portly chimp, it was thought, had been invited because he bore a striking resemblance to Barry Wall, McAllister's rival as a dandy, who, disapproving of the new trend in New York society, had moved to Paris where he posed as a Beau Brummel of the race tracks and the boulevards until his death at an incredible age on the very day that the Nazis marched down the Champs-Elysées in June 1940.

Lehr thought that most human beings were fools and to live with them harmoniously one must pander to their stupidity. "They overlook almost anything if you can make them laugh," he philosophized, and he practiced his doctrine with a deliberately destructive delight. But other affluent New Yorkers made themselves equally ridiculous in the delusion that they were impressing the masses with their dollars.

C. K. G. Billings, "The American Horse King," gave a Horseback Dinner for the discomfort of thirty-six guests. Transforming Sherry's ballroom into a woodland scene and providing mounts for the invited from the local riding academies, his soirée commenced with the sounding of hunting horns. His friends, in answer to tally-ho call, swung into their saddles on the pommels of which they found miniature tables. Dinner was served by waiters dressed as grooms of a hunting party and oat filled feeding troughs were set before the patient equines who dined with their riders.

These — and similar foolish festivities — received heavy coverage in the newspapers and magazines, for the public at that time followed the activities of the smart set as avidly as the public was later to follow the activities of movie stars.

The tone of this New Society sounded the vulgar defiance of the parvenu, sometimes expressedly, sometimes by error. At the

Metropolitan Opera on Monday nights, Mrs. William Astor still ruled the golden horseshoe, but elsewhere her influence was no longer felt nor wanted. When she died at seventy-seven in the autumn of 1908, the world over which she had so long reigned, the world that Edith Wharton and Henry James pictured in their New York novels, the old society world of the 1880s and the early 1890s, had already vanished.

Nathan, at twenty-five, preferred the company of the well-bred and the well-fed and undeniably was a bit of a snob. He looked on the grandiose foolishness of the nouveaux riches with disdain and had no wish to ally himself with the frivolity with which they tried to fill the vacuum of their empty lives. And there were other aspects of the New York circles in which he moved that he found equally distasteful.

He enjoyed wine, women, and song, but was disgusted with the common mistranslation of those pleasures: swilling, prostitutes, and drunken howling. Refined by nature, he had no nostalgia for the gutter. This was an unusual trait in a member of the younger literary generation that had defiantly embraced low life, mistakenly seeing in the squalid *laisser-aller* of the cheap saloons an existence that contradicted the hated conventions of middle-class morality.

The artist — or the would-be artist — of the era felt himself an outcast and gloried in his exile. Stephen Crane, a decade earlier, had made the Bowery his home and written of it realistically but with obvious affection in *Maggie, a Girl of the Streets*. The golden-hearted streetwalker, the barkeep with a profound philosophy (imagined comically by Finley Peter Dunne in his "Mr. Dooley" column, but later to receive extended appreciation from O'Neill, Hemingway, Saroyan and Robert Sherwood), the potentially fine man crushed by the ugly, hypocritical standards of bourgeois society — these were romantic figures to the rising writers.

Jack London, visiting New York, sat in an alcoholic daze at Mouquin's, staring vacantly ahead of him as he mumbled to his tee-totaler companion, Upton Sinclair, about the wonderful freedom of the frozen north he had found in the Klondike during the Gold

Rush, far from the corrupting cities, where men were men and women were glad of it.

The He-Man cult in American literature — of which Mark Twain, Bret Harte, and Ambrose Bierce were godfathers — was paralleled in London by Kipling. Eugene O'Neill ran off to sea in the hopes of becoming one of London's two-fisted sailors. The barroom, "the poor man's club," was the shrine of the young literary aspirants. The Haymarket, a lurid dance hall at Sixth Avenue and Thirty-fourth Street, where a variety show and feminine companionship were provided the customer, was a haunt of O'Neill, when home from the sea and under the guidance of his dissipated brother, Jamie. Diamond Jim Brady often entertained his out-of-town friends there, but even Brady, a police-protected rounder, found it advisable to leave his jewelry at home when undertaking such an expedition.

The barroom and its ballads made a lasting impression on the literati in revolt. O. Henry's last words as he lay dying in a hospital bed were: "Turn up the lights, I'm afraid to go home in the dark." O'Neill was to work many of the old songs into his plays. The maudlin tear-jerker, "In the Baggage Coach Ahead," was employed forty years later as a running theme in *A Moon for the Misbegotten*. The jaunty "Bedillah" was written into the saloon scene of *Ah! Wilderness*, as were two others — "Waiting at the Church" and "Dearie" — and a whole album of 1900–10 tunes was used for purposes of quick characterization in *The Iceman Cometh*, with the rejected ward heeler bawling out "Tammany," the bartender singing "All I Got Was Sympathy," and the saloon proprietor calling vainly for "The Sunshine of Paradise Alley," a cockney favorite of the mid-1890s.

The underworld then as now touched Broadway. Over the Maine lobsters and amid the ragtime din at Shanley's in Longacre Square, theatrical celebrities sat cheek by jowl with the city's most notorious gang leaders. At Rector's, too, there was a similar elbow-rubbing.

Herman Rosenthal, the proprietor of a gambling house in the West Forties, had taken into his partnership Police Lieutenant

Charles Becker, head of the Gambling Squad, but the two had subsequently quarrelled. Becker, threatened with exposure, wanted Rosenthal silenced forever. He arranged for Big Jack Zelig, a redoubtable killer, and Bald Jack Rose, another gambler, to undertake the murder. Zelig deputied four of his gunmen to carry out the assignment and Rosenthal was machine-gunned as he left the Metropole one morning.

Perhaps the most characteristic and colorful personality of the half-world between the nightlife and crime was the giant playboy, Wilson Mizner. Nathan knew him at the beginning of his career as a playwright and praised his melodramas: *The Only Law*, a grim tale of a street-walker and her protector, and *The Deep Purple*, a bold exposé of clever corruption and vice.

Born in San Francisco of an old California family, Mizner left college to join a medicine faker and quickly learned the easy exaggeration that was to carry him through life. Mizner found no gold in the mountains of Alaska and his takings at poker (he always won), though large, were ephemeral. He was a showy spender and liked to live high. As a professional gambler he had crossed the Atlantic countless times and was the type of card player that the management of liners warns its travellers to avoid. Later, Mizner incorporated his experiences as a ship gambler into another play, *The Greyhound*.

Fortune came to him briefly when he married the widow of C. T. Yerkes, the Chicago traction magnate. Mizner was thirty; his bride was seventy. She was enchanted by his facility at the piano and he was forced to play the popular song "Dearie" over and over again. There were so many complications and so many requests for "Dearie" that Mizner sued for divorce. His lawyer asked him the grounds for the suit. "Isn't marriage sufficient?" inquired the indifferent husband.

At the time of Nathan's journalistic apprenticeship Mizner ran a dubious hotel in the Broadway district. Renowned for its informality, he placed a sign in its seedy lobby: "There are no house rules, but please don't smoke opium in the elevator."

But this desperate, violent world which attracted so many of his literary contemporaries held no allure for Nathan. He was equally disdainful of sentimentalizing about poor little rich girls and Bowery panhandlers. In philosophy he substituted his own "Be Indifferent!" for the militant "Be Hard!" of Nietzsche. In music he preferred, among the moderns, Richard Strauss, Stravinsky, and Rimski-Korsakov to "Only a Bird in a Gilded Cage" and "The Curse of an Aching Heart." In drama — but his preferences there he was already making clear whenever the call for an additional critic was heard in the *Herald* office.

PART TWO

"Above all, beware of journalism!" André Gide once cautioned young writers. The warning is astonishing and, when one examines the statistics, nonsense. Some of the foremost French writers of the generation that preceded Gide's were graduates of journalism. Zola, Anatole France, and Proust made their entrances into literature through the newspapers. In the United States beginning as a journalist had almost become a rule. Such diverse authors as Mark Twain, Henry James, Ambrose Bierce, Willa Cather, Theodore Dreiser, H.L. Mencken, Jack London, O. Henry, Ben Hecht, Ernest Hemingway, and Eugene O'Neill began—as Nathan did—by contributing to the newspapers and most of them—like Nathan—had their start as common reporters.

However, Gide's advice might have fallen on receptive ears had Nathan heard it after his initial year on *The Herald*. The novelty of the job soon wore off and he began to feel he was lost in a blind alley.

William C. Reick, *The Herald*'s Managing Editor, was remembered by Nathan as "An atheist so far as paying salaries was concerned and held them down to the Chinese coolie rate." No matter how many stories Nathan covered, and no matter how well, his salary remained at the $30-35-a-week standstill.

The Herald was a mere business office and, editorially, a joke. James Gordon Bennett considered his big advertisers first and his readers second. There were so many "Don'ts" that a reporter had to be a vaudeville mind reader to remember them all in composing an article:

Don't call a theatrical performance a "show."

Don't use "New Yorker."

Don't use "week-end" or "over Sunday."

Don't use "gang" or gangster."

Don't use "house guest," "house party," or "reception guest."

In addition, there was a list of names on the city-room bulletin board of people who, having offended Bennett, were never to be mentioned in *The Herald*. This blackball roll call grew almost daily. Nathan, unlike his uncle, could muster no admiration for Bennett.

Bennett was the caricature of the ruthless press lord and gloried in his tasteless eccentricities and his mania to control everything and everyone by the power of his wealth.

His father had founded *The New York Herald* and early in life Bennett Jr. had sought to crash society. The winning skipper of the first transatlantic yacht race, he became a Commodore of the New York Yacht Club at twenty-six. To attract further attention he had ridden his horse into an exclusive Newport club.

At thirty-five he had been banned from polite society in New York. Arriving at his engagement party drunk and feeling an irrepressible call of nature he had — in view of his fiancée, her father, and their guests — urinated into the fireplace. Finding himself ostracized as an impossible barbarian in New York, he fled to Europe.

From his mansion on the Champs-Elysées he directed the operations of his New York paper by cable. It was he who sent Stanley as his reporter to Africa to find Dr. Livingstone, though afterwards, envious of Stanley's fame, Bennett broke with him and persecuted him in brutal fashion.

In 1888 Bennett began to publish a Paris edition of *The Herald* and his visits to his native land were few and hasty. They inevitably threw his employees into a state of panic. His arrival in the United States was usually kept secret and then, often during the night shift at *The Herald*, he would suddenly swoop down on the office. Bleary-eyed and drunk, he would appear in the city-room and shout out erratic commands, firing harmless old-timers and promoting copy-boys to reporters and editors. The morning after these angry and confused whims of the small hours would often be forgotten, but sometimes the drunken decisions would be strenuously enforced.

Though bold in his personal behavior, Bennett's cowardice as a publisher extended to all departments of *The Herald*. The drama editor trembled hourly that some unfavorable comment by one of his reviewers might offend one of the theatrical managers and cost the paper a slice of its advertising revenue. There was a minimum of honesty permitted the critics and the dramatic policy of the paper was absolutely dictated by the theatrical syndicate then at the zenith of its octupus powers. Nor was the general news treated more outspokenly. Each story was carefully scanned and edited to make sure that it would contain nothing at which any segment of readers might take offense.

One rainy winter night Nathan was sent out to report the story of a man and a woman who had been found asphyxiated in a bedroom of a shabby hotel on East 17th Street. It developed that the man, discovered lying dead in the arms of the naked woman, had been a priest.

Nathan hurried back to the office in Herald Square and wrote the story in the style of a fledgling realist. After handing in his copy he headed up Broadway in the deep winter drizzle to the Hotel Knickerbocker at Forty-second Street for a stiff whiskey or two to dispel the chill of the dank night and his gloomy investigation. At the bar — where Maxfield Parrish's portrait of King Cole and his attending minstrels beamed soothingly down on the assembled — Nathan came on a group of his *Herald* colleagues. What had he been up to? they inquired. Had he been out to Brooklyn to see some girl and been caught in the downpour?

No, he replied, he had been working. A jeer of incredulity rose in the high-ceiling barroom. Yes, he insisted, he had been sent out on an assignment and had just written a strong story, something worthy of Frank Norris or Stephen Crane, something that would set the town talking. It was about time a note of fearless truth penetrated into the sickening sycophancy of *The Herald*'s pages. His companions agreed that he was theoretically correct, but loudly aired their doubts that any realistic story would survive the editorial blue-pencils. This one would, Nathan told them and advising them to watch for the late editions he departed for bed.

Next morning over his breakfast coffee Nathan searched in vain for his story. At the bottom of page 4 he found a short note on the double suicide of the night before, but reference to the male victim's calling had been omitted and Nathan's graphic description of the sordid hostel and the underlying motives of the tragedy had been stricken out.

Nathan angrily crumpled the paper and sitting back, emitted a sigh. To protest such editorial censorship would be futile. He decided it would be best to not even mention the incident for he understood its implications. But he never forgot this frightened misrepresentation of the news which symbolized for him the hypocrisy of Bennett and his practices. Years later, in 1929, he told a London interviewer: "I left *The Herald* when I grew tired of lying every day."

Nathan's unblinking account of the double suicide on East 17th Street, though unpublished, was read with admiration by *The Herald*'s editors. Leo Redding, the city editor, remembered Nathan's gripping coverage of murder trials, and asked him to take on the police news until the regular man returned from vacation.

At this Nathan bridled; he was, he haughtily announced, now above such cub-reporter chores. Redding accepted his refusal with good grace, but disapproved of his attitude. "Why, covering the police courts is the greatest and most valuable experience a man can have in life," Redding boomed. To which Nathan replied with a contemptuous sniff, "That is one of the favorite schnitzels of buncombe with which newspapermen delude themselves."

Redding greeted this retort with a wry smile and mentioned it to Gordon Bennett, who had just arrived on one of his rare visits to his homeland.

The business which had brought Bennett across the Atlantic on this occasion left him no time for his customary nocturnal terrorizing of the city-room. *The Herald* had stoutly opposed William Randolph Hearst's bold bid for political power. Hearst a few years before had financed a noisy and gaudy campaign to elect himself governor of New York, a likely springboard to the presidency. *The Herald* waged all-out war on Hearst, and, after he lost the election to Charles Evans Hughes, he was determined to avenge himself on Bennett who had pricked his bubble reputation as a statesman.

Hearst secret agents were put on the case and soon discovered a weak spot in *The Herald*'s armor of self-righteousness. The paper's personal columns were being used by prostitutes and brothels (thinly disguised as Turkish baths and Swedish massage parlors) for the soliciting of clients. When sufficiently damaging evidence had been harvested, the Hearst press began a loud moral crusade to attract the Comstocks and bring them down on Bennett. In a very short time there was a federal indictment against *The Herald*.

Bennett had come to New York to settle the matter in person. He went directly from the dock to the criminal branch of the United States Circuit Court, pleaded guilty, and was fined $30,000. Learning these terms, Bennett, with a sweeping gesture, drew a swollen wallet from his pocket. Quickly counting out $30,000 in cash, he slammed the bills down and stalked grandly from the courtroom.

After this imperious exhibition, which summarized his contempt for moral snoopers and their present spokesman, Hearst, Bennett drove to Herald Square to confer with his editors. When Redding brought up the Nathan case among other business, Bennett, always amused by impudence, pricked up his ears and asked to see the cheeky upstart.

The young Nathan was formally ushered into the Commodore's study to find the Great Man ensconced behind an eighteenth-century French desk and looking more imperial than ever. On being summoned Nathan had visions of being fired personally by his boss. But here was Bennett virtually purring at him across his worktable, crowded with antique inkwells.

Bennett had read Nathan's stories and reviews and was a good enough newspaperman to appreciate their style and originality. Would Nathan consider a post on *The Paris Herald*? Paris, Bennett believed (as did Huneker later), was the place for Nathan. The offer tempted Nathan for a moment, but he was already sufficiently shrewd to ask one question. What would his wages be?

"Why, you'll have exactly the same salary as you are getting now," replied Bennett heartily as though this were a reassurance.

Nathan pretended to be meditating and then politely declined.

He thought it best that he remain in New York where he was slowly gaining a foothold. An interruption of his present work... The audience was over. Shortly after this Nathan, seeing opportunities in the magazine field, resigned from *The Herald.*

Increasingly restless, and realizing that such an intellectually subservient newspaper was by its nature the enemy of free expression, Nathan had begun to do outside writing before submitting his resignation.

He'd had a one-act play of his, *That Affair at Huntley's,* produced in the autumn of 1907 at a benefit matinée at the Hudson Theater, where it shared the program with Ethel Barrymore in *Carrots,* Arthur Sutro's Englishing of Jules Renard's miniature tragedy of childhood, *Poil de Carotte.* The Nathan playlet received favorable notices not only in *The Herald*—where he had become a hero of the younger men—but in the other New York dailies as well, and there were kind words in *Variety* and *The Dramatic Mirror,* too.

That Affair at Huntley's is a curious little piece and, though it belongs to its period and is somewhat dated, it reveals—as did Nathan's collegiate stabs at dramaturgy—a thorough comprehension of stagecraft.

A well-born young bachelor invites some of his university classmates to a stag dinner in his elegant New York flat. The party begins with some reminiscences of college days and flirtations, but suddenly a sinister shadow falls across the gay chatter. The host informs his guests that his fiancée is dead and artfully wrings a confession from the man who has seduced her and caused her death. Murder brings down the curtain on this drawing-room melodrama, a peculiar combination of Pinero punctilio—with a Japanese manservant lighting the candles of the dinner table at the start and extinguishing them after the crime—and Grand Guignol bloodletting.

Lynn G. Wright, a Cornell Alumnus and a former editor of *The Cornell Daily Sun* (on which Nathan had also served) attended the matinée, liked the play, and remembered Nathan. Wright was now editing the Knapp magazines, *Outing* and *The Bohemian,* and he left a note for Nathan at the Cornell Club suggesting that he take over the dramatic departments of those periodicals. Nathan accepted and celebrated his liberation from *The Herald* with a sizzling and penetrating essay on Bennett and his methods: "James Gordon Bennett, the Monte Cristo of Modern Journalism." It caused loud laughter among the slaves at *The Herald* and a thwarted gnashing of false teeth when Bennett came upon it in his Champs-Elysées residence.

Established at twenty-five as a dramatic critic, Nathan now moved to new quarters in the theatre district, taking an apartment in the Hotel Royalton at 44 West 44th Street. This was to be his home for the rest of his life, and though he traveled a great deal, he always retained rooms at the Royalton.

George Hobart, editor of *Burr McIntosh's Magazine*, was struck by the zest and bounce of the Nathan reviews and feature articles and invited him to contribute to the magazine. Its founder, Burr McIntosh, was a pioneer in the art of photography and the magazine, printed on glossy paper and filled with excellent photographs, was handsome and unique, a forerunner of *Vanity Fair* and *Vogue*. McIntosh later sold it to Julian Ripley when he became interested in the motion pictures. It was the photography of the cinema that first drew him, but his face, so full of character and determination, proved irresistible to the casting directors, and he became an actor. (He is probably best remembered as Squire Bartlett, the Puritanic farmer who turned Lillian Gish out into the snow, in D. W. Griffith's film *Way Down East*.)

The pages of Munsey's popular magazines were opened to Nathan by the clever journalist, Robert H. Davis, one of the first of the modern columnists. Davis became a close friend of Nathan. Munsey, who bought *The Herald* after Bennett's death and was generally despised as an uncouth and money-grubbing oaf, was preferred by Nathan to his former employer.

The Munsey magazine offices were then in the Flatiron Building and Munsey's own sanctum had the luxury of a movie by Cecil B. De Mille.

"It was his practice," Nathan recalled, "to sit at a large desk on a platform raised three or four steps above the floor level, and when a man had audience with him, to stand at the top of the steps and treat the fellow to a large dose of Napoleonic dignity. I had written an article for 'Munsey's' on the Department of the Interior, some of the facts of which had interested Munsey. He called me to discuss further the facts before the article went into type. Contrary to the general opinion of him, he was anything but a sourball. He was, indeed, a very amiable fellow."

Another meeting of a year before proved significant. While still in the employ of *The Herald*, Nathan was introduced by his Uncle Fred to James Gibbons Huneker, the self-styled Steeplejack of the arts and the most influential American commentator on music and letters of his time. Nirdlinger and Huneker were old friends and had been associated professionally in the editing of *The Criterion*, a daring and short-lived attempt to flavor an American magazine with the "decadent" sophistication of the English *Yellow Book*.

One evening, Nirdlinger invited his nephew to accompany him to Scheffel Hall, a *Bierstube* near Union Square where Pilsner and most of the other Mittel-Europa malt beverages were on tap. Twice weekly Huneker — "Lord Jim" to his intimates — sat at his *Stammtisch* in Scheffel Hall, surrounded by his cronies, making the rafters ring with his talk. These informal gatherings had their private jokes. At the stroke of eleven, the perspiring *Ober* would always pretend that his right arm had grown lame with the carrying of the seidel-laden trays and Lord Jim, answering the call of comic ritual, would make a great show of massaging the over-worked limb as though he were in terrible fear that a drought might ensue and cut the evening short.

Huneker, a man of enormous gusto, was in the flush of his middle years and the absolute autocrat of the beer-table. He was a non-stop talker and held his audience in rapt attention. As a critic it was his habit to mix gossip into his essays, and Max Beerbohm, angered by his indiscretions, had once denounced him as a "yellow journalist." It was said he could never make up his mind about a new symphony until he had seen the composer's mistress, or at least a good photograph of her. He had travelled widely and had known all the leading figures of the modern movement: Liszt and Richard

Strauss, Tolstoy and Oscar Wilde, Flaubert, de Maupassant and Huysmans. He knew all the scandal about them, too, but as libel laws, alas, govern the published word he was limited in his critiques. These critiques were but cautiously watered-down versions of his uninhibited discourses over the foaming steins.

A Huneker monologue was a torrent of amazing tittle-tattle, weird learning, and startling speculations. Nathan had never heard anything like it. Art and the personal idiosyncrasies of artists fascinated Huneker equally for he believed — as did his French forerunner, Sainte-Beuve — that a man's private life played a dominant part in what he created. The verbal fireworks shot off in every direction:

> Berlioz and the question of the clang-tint of the viola, the psychopathological causes of Tschaikowsky's suicide, why Nietzsche had to leave Sils Maria between days in 1887, the echoes of Flaubert in Joseph Conrad, the precise topography of the warts of Liszt, George Bernard Shaw's heroic but vain attempts to throw off Presbyterianism, how Frau Wagner saved Wagner from the libidinous Swedish baroness, what to drink when playing Chopin, whether girls educated at Vassar could ever really learn to love, the origin of the theory that all oboe players are crazy, the sheer physical impossibility of getting Dvorak drunk...

are some of the subjects recalled by a listener.

Nathan had read and admired Huneker's books, but this initial encounter with the joyous Light-Bringer surpassed his expectations and guided his ambitions. Never had he heard anything to equal this talk. He set Huneker down as the greatest conversationalist of the age. In the years to come, Nathan was to make the acquaintance of almost all the eminent literary men of the first half of the century — H. G. Wells, Yeats, George (AE) Russell, Lord Dunsany, W. Somerset Maugham, Claudel, Schnitzler, Hauptmann, Max Beerbohm — but none of these, not even the fabled gabbler, Frank Harris, could eclipse the memory of Huneker, relaying audacious information about the arts and the artists in Scheffel Hall. "All criticism is a form of gossip," announced Huneker, remembering his idol, Sainte-Beuve, and Nathan gave an approving nod.

The old critic and the young critic became fast friends and remained mutual admirers until Huneker's death in 1921. The grand
dandy of American literature had been slain by the horror of Prohibition, his friends believed, and Nathan composed a revealing
tribute to his mentor when the sad news came:

> He was the greatest of American critics... He was the only
> inspiration that we younger men had in our unimportant lit-
> tle skirmishes on the outskirts of his own great battlefield. A
> man of no country and no people, save that of beautiful
> things and those who loved them, he made possible civilized
> criticism in this great, prosperous prairie. He taught us many
> things, but first of all he taught us cosmopolitanism, and love
> of life, and the crimson courage of youth. He is dead at 61,
> the youngest critic America has known.
>
> Huneker's books are our foremost university. The man
> himself was our foremost cultural figure. One likes to visualize
> his spirit in the years of the future, holding up that now equiv-
> ocal light on a more meaningful Bedloe's island. He did more
> to free America from slavery than any Lincoln. He liberalized
> American taste; he threw open to these insular eyes the gal-
> leries and concert halls and libraries and theatres of Europe.
>
> He looked upon all art with his twinkling eyes and made
> it glow and glitter afresh. A comedian of comedians to the
> end, he saw that nothing matters in this world but pleasure,
> and the sound of the pleasures of the four B's — Bach,
> Beethoven, Brahms and Beer. To these he consecrated his
> happy days.... His hair was gray and his mind was a great
> storm-lashed cathedral of experience, but his heart was the
> heart of Huck Finn.

At the time of this meeting with Nathan, Huneker was acting
as music and drama critic of *The New York Sun*. In this dual capacity he was less interested in reporting on local concerts and plays
than in filling his page with lively and stimulating propaganda for
the New Movement in Europe, a cause he had forwarded bravely
in American magazines and newspapers since the early 1890s. He
wrote excitedly of Richard Strauss, George Bernard Shaw, Ibsen,
Maeterlinck, Hauptmann, Suderman, Brieux, and Strindberg, all of

whom the older critics of the Genteel Tradition in the United States frowned upon.

The protest against these innovators was not limited to critical frowning. The New York police actually closed Shaw's play, *Mrs. Warren's Profession*, in 1905 and dragged its actors into court. When Mary Garden sang Richard Strauss's *Salome* at the Metropolitan in 1907 there was a furor over the Dance of the Seven Veils and public reminders that the opera was based on a play written by "that condemned degenerate, Oscar Wilde." The police threatened action again when Richard Bennett dared to stage Brieux's *Damaged Goods*, which dealt with venereal disease and was, in fact, a stern, moral warning against prostitution. Veneral disease, though widespread at the time, was not to be mentioned. Such was the Puritan logic.

But Huneker never descended to arguments with the Right Thinkers. He believed art to be "The Joyous Science," in the phrase of another of his idols, Nietzsche, the philosopher most hated and feared by the Old Guard. Huneker wrote for the civilized minority and to interest the young in the art of far-away Europe.

In 1908 Nathan began to contribute to *Harper's Weekly*. There his pungent comments on the theatre came to the notice of Norman Boyer, managing editor of *The Smart Set*, who was hunting for a critic. Channing Pollock, *The Smart Set*'s theatrical reviewer, had been tempted away by a more lucrative offer at *The Green Book*.

Pollock had had considerable practical experience in the theatre. His dramatization of Frank Norris's novel *The Pit* had toured America and become a stock-company favorite. *The Green Book* gave the theatre more space than *The Smart Set*, publishing extracts from plays and Pollock was anxious to write more plays. He wrote a score of them — *The Fool, The Enemy, Such a Little Queen*, and *The House Beautiful* (remembered chiefly for Dorothy Parker's brief criticism of it: "The Play Lousey"). Some of these marched to box-office glory, but Pollock's successor at *The Smart Set* was never able to muster much enthusiasm for any of them. When Pollock finally retired from play-manufacture he announced that it was his old profession — criticism — that had forced him out. "I am tired of sitting up all night to find out what Richard Watts, Jr. thinks of me," he remarked sourly, and devoted his last years to a bulging book of memoirs.

In 1908, however, Pollock had had but one authentic theatrical triumph—his dramatization of *The Pit*. His career as one of America's most prosperous playwrights still lay ahead. The offer from *The Green Book* with its guarantee of higher wages and more space was irresistible. He told Boyer that he was resigning from *The Smart Set* and that his theatre article for the June issue would be his swan song for the magazine. Boyer consulted with the editor, Fred Splint, on this unforeseen crisis and wrote Nathan at *Harper's Weekly*, asking him to drop by and discuss the prospect of becoming the dramatic critic of *The Smart Set*.

The appointment was set for an afternoon in early May. When Nathan arrived in Boyer's office he found the managing editor chatting with a cherub-faced, snub-nosed young man whose golden hair was parted in the middle and slapped down like a butcher's on Sunday morning. The stranger's clothes—a stiff, starched collar, gaudy strawberry tie, checkered suit, and yellow shoes—typified a provincial dandy or race-track tout.

On seeing Nathan the man leapt to his feet and thrust out his hand. "I'm H. L. Mencken of Baltimore," he exclaimed, his bright, blue eyes sparkling. "I'm the biggest damned fool in Christendom and I don't want any boastful reply that you claim the honor."

Mencken then drew a cigar from his vest pocket and, handing it to his new acquaintance, informed him that it was a product of the family tobacco factory, a genuine "Uncle Willie" (a brand of popular, five-cent cigar). Nathan accepted the token of esteem with a courtly nod and, instead of biting off its end, took a gold cutter from his watch-chain and neatly snipped off its tip.

Both men seated themselves on the gilt chairs before Boyer's ornate desk and gave the editor their attention. Boyer launched into a leisurely discourse on *The Smart Set*, relating its history and explaining its present aims.

The Smart Set had been founded in 1900 by Colonel Mann, publisher of the shady *Town Topics*. Fat on the profits of his scandalmongering weekly and his blackmailing of prominent New Yorkers, the colonel was inspired by a new idea of making money out of Manhattan's elite. Why not a monthly magazine reflecting the mores and codes of Fifth Avenue society written chiefly by its members? The novels of Henry James and Edith Wharton were selling well and perhaps there were other talents among the well-born.

The colonel was over-optimistic. There were many literary aspirants in the smart set, but few of literary ability. Dowagers and debutantes tried their hand at the game, but their work was so amateurish, and often so illiterate, that the colonel began to suspect that the manuscripts emanated from the servants' quarters of the fine mansions from which they were sent.

Only one authentic member of the 400 emerged as a "find": Alice Duer, later Alice Duer Miller. Miss Duer was a high-born lady who could actually write and write extremely well. Her first stories were published in *The Smart Set* and long before World War I she had become one of the most popular magazine authors in the country. Later dramatizations of her serials — *Come Out of the Kitchen*, *The Charm School*, and *Gowns by Roberta* (the basis of Jerome Kern's operetta *Roberta*) — were very successful in the theatre.

Arthur Grissom, the first editor of *The Smart Set*, displayed a discernment that formed the policy of the magazine. He soon engaged as his assistant a young poet from Louisville, Kentucky, Charles Hanson Towne. As their budget was limited, they sought out fiction by unknown writers whose work showed promise and originality. From the start the magazine had a freshness and a youthful impertinence.

The Smart Set in those days paid a cent a word. One day Grissom and Towne received a story by a young man called William Sydney Porter from Pittsburgh. His story, "By Proxy," was only 1,700 words in length and he was duly mailed a check for $17. Then came an envelope from him containing a 6,000-word story and a note saying he would take a $10 discount if the money were sent immediately as he wanted to come to New York and needed the railway fare. The editors dispatched the full $60 in a rush mail order. Porter, who wrote under the pen name O. Henry, came to New York, but Grissom and Towne heard no more from him, though they tried to locate him. O. Henry's cent-a-word days were behind him.

Also among the early contributors to *The Smart Set* were Damon Runyon, Jack London, Susan Glaspell, John Erskine, Theodore Dreiser, and Hugh Walpole. Poetry was also a feature of the magazine and verse by the likes of Louis Untermeyer and Ezra Pound adorned its pages.

The budding iconoclasts among the younger writers viewed *The Smart Set* as a showcase for their wares. Its pay rates were low, but they had few other outlets. The big-circulation magazines knew the popular market and filled their pages with the fiction of Harold Bell Wright, Robert W. Chambers, Rupert Hughes, Rex Beach, Irvin S. Cobb, and John Fox, Jr., all manufacturers of "glad" romances. *The Rosary* was a best-seller; Robert Service, bringing Kipling's style to his ballads of the Alaska Gold Rush, was hailed as a great poet; Pollyanna was a national heroine.

On the other hand, the literary periodicals were ruled by such men as Richard Watson Gilder (who had actually refused to publish Robert Louis Stevenson because it was rumored that Stevenson was "a cad where women were concerned"), Henry Van Dyke, Paul Elmer More, Brander Matthews, and William Dean Howells, a pioneering, though extremely cautious, realist who sat in the editor's chair at *The Atlantic Monthly*. (Howells, having been accepted by the Puritans, was afraid that he might lose their favor. He had become so timorous that he apologized for Mark Twain's atheism in his biography of his old friend. This set of editors and critics had sworn to maintain the "moral" line. They deplored Stephen Crane's vivid stories of the Bowery and rang a general alarm when Frank Norris tried to follow in the foot-steps of Zola. Zola, who was to exercise such an influence on the coming generation, was the *bête noire* of the old guard critics. In *The New York Times Book Review*, Theodore Dreiser was warned that Zola "had died in his own vomit" and his American disciple had better take heed.

Fred Splint and Norman Boyer had replaced Grissom and

Towne as editors of *The Smart Set*. Splint had worked under Theodore Dreiser, who was then editing the Butterick Publications, and it was Dreiser who had suggested that *The Smart Set* introduce a book department and had recommended Mencken as a likely candidate for the post of reviewer. Mencken had come to Dreiser's notice not as a literary critic but as a rewrite man. Dreiser had abandoned creative writing after the scandal his first novel, *Sister Carrie*, had caused in 1900. The manuscript had been highly praised by Frank Norris, who was a reader for Doubleday, and was accepted for publication by that house. Shortly before it was to appear the wife of the publisher had read it and had been profoundly shocked by its objective, realistic treatment of a "fallen" woman. Mrs. Doubleday was an important figure in various societies devoted to the improvement of public morals and her opinion of the book threw the Doubleday office into a panic. The directors eventually came up with an odd compromise: To avoid being sued by Dreiser, the house technically fulfilled its contract. A short run of *Sister Carrie* was printed, but the book was withheld from distribution, a few copies going to the reviewers while the rest moldered in the Doubleday storerooms. Discouraged by this tricky maneuver, Dreiser, who had been a newspaperman in both Chicago and New York, returned to journalism to earn a living. He secured himself a berth at the Butterick Publications and rose to the position of managing editor.

One day, a Baltimore physician, Dr. Leonard K. Hirshberg, wrote to Dreiser outlining a series of articles for the Butterick magazines on recent developments in medical science. These pieces would be written not in the style of the medical journals but for the layman. Being a medical man rather than a writer, Hirshberg suggested that the writing be done by a young newspaperman on *The Baltimore Sun*.

Dreiser, dubious about the project, requested a sample article before making a final decision. In less than three weeks he received the most refreshing and colorful bit of semi-scientific exposition that he had read in years. He was so pleased that he wrote Hirshberg immediately, forwarding a contract for the doctor and his friend. Some weeks later a ruddy, blue-eyed youth of twenty-eight appeared in Dreiser's office — it was Hirshberg's collaborator, Henry L. Mencken. Many years later, Dreiser recalled:

> More than anything he reminded me of a spoiled and petted and possibly over-financed brewer's or wholesale grocer's son who was out for a lark. With the sangfroid of a Caesar or a Napoleon he made himself comfortable in a large and impressive chair which was designed primarily to reduce the over-confidence of the average beginner. And from that particular and unintended vantage point he beamed on me with the confidence of a smirking fox about to devour a chicken.
>
> After studying him in that almost arch-episcopal setting which the chair provided, I began to laugh. "Well, well," I said, "if it isn't Anheuser's own brightest boy out to see the town."
>
> And with that unfailing readiness for any nonsensical flight that has always characterized him, he proceeded to insist that this was true. All thought of the original purpose of the conference was at once dismissed and instead we proceeded to palaver and yoohoo anent the more general phases and ridiculosities of life, with the result that an understanding based on a mutual liking was established.

Subsequently, Mencken visited Dreiser's apartment when he came to New York, and when business took Dreiser to Baltimore the two joined forces in noisy, roistering parties.

Acting on Dreiser's advice, Splint had written to Mencken, and the latter came to New York to discuss the proposed book department.

After his lecture on the magazine's history, Boyer turned to business. Mencken would begin his book reviewing in the September issue and Nathan, who was leaving for a summer holiday in Europe, would provide his initial critique on the theatre for the magazine in time to appear in the October issue. Boyer rose, shook hands with his new associates, wished them well, and bowed them out. Together the two went downstairs and strolled in silence to the corner.

Suddenly Mencken, who had been horribly bored by Boyer's

meandering monologue, burst out with, "What a horse's ass that Boyer is!"

"A complete and utter horse's ass," Nathan agreed. "Now let's have a drink and some intelligent conversation."

Mencken hesitated. He had intended to board the late afternoon train for Baltimore. But he was rather intrigued by this dapper, handsome, young man, with his worldly manner and his gold cigar-scissors, who had sat so stoically as Boyer rambled on and on. Mencken consented, and the two made off for the Holland House.

The mahogany-panelled bar of the Holland House on lower Fifth Avenue was a relaxing retreat for millionaires homeward-bound from Wall Street. It was also — at the same late-afternoon hour — the breakfast-room of men-about-town and affluent actors who had just rolled out of bed.

"Bet-a-million" Gates was a regular and loudly shouted out some of his more preposterous wagers from his *Stammtisch* near the door. And the men's room attendant had gained a certain notoriety for his indiscreet gossip about the private lives of the mighty. One of his heroes was Maurice Barrymore, the matinée idol of the 1890s and the father of Ethel, Lionel, and John. On one occasion, it seems, the elder Barrymore, who detested critics, found himself occupying a urinal next to one of the hated tribe. The ancient enemy, Barrymore noted with satisfaction, was straining painfully to negotiate a natural function. "Ah, ha! I now understand what is meant by the strictures of the press," exclaimed the actor sarcastically in a stage-whisper that boomed so resoundingly that it would be heard in the adjacent barroom.

Mencken needed little prompting. His blue eyes took on a frosty twinkle and his eyebrows assumed the shape of Turkish crescents as he rolled forth with a hearty and humorous shove the story of his life.

He was, as he had already informed Nathan, a native of Baltimore, and his late father had been a cigar manufacturer (though "Uncle Willie" was not one of his "relatives," as he had facetiously boasted to confound Boyer). Mencken sprang from staunch, Teutonic stock. There was a tradition of learning and scholarship in the family — several of his ancestors (as far back as the seventeenth century) had been professors at the University of Leipzig. He was proud of the noble blood that ran in his veins and of his family connections with the Prussian aristocracy: Louise Wilhelmine Mencken, a great-great-aunt, had married Karl William Ferdinand von Bismarck, a cavalry officer, and in 1815 she gave birth to a son, Otto, the future Iron Chancellor.

Burchard Ludwig Mencken, the present Mencken's paternal grandfather, had come to the New World from Oschatz, Saxony, in 1848 because, his grandson used to say, he wanted to see the preposterous comedy of democracy in action at first hand. It is more likely that the economic pressures in Europe had made the voyage inevitable. In any case, Grandfather Mencken had settled in the German section of Baltimore, starting as a cigar maker. Afterwards he had managed a general store and finally became a tobacco wholesaler. His son, August, expanded the business, owning a factory in Baltimore and warehouses in Maryland and Pennsylvania.

Henry Mencken had been educated at a German private school and at the Baltimore Polytechnic Institute, from which he had graduated at eighteen. An English professor at the Polytechnic had awakened his interest in Shakespeare. With characteristic gusto and thoroughness he went through the whole canon of the plays and began to write a novel about Shakespeare. He abandoned the project after three chapters, defeated by his lack of knowledge of the Elizabethan era. But his enthusiasm introduced him to other great Elizabethans, Marlowe and Jonson.

His interest in all literature was insatiable. In one winter he read the whole of Thackeray and then proceeded backward to Addison, Steele, Pope, Swift, Johnson, and the other magnificoes of the eighteenth century. Keats, Swinburne, Shelley, and Tennyson were his favorite poets, although the vigorous, bracing verse of Kipling had its influence on him, as it did on most literary-minded boys of the era.

Like Frank Norris, Mencken suffered an acute case of Richard Harding Davis during his adolescence and he began to write short stories when he was still in school. But the greatest influence of all was his discovery of Thomas Henry Huxley, Darwin's bulldog. Mencken was enchanted by the purity clarity, and persuasiveness of Huxley's prose and wondered if science might not be his field. He thought of becoming a chemist, running explosive experiments in the family's backyard shed.

After graduation, his father wanted him either to study law or engineering at Johns Hopkins or to join him in the tobacco concern. As several of his short stories had appeared in magazines, Mencken wanted to become a journalist. His father objected to this and as a result he went to work in the cigar factory, but he was unhappy and bored there. Then, during an annual physical, the family doctor thought he detected a weakness in the young man's lungs. A vacation in sunny climates was recommended and Henry was sent off on a cruise to the West Indies. Shortly after his return his father died suddenly. His father's death set him free to do as he pleased and he applied at once for a job as cub reporter on *The Baltimore Herald*.

He rose rapidly from reporting on neighborhood fires and covering the police beat. Informed, energetic, and fearless, he was in turn drama critic, Sunday editor, city editor, managing editor, and, at twenty-five, editor-in-chief. A year later, in 1906, *The Baltimore Herald* folded. He was immediately engaged by *The Baltimore Sun-papers* as Sunday editor, drama critic, and editorial writer.

Later he added a daily column, "The Free Lance," in which he sharpened his claws as a satirist of public mores. In this space he lashed out against grafting politicians, the city "boomers," Prohibitionists, the circus evangelists (such as the Rev. Billy Sunday), quack medicine, literary censorship, and bigotry of every sort. "The Free Lance" was chiefly concerned with local matters, but it was Mencken's training ground as a future national prophet. It appalled the guilty and made conservative Baltimoreans uneasy. It also boosted circulation and brought more letters — most of them sizzling with indignation — to the *Sun* offices than any other feature.

Mencken never attended a university, scorning the American college system and most of its presidents and professors, although he was on friendly terms with many members of the Johns Hopkins faculty. He was self-taught and continued his wide reading while tied to a newspaper desk. Ibsen, Nietzsche, Wilde, Wells, Shaw, Conrad, and, above all, Huxley, were his gods during these years.

An indefatigable worker, he had found time for writing aside from his journalistic chores. While on *The Baltimore Herald* he had had two books published: a volume of Kipling-like poems, *Ventures in Verse*, and *George Bernard Shaw: His Plays*, the first study of the Irish dramatist in book form. A new book, *The Philosophy of Frederich Nietzsche*, a tribute to another of his idols, was in press and would be published in the autumn.

Nathan had read Mencken's little book on Shaw and considered it of value as a pioneering effort, clearing the way for the new drama. The man himself rather puzzled him. What was the dynamic drive behind all this jubilant enthusiasm? He liked his new companion, but he wanted to know more about his motives and opinions. It was nearing eight o'clock and he suggested dinner. At the Beaux Arts Restaurant, on the roof of a building at the corner of Sixth Avenue and Fortieth Street, they could dine in the continental summer fashion, in the open. Mencken gave one last, loving glance at the Bouguereau nude above the Holland House bar, blew it a roguish kiss, and they were off.

As they dined Mencken, having related much of his past, now outlined his aims as a writer. It was an ambitious program.

"My aim is to combat with ridicule and invective American piety, stupidity and tin-pot morality: progressives, professional moralists, patriots, Methodists, osteopaths, Christian Scientists, socialists, the single-taxers and the advocates of the initiative, the referendum and the recall," he proclaimed. "In brief, I am tackling the whole doctrine of democracy."

Nathan was amused by this grandiose outburst, but what, he wanted to know, had these things — dubious osteopaths, fraudulent seers, and noisy rabble-rousers — to do with literature? An artist — or a would-be artist — should stand aloof from the sordid preoccupations of the mob. Mencken debated the point.

"In the *Sun*," Mencken proclaimed, "I have advocated the tax of a dollar a day on bachelors, on the grounds that it's worth it to be free. I have drafted laws providing for the assassination of public officials and the regulation and licensing of uplifters. I am in favor of votes for women because it is the reductio ad absurdum of democracy."

He took as an example a critic both men admired, Huneker. Certainly, Huneker was non-political. Certainly, Huneker was uninterested in blowing up the White House or Brooklyn Bridge or selling girls into the white slave trade (one of the bugaboos of the day). Yet Huneker had been forced to fight, single-handedly, against the silliest sort of opposition. Most of the French authors he glowingly recommended — Flaubert, Baudelaire, Verlaine, Huysmans, de Maupaussant, Stendahl, even Balzac and Daudet — were proscribed in the libraries, and some of them were forbidden publication in translation in the United States. Anyone who published them or sold them could be fined and sent to jail for years, as in England had happened to poor old Vizetelly for publishing Zola.

The battle of "tin-pot" morality had even been carried into the field of music to further harass Huneker. While his colleagues among the music critics were still undecided whether or not Wagner was a respectable composer, Huneker had brought another mud-bath on himself by advocating the introduction of Richard Strauss and Stravinsky. The abusive adjectives that were flung at a pioneering critic were always the same, coming from the standard vocabulary of Puritanism — "immoral," "degenerate," "morbid," "godless." The New York drama critics uttered no audible word of protest and the editorialsists of the great New York dailies, who were forever blathering about freedom of speech and the crusade for progress, were suddenly mum. That was, Mencken held, the reason the arts were in such a low state in America. It was time someone remedied matters and perhaps in his forthcoming book pages in *The Smart Set* Mencken could gain, if not a national audience, at least the attention of the civilized minority.

With this reasoning Nathan was in full accord. Censorship by the ignorant and the biased held the American theatre and its critics in chains and prevented the production of the more advanced European plays.

Ibsen was judged a foul Scandinavian ogre, an enemy of home, virtue, and morality. Theodore Roosevelt, who fancied himself as a literary arbiter, had accused Zola of writing of the unmentionable and Ibsen, who had dared to write a play about syphilis, was open to the same charge. The revered dean of the American drama critics, William Winter, kept in his old age by David Belasco, led the hymn of hate against the monster of the North.

Criticism in America had no courage. It lagged behind the fogies, backward-looking prophets such as Winter, and the vice squad. The theatre people themselves had to lead the way. Mrs. Fiske gave special matinées of *Rosmersholm* and *Little Eyolf*. Charles Frohman presented Ibsen's *A Doll's House* with Ethel Barrymore. Arnold Daly and Richard Mansfield acted the plays of Shaw over critical protest. The Shuberts discovered a handsome, auburn-haired Russian actress, Alla Nazimova, playing in a Yiddish theatre on the East Side and brought her to Broadway in *Hedda Gabler*.

Yes, a critic should forward the cause of the novel and daring in the arts, Nathan agreed. But as for attacking the entire doctrine of democracy, as Mencken boldly proposed — why bother? All governments were more or less idiotic, systems to hold the majority in servitude, and Nathan had little interest in the world outside the arts. Mencken, on the other hand, was fascinated by the farce of politics.

This difference between the two men could hardly be better exemplified than by their plans for the coming summer. Mencken was off, as correspondent of *The Baltimore Sun*, to cover the Republican and Democratic conventions. After that he would trail the candidates (they turned out to be William Howard Taft and William Jennings Bryan) on their campaign tours. Nathan was sailing for Europe to see the new plays in London, Paris, Berlin, and Vienna.

But they had much in common: They had like tastes in literature and music. They were united in a belief that critical standards in America must be changed, taking those of Europe as a model. Their disdain for the conventional and for the idols of the crowd made them brothers.

It was after midnight when the two men strolled up Sixth Avenue. Mencken decided to walk Nathan back to the Royalton before boarding the night train for Baltimore. A comic malcontent, he was now complaining about his summer duties at the conventions. He, too, would like to take an ocean voyage and travel about Europe. Perhaps some summer they could make the trip together. In any case, they would be in close touch and he expected that he would be in New York more often — at least once a month for a few days — when he began his contributions to *The Smart Set*.

They parted with fraternal adieux before the Royalton.

PART THREE

Mencken made his debut in *The Smart Set* pages in the November 1908 issue. During the summer he had sweated through the political conventions and reported merrily upon them in *The Baltimore Sun*. Now with William Howard Taft elected president, it was time to turn to literature.

In the back pages of the magazine he reviewed some of the latest books, using them as springboards for his own ideas on social and literary matters. He wrote roughly of Upton Sinclair's *The Money-changers*, expressing disappointment at the course its author was taking:

> When he started out he loomed big. There seemed to be something of the vigor of Frank Norris, even of Zola in him. He appeared to sense the sheer meaninglessness of life — the strange, inexplicable, incredible tragedy of the struggle for existence. But then came the vociferous success of *The Jungle* [Sinclair's sensational exposé of the Chicago stockyards which persuaded President Theodore Roosevelt to demand better conditions in the meat industry]. The afflatus of a divine mission began to stir in Sinclair and he sallied forth to produce his incomprehensible jehad.

Sinclair, Mencken felt, had confused the job of the novelist with the job of the crusader and the result was bad art.

Nathan made his first appearance in the October 1909 issue with a frivolous essay, "Why We Fall In Love With Actresses," a warm-up piece for his regular theatre column, which he began the following month. Nathan's reviews thereafter preceded Mencken's book department on the last pages. This arrangement was continued throughout their years on *The Smart Set*. Nathan's November contribution, "The Drama Comes Into Season," likened the theatre year's choice months to those of the oyster season — only months containing "R" being trustworthy. This introduction was followed by an account of what September had brought Broadway.

To appreciate the immensity of the task Nathan imposed upon himself — that of elevating the theatre — it is necessary to recall the primitive, backward state in which he found the national theatrical situation in the early 1900s.

In Europe an evolution in the drama had begun at about the time that Nathan was born. During the 1880s, Ibsen's realistic plays had invaded the continent to sweep away the faded romanticism that lingered in its theatres. But the turmoil that had been rocking the theatres of Europe to their foundations for two decades caused only a faint, underground rumble on the other side of the Atlantic. Ibsen was still little more than a name, a bad word connoting foreign morbidity and immorality to the general public. Richard Mansfield, the London-born actor-manager, presented *Peer Gynt* as his last production at his Madison Square Theater after two Shaw plays, *Arms and the Man* and *The Devil's Disciple*. Mansfield was a curious specimen, a bombastic, vainglorious star, an imitation of Henry Irving, who had an inkling that the drama was undergoing a change. He made some efforts to keep up with the times. He tried a dramatization of Dostoevski's *Crime and Punishment* (under the unwieldly title, *A Fool Hath Said in His Heart: "There is no God"*), Alexis Tolstoy's *Ivan the Terrible*, the wistful German romance *Old Heidelberg*, and Rostand's *Cyrano de Bergerac*. These were concessions to modernity, but his instinct for the new was uncertain. He rejected *Caesar and Cleopatra*, which Shaw urged upon him and felt more secure in his standard popular favorites, *A Parisian Romance*, *Beau Brummel*, *Dr. Jekyll and Mr. Hyde* (its hair-raising transformation scene was always greeted with wild applause), and *Monsieur Beaucaire*, which he alternated with Shakespeare, Schiller, and an adaptation of Molière's *Misanthrope*.

In the United States, as in Europe twenty years earlier, the new drama was slowly, almost clandestinely, infiltrating. Actresses and actors understood its importance and led the way, while the impresarios lagged behind, cursing "the new-fangled nonsense" that threatened their prosperous trade in old-fashioned nonsense.

Mrs. Fiske gave special performances of Ibsen and Ethel Barry-more, temporarily abandoning trivial comedies, played Nora and the bedraggled scrubwoman of John Galsworthy's first play, *The Silver Box*. A young understudy of John Drew, Arnold Daly, staked his savings on a matinée of Shaw's *Candida*. The audience responded and *Candida* achieved a run. Encouraged, Daly continued his Shavian course with *The Man of Destiny* and the sequel to *Candida*, *How He Lied To Her Husband*. But the critics of the day were as opposed to the new movement as the established producers. When Daly produced Shaw's witty contrasting of Irish and English temperaments, *John Bull's Other Island*, Alan Dale of the Hearst press referred to it as "a thick, glutinous and imponderable four-act tract."

Warner Oland, a Swedish immigrant of high theatrical ideals, rendered the first English translations of Strindberg, and backed performances of *The Father* with his own capital. The experiment was a failure and he quit the theatre to accept film work (as an oriental menace he pursued Pearl White in the movie serial, *The Perils of Pauline*, and later became a famous face of Hollywood).

Such continental plays as were imported by the commercial managers — the farces of Feydeau, the problem plays of Bataille and Bernstein, *Zaza* and Sardou — underwent a sort of customs inspection and "cleaning up" process. They were emasculated by their American adapters lest the untarnished original offend the sensibilities of the pure Broadway public or those of the Tammany police force. As the majority of critics and their editors were in the Puritan camp, progress appeared to be blocked on every side. When the old-fashioned, native playwright, James A. Herne, tried clumsily to write in the Ibsen vein in *Margaret Fleming* he was informed by a reviewer that there was no pleasure to be found in "the details of unpleasant and unhealthy forms of unruly life."

That dreary octogenarian, William Winter, was dean of the American critical fraternity, holding rank as the great authority on the drama. He had been contributing essays, in which prudery and pedantry were combined, to *The New York Tribune* since the Civil War. Winter violently denounced Ibsen and Shaw and decried distinguished continental actresses who came to tour the United States as brazen strumpets. Winter retired from his long service at

The Tribune in 1908, the very year that George Jean Nathan was engaged to write for *The Smart Set,* but the Winterish attitude did not disappear with its originator.

James Huneker, while a drama critic, had acted as an antidote to Winterism. There was a gusto and panache to his writing and he expressed his audacious opinions without consideration of Sunday school decorum. He was a strong advocate of Ibsen, Shaw, d'Annunzio, Henri Becque, and of all the European innovators in the arts. But Huneker, bored with the coverage of the Broadway theatre, withdrew to concentrate on music criticism and his books. And Mencken had been excited by the new, intellectual drama. Aside from writing a book on Shaw, he had edited translations of Ibsen's *A Doll's House* and *Little Eyolf* but, disgusted with the average American play, he restricted his play-going to burlesque shows. The Broadway theatre of the 1900s seemed at first glance a dull, despised, and barren field for a young man with taste, talent, and fresh ideas.

The theatre, however, amused Nathan whether it was good or bad. "A bad painting is simply a bad painting, and so fit only for the gallery of a rich American meat-packer," he wrote, "but a bad play acted by impossible hams is often a joy and delight for kings and emperors. Let a man of unimpeachable taste tell the truth and he will tell you that he has had ten times the pleasure at a No. 3 company's performance of *Uncle Tom's Cabin* than he has had at any No. 1 company's performance of the best play that Charles Rann Kennedy [a sanctimonious, pre-1914 dramatist given to maudlin religiosity and the author of *The Servant in the House*] ever wrote."

Some observers before him were keenly aware of the sorry state of the national theatre, but they had been unable to proceed. It may be that the hour was ripe for change and that had Nathan begun his tussle with the dismal situation a decade sooner he, too, would have found himself crying in the wilderness; that he, too, would have encountered defeat. However, a glance at the theatrical scene *circa* 1908 reveals that the worn traditions were still firmly entrenched.

The American theatre as Nathan found it was in great measure a replica of the European theatre of about 1860. Stars strutted in bowlderized adaptations of the classics; playwrights, steering close to the "moral" coast, wrote preposterous melodramas and childish farces; and there was an occasional society comedy to break the monotony. Stock companies across the nation were still barnstorming in *East Lynne* and *Camille*. The rural uplift piece *The Old Homestead* by Denham Thompson, which preached the homely virtues of life on the farm and denounced the corruption of the cities, was an example of the dramatic output that had far-flung appeal (Thompson accumulated a huge fortune with tours of this vehicle between 1886 and his death in 1911) and "Tom" (for Thompson) shows roamed from one county to another.

The monopolistic stranglehold of the Theater Syndicate (an alliance of such managers as A. L. Erlanger, Marc Klaw, Nixon and Zimmerman, and Charles Frohman) which had controlled the majority of American playhouses, had just been broken by the defiance of independent stars and producers who refused to accept its exorbitant booking terms. Sarah Bernhardt had balked at the demands of the Syndicate, preferring to play in tents under the auspices of the Shubert brothers rather than patronize the Syndicate's theatres and submit to its shakedown practices.

Charles Frohman was the arbiter elegantiarum of the American theatre. His name was an assurance against cheapness and vulgarity, and the premieres at his theatre — the elegant Empire at Broadway and 40th Street — were attended by society's 400, lending all he did snob appeal.

It was Frohman who discovered Maude Adams when she was playing a bit role in *The Charity Ball*, a melodrama of the 1890s. He at once saw the star potential in this frail, wistful girl. A decade later she was America's most beloved actress. Maude Adams became a theatrical legend, largely due, Nathan believed, to Frohman's shrewd showmanship. Frohman invented a personality for her.

Frohman had strict rules for young actresses in his company. They were to remain remote from the public gaze outside the theatre. They were never to dine in restaurants or to attend theatrical parties. Nor were they to associate with actors. Marie Doro one day took a stroll with an actor whom she subsequently married. For this offense she was promptly dismissed by Frohman.

Frohman, an exponent of romance and glamour, wrapped his actresses in a dreamy haze of mystery. His methods had the air of anti-publicity. With Miss Adams the policy of offstage invisibility was perfected. Interviews with her were virtually impossible to obtain. The Frohman press agents would postpone the appointments again and again until journalists gave up in despair and begged their editors to assign them the easier task of interviewing the Pope. Miss Adams hid her face in veils even when she took the few steps from the stagedoor to her carriage waiting at the curb. When on tour she was accompanied by a chaperon, resided secretly in the most exclusive hotels, and took all her meals in her rooms. All this excited the public imagination. She was the Greta Garbo of 1905.

Frohman, a sentimental Frankenstein, labored tirelessly on his creation. He selected her roles with utmost care, persuading James Barrie to dramatize his novel, *The Little Minister*, so that Miss Adams might play Lady Babbie. Barrie grudgingly complied, very doubtful of such a project, but the play became a record success. It was in another Barrie play that Miss Adams rose to the pinnacle of her career as Peter Pan, the boy who never grew up. The delicate Barrie pathos was in harmony with the wistful Adams charm. She was the ideal heroine for his *What Every Woman Knows*. Her personality was in tune with the work of the romantic Rostand, too, and she garnered praise for her performances as the eloquent rooster who sings the sunrise in the farm-yard fantasy *Chantecler*.

Frohman, in common with his affluent colleagues, viewed Ibsen as the enemy, and he had probably never heard of Strindberg. To Frohman, the theatre was a temple of elegant escape, a soothing never-never land, an enchanting retreat divorced from ugly reality, hence his practice of turning his actresses into veiled goddesses who had no existence beyond the footlights. He met increasing difficulty in imposing his strictures, however, for not all his protégées were as docile as Miss Adams. He had abruptly dismissed Miss Doro for being seen with an actor, but he was unable to keep Ethel Barrymore similarly caged. When, in defiance of his commands, she went out to lunch one day at Delmonico's with the debonair journalist, Richard Harding Davis, he realized that, as she was an established audience favorite, there was nothing he could do.

Once in London he had sponsored a repertory season of Pinero, Shaw, and Granville Barker. This experiment had failed dismally and soured him on highbrow drama. His audience wanted impossible golden dreams, not dramatized editorials, he concluded. But he was always diplomatically polite, upholding his reputation as the American theatre's first gentleman. Then, too, who knows what the future may have in store and what tomorrow's play-goers may demand? When an inquiring reporter cornered him for a statement on his play selection, he replied with a friendly smile, "There are plays that I like and produce and there are plays I like and don't produce."

In 1915 he was aboard the London-bound Cunard liner, the *Lusitania*, when it was torpedoed by German submarines off the Irish coast. Fellow passengers remembered him as a squat little old man wrapped in a greatcoat, standing calmly on the deck as the vessel sank and others scrambled frantically for the lifeboats. "Why fear death? It must be a great adventure," he quoted from *Peter Pan*, before going to a watery grave.

David Belasco, of chalk-white face, flowing silver mane, and glowing brown eyes blazing beneath bushy eyebrows, was reverently respected as a superb theatrical artist until Nathan came along. Even Huneker had kind words for Belasco, explaining away his hostility to the modern problem drama by comparing his scorn for Ibsen to the conservative connoisseurs of painting who preferred the mellow coloring of Zoffany, Turner, and Gainsborough to the jolting splashes of the Futurists coming to the fore.

Like Frohman, Belasco was a star-maker. He took David Warfield, a low comic of the Weber and Fields music hall, and transformed him into a celebrated actor. Warfield made his legitimate stage debut in Charles Klein's *The Auctioneer*, where a Lower East Side junk shop served as decor. A specimen of Belasco's zeal for the authentic, it was "real" down to the last pair of tattered trousers that hung from its walls. Warfield subsequently starred in Belasco productions of *The Return of Peter Grimm* and *The Music Master*, both resounding hits. Many years later, Warfield retired from the boards a millionaire.

The auburn-haired Mrs. Leslie Carter was another of Belasco's discoveries. She was involved in a much publicized divorce case when she opened in *Zaza*, which Belasco had adapted from Réjane's Parisian success and produced to give vivid glimpses of life backstage at a French music hall. Mrs. Carter was trying to obtain the custody of her child from her society husband, who resented both her taking to the stage and her use of his name. The news that she had won her suit came during the premiere performance, and at the evening's end Belasco, appreciating the sentimentality of his audience, went before the curtain and announced in a quavering voice that Mrs. Carter and her child would be reunited.

Henrietta Crossman, Blanche Bates (for whom he wrote *Girl of the Golden West*), Frances Starr (for whom he wrote *Rose of the Rancho*), and Judith Anderson were actresses who benefited from his sponsorship. Ina Claire, fresh from the *Ziegfeld Follies*, joined the Belasco entourage and developed into America's finest light comedienne.

The established playwrights of the epoch were Augustus Thomas, who wrote a series of popular plays beginning with *Alabama* in 1891; Charles Klein, author of social melodramas; Clyde Fitch, who confected pseudo-historical costume pieces — *Barbara Frietschie* for Julia Marlowe, *Major André* and *Beau Brummel* for Mansfield, *Nathan Hale* — adapted comedies from the French and German and provided light comedies about New York's smart set.

Some young men — and a young woman, Rachel Crothers — arrived to challenge the old guard.

George M. Cohan was starring in comedies and musical comedies which he wrote and for which he composed the music: *45 Minutes from Broadway*, *Broadway Jones*, *A Prince There Was*. The dour critical fraternity dismissed him as an escaped music hall clown who had crashed the legitimate theatre; an out-of-order, flag-waving vulgarian. But Nathan appreciated his theatrical vitality and his knack for playwriting, and Arnold Bennett, visiting the United States, declared that Cohan was the nimblest American dramatist.

Rachel Crothers wrote of the problems of young women in *The Three of Us*, and about the double standard in *A Man's World* and *He and She*, beginning a playwriting career that continued until the eve of the Second World War. Edward Sheldon, a well-to-do New Yorker just out of Harvard, was to be almost as prolific a playwright during the coming decades. He made his debut with *Salvation Nell*, which had a barroom setting and uplifting overtones, telling of a bedraggled working girl's redemption of the man she loved. William Vaughn Moody, a university professor of English, contributed a melodrama of the Western plains, *The Great Divide*, in which Henry Miller as a rugged he-man of the open spaces wooed Margaret Anglin as a prim New England maiden whom he has won from her abductor in a poker game.

There was still a great divide between American letters and the American theatre. Moody already had a considerable reputation as a poet when he was teaching at the University of Chicago. Miss Anglin, who had played Roxane in Mansfield's *Cyrano*, was sent the Moody script by Donald Robertson, a theatre leader of that city. She read it through at a single sitting and, deeply impressed, wired Lee Shubert, advising him to produce it, and telephoned Henry Miller to tell him that she had found him a magnificent part. Shubert and Miller agreed with her verdict of the play, but Miller, already a star, inquired, "Who's Moody?" When Moody was informed that Shubert and Miller had agreed to do *The Great Divide*, he asked at once, "Who's Miller?"

Two young European playwrights, Ferenc Molnár and W. Somerset Maugham, each of whom was to have a new play almost every season in the next decades, were first represented on Broadway in 1908. There had been an unresolved legal squabble over the American rights of Molnár's comedy, *The Devil*, with the result that two different versions of it opened on the same evening in different theatres. Maugham's *Lady Frederick* had had difficulties in getting produced in England because in its third act its heroine had to appear dishevelled, without makeup, and have her hair done while arranging her face before the audience. No British actress wanted to play it, but Ethel Barrymore was willing to take on a role that was not altogether glamorous.

Such was the theatre that Nathan was called upon to review. It was scarcely intellectually inspiring. Broadway stage, if not Broadway dramaturgy, displayed some promising blossoms — especially its musical shows, which were soon to exceed in verve and invention those of Paris and London. Florenz Ziegfeld, in whom Nathan detected an artist, had just begun his annual editions of *The Follies*, and the melodious operettas of Victor Herbert — *The Red Mill, Babes in Toyland, Mlle Modiste* — were the equal of those by the Viennese Oscar Strauss, Leo Fall, and Franz Lehár.

Nathan had settled in a comfortable, three-room suite in the Hotel Royalton, only a step from Times Square. He spent his mornings reading, his afternoons writing, and most of his evenings at the theatre. His writing hours were devoted to magazine articles, the concoction of a Sunday feature for *The Philadelphia Ledger,* and, now and again, a weekly piece for one of the local newspapers.

Nathan's mother and younger brother Fred now resided in Philadelphia, having moved there after Charles Nathan's death. Mrs. Nathan lived in the Ritz Hotel and Fred was employed as house manager of the Nixon Theater. George Jean, who remained close to them, spent a weekend each month in Philadelphia, time permitting.

His byline was beginning to attract attention and comment. His three-barreled name was becoming familiar and was already an assurance of worldly wit and defiant independence. None of his rivals could write as well or as entertainingly. Professional graybeards such as Clayton Hamilton and Brander Matthews churned out stodgy essays on the drama in academic journals. The newspaper's review posts were held either by similar ancients, exponents of neo-Winterism, or by callow youths just out of college. The latter, like the former, were Puritans either by nature or by orders from their conservative editors, who were always wary of offending important advertisers or belligerent church groups eager for evidence of the theatre's immorality.

Nathan's acquaintance with those in the theatrical world began to broaden. His appreciative notice of a deftly devised farce, *Baby Mine*, brought him three new friends: its author, Margaret Mayo;

the actor Edgar Selwyn, Mayo's husband; and its heroine; Marguerite Clark, a petite, doll-like brunette who scampered with dainty grace through the innocuous romp about exchanged infants.

Miss Clark's childlike loveliness had impressed many playgoers, including Nathan, when she appeared in the musical comedy *The Wild Rose* a few seasons earlier. The comedienne and the critic were soon to be seen dining together at the Beaux Arts restaurant and Delmonico's, and were a familiar pair at theatrical gatherings. Shortly thereafter, Miss Clark became a motion picture star, making her screen debut in an early celluloid version of *Snow White and the Seven Dwarfs*.

The critic's evaluation of *Baby Mine* was equally prophetic. It prospered on Broadway and is still — after a century or so — revived in summer stock. Weedon Grossmith, seeing it in New York, purchased the English rights and produced it in London, playing in it himself for a long engagement. Maurice Hennequin, the Belgian author and a collaborator of Feydeau, adapted it for the French stage and it was a favorite of the Palais-Royal repertory for several decades, though Nathan complained that Hennequin had "dirtied it up" in his revision to such an extent that it was indistinguishable from the washroom of a third-class railroad coach. It has been frequently revived in France, as well.

Selwyn, whom Nathan liked at once, was amusing and self-assured, sporting the devil-may-care air of a Broadway D'Artagnan, but, despite this cavalier pose he was a shrewd and practical showman. He was the son of an Polish Jewish immigrant named Simon, who in his trade had traveled from New York to Cincinnati and from Alabama to Canada. When Edgar was in his teens his father settled in Manhattan and secured his son a situation as a necktie salesman. In the evenings, however, his passion for the theatre led him to take a job as an usher at the Herald Square Theater where Richard Mansfield, the imperious, English-born actor-manager, played Shakespeare, Rostand, and Shaw.

Selwyn sought out a position at that playhouse because Mansfield was reputed to be the finest actor since Booth. However, differing verdicts on Mansfield's histrionic abilities have come down to us. Nathan was skeptical of his acting, especially in the more ambitious ranges, comparing it unfavorably with that of the foremost European actors. The public, on the other hand, believed him to be a great actor and a great man. He was undeniably an extravagant personality and assiduously cultivated his public image. He gave learned discourses on the drama, received interviews with lofty condescension, and photographs of his imperial private railroad car and palatial country estate probably enhanced his fame in the provinces more than his bombastic acting.

Mansfield's nationwide tours were lucrative and he was keenly aware that he must retain respect and prestige in the hinterlands, so, like Belasco, he had developed a system for silencing adverse criticism. If a reporter covering the theatre for the paper of one of the smaller cities voiced derogatory opinions of his performances, the actor-manager would invite the reporter to his regal Pullman car for a chat. Mansfield would then thank the $20-a-week reviewer for his enlightening comments and beg him to join his staff as an artistic advisor. The ruse rarely failed. The flattered reporter would throw up his local newspaper job and become a member of the Mansfield entourage. Once the company had moved on to some distant city and said reporter had severed all ties with his hometown paper, Mansfield would discharge him, leaving one less critic to speak negatively of his art. A critic, Mansfield once pointed out, is only a critic as long as he has a job.

While Edgar Selwyn was showing playgoers to their seats in the Herald Square Theater, he befriended a fellow usher, Winchell Smith, the future author of *The Fortune Hunter* and other Broadway hits. Smith and Selwyn both hoped to become actors and in their spare time would coach each other in scenes. One night after a performance, the two were busily clowning around at the rear of the deserted theatre. Selwyn was in the midst of an imitation of Mansfield as Beau Brummel when Mansfield himself stepped from the shadows. He ordered both young men to report to his office the next day and stalked off. Smith and Selwyn were aghast, assuming that Mansfield would certainly dismiss them and had merely postponed the bad news out of sadism. To their surprise, when they went before him the following afternoon he informed them that he thought they should have a try at professional acting and allotted them walk-ons in his productions. A year later Smith was playing with William Gillette in the Civil War melodrama *Secret Service*, while Selwyn had a plum role in Augustus Thomas' *Arizona* in a cast that included Eleanor Robson, Vincent Serrano, and Theodore Roberts.

Subsequently Selwyn played Foreman in *Sherlock Holmes* with Gillette, Telemachus in Stephen Phillips' *Ulysses* with Tyrone Power, Sr. as the roaming warrior, was Maude Adams' leading man in *The Pretty Sister of José*, and Ethel Barrymore's acting partner in *Sunday*. With his brother, Arch, he founded a producing company, of which Henry B. Harris was also a partner, and wrote plays in which he starred. One of these was *Pierre of the Plains*, a dramatization of Sir Gilbert Parker's novel of the Canadian wilds. Another was *The Arab*, in which Selwyn appeared as a Bedouin sheik who wins the heart of an American girl after rescuing her missionary father from desert banditti.

It was during the prosperous run of *The Arab* that Selwyn's ambition to be the neo-Richard Mansfield burnt itself out. Acting, especially the acting of romantic heroes, ruffled his patience and tried his sense of the ridiculous. He hated smearing his face with nut-brown grease every evening to impersonate the daring Arab, and on matinée days he had to endure the ordeal twice. One Saturday evening, after such double duty, he sat staring at himself in brown-face and Arabian headdress in his dressing-room mirror. "What a God-damned fool!" he exclaimed as he studied his image. He immediately scribbled a note that the play was closing, tacked it to the call-board, and never set foot on a stage again. He often remarked that he had not the slightest regret about the retirement made in a moment of good taste.

He later sold the movie rights of *The Arab* and it was filmed twice, once by Cecil B. De Mille in Hollywood and later by Rex Ingram on location in Cairo with Ramon Navarro in the romantic leading role.

Selwyn became an eminent Broadway impresario and a millionaire. He built three theatres on 42nd Street: the Selwyn, the

Apollo, and the Times Square. He was also involved with Major Bowles in the construction of one of the first movie palaces: the Capitol, designed to accommodate four thousand spectators at each of its five daily shows, which opened its bronze doors in 1917.

During his early days on *The Smart Set* Nathan met Avery Hopwood, a gangling, yellow-haired young man from Ann Arbor, Michigan, who was intent on conquering Broadway. The success complex spurred Hopwood mercilessly and he responded to its jabs by writing day and night. In the course of his career he amassed the largest fortune earned by any American playwright. As prolific as Clyde Fitch, Hopwood outdistanced him in money-making. Fitch, dying in 1909, never benefited from motion picture sales as Hopwood did, and Fitch's polite parlor entertainments had more limited appeal than Hopwood's uproarious farces.

Hopwood's first play, a serious problem piece, had been an instant failure. After its closing he vowed that he would henceforth write only hits, a boast which he fulfilled. Never again was he to encounter defeat at the box-office, though his writing deteriorated and his humor coarsened in his eager chase after the dollar.

His speciality was the breezy sex farce, as salacious as the "Comstocks" would permit. Sometimes he went too far and the censors wagged warning fingers. *The New York Times* refused to accept advertising for his play, *The Demi-Virgin*, complaining that its title was obscene. Actually, it was a within-the-blue-law-bounds account of the unconsummated marriage of two movie stars. *Getting Gertie's Garter* was denounced from the pulpit by blushing clergymen who were offended at its strip-poker sequence in which a pretty girl, Hazel Dawn, joining the game and losing, was asked to pay the penalty. Police interference threatened but failed to materialize, and the loud clerical disapproval augmented the box-office takings.

Nathan found Hopwood's early comedy writing of exceptional merit — fresh, fertile, and very funny. *Fair and Warmer, Sadie Love, Our Little Wife,* and *The Gold Diggers* belong to this phase. Hopwood was also an invaluable collaborator and an expert play doctor. He collaborated with Channing Pollock on *Clothes*, a star vehicle for Grace George, and aided Mary Roberts Rinehart in adapting her detective novel, *The Bat*, for the stage. *The Bat* broke long-run records and is still revived. When David Gray, a New York socialite and a cousin of Mrs. Franklin Roosevelt, wrote a society comedy, *The Best People*, Hopwood took it over, revised it, and made it stage-worthy. It emerged as a Broadway success and was sold to the movies. "He is as Parisian as Guitry," wrote Nathan of Hopwood. "He is the only man writing risqué farce in America today whose work has any finish, any style, any metropolitan flavor."

American comedy seemed to Nathan immeasurably superior to the "serious" American plays of the time. He insisted — much to the consternation of the critical establishment — that George Ade, George M. Cohan, Montague Glass, and Hopwood were far better writers than Augustus Thomas, David Belasco, and Charles Klein.

When Nathan was a boy in Cleveland, his uncle, Charles Frederick Nirdlinger, had taken him to the state fair and introduced him to Charles T. Hoyt, whose theatrical company was one of the fair's attractions. Hoyt had been a music and drama critic on *The Boston Post* before writing a series of nationally popular plays. The models for these were the Harrigan and Hart extravaganzas of the 1880s, *The Mulligan Guard Ball* and its sequels. The title of each Hoyt play was prefixed by an "A," and each burlesqued some fad of the day. *A Temperance Town* poked fun at the Prohibition advocates. *A Texas Steer* related how a Lone Star state bumpkin, elected to Congress, went to Washington and discovered the chicanery practiced by politicians there. *A Milk White Flag* chose the National Guard regiments as its target. *A Trip to Chinatown*, which featured "slumming parties," played 650 performances at the Madison Square Theater in New York and had a lucrative tour before becoming a stock favorite. It was probably the most popular show of the 1890s, debuting Charles K. Harris' mournful ballad, "After the Ball," and Percy Grant's jolly, jaunty "The Bowery."

Hoyt's plays were a combination of broad farce, broad spoofing, and song and dance. They were typically American in their humor, subjects, and settings, and Nathan believed them valuable contributions to national folklore.

Hoyt's theatrical descendants were George Ade, George M. Cohan, Booth Tarkington, and Harry Leon Wilson who, emulating their forerunner and similarly seeking the conquest of a wide market, good-naturedly caricatured American mores, American types, and the American middle-class ideals and institutions, and their characters spoke in a racy American idiom. Their plays were praised as being "clean as a whistle," "wholesome family entertainment" like the serials in *The Saturday Evening Post*. They were often cleverly devised, but were as devoid of any deep probing of "the American way of life" as they were of "dirt."

Hopwood, on the other hand, took as his models the comedies of the wicked Parisian boulevards, developing another branch of native humor in which a continental attitude toward sex was introduced. His adaptations of French farces and his own plays written in imitation were snapped up by A. H. Woods, a picturesque impresario, who shared Hopwood's ambition to get rich quick. Woods was an exuberant figure, flashy and expansive, a very cartoon of the flamboyant, Barnum-type showman. He wore loud checked suits and perpetually smoked a mammoth cigar, hailing all and sundry with a "Hello, Sweetheart!" He was cocky and cockeyed, too, one of his eyes being of glass. Woods amassed a fortune in the theatre, before losing his major stars to the movies and the bulk of his money in the stock market crash of 1929. During the bleak 1930s his name reappeared as a producer, but he seemed to have more downs than ups, his former flair of anticipating what the public wanted had vanished with his savings.

Nathan's friendship with Hopwood began when they discovered that they had both spent their boyhoods in Cleveland. Each spring Nathan would visit Paris and usually found Hopwood staying at the same hotel: the high-ceilinged, marble-halled Continental on the Rue de Rivoli. The hotel's front suites commanded a view of the leafy, flowering Tuileries, wistfully lovely in April and May. Together Nathan and Hopwood would saunter forth to do the theatres, the critic in search of copy and the dramatist looking for saucy situations in the boulevard farces that he might filch for Broadway.

One evening Nathan and Hopwood booked seats to hear

Tristan at the Opera but, lingering over dinner at Foyot's, they arrived to find they had missed the first two acts. "No matter how late one gets to Wagner, there is always another act," quipped Hopwood. "The difference between us," he said on another occasion to Nathan, "is that you respect the theatre and I see in it only a way of making money."

Nathan's repeated opinion that Hopwood's writing possessed more theatrical merit than that of any other American playwright in active practice scandalized the critical establishment. Even such critics as were secretly in accord with the Nathan verdict were prevented by the commercialism of their editors from expressing such a view. "I agree with you that this last naughty farce of Hopwood's is awfully funny stuff," a New York newspaper reviewer told Nathan. "I laughed at it until my ribs ached; but I don't dare write as much. One can't praise such things in a paper that has the kind of circulation ours has."

Hopwood grew rich, but success left him dissatisfied. He took to heavy drinking and when in his cups would bemoan sacrificing his gifts to money-making. The quality of his work declined and his later comedies were stale repetitions. Nathan perceived this falling-off and criticized him severely, accusing him of bringing 14th Street burlesque shows uptown and simply advancing their prices, replacing the gold-toothed burlesque queens with more comely girls.

Hopwood had a tormenting personal problem. He was persecuted by a female relative who was determined to "reform" him — to stop his drinking and the sinful life she was certain he was leading in wicked New York. She made periodic surprise raids on his bachelor quarters. At first, he tried to laugh away her behavior by writing his pestering relation into his farces. She was the visiting nuisance in *The Alarm Clock*, his adaptation of the Romain Coolus comedy about a misbehaving man-about-town. The intruding uplifter brought roars from thousands of playgoers, but its model was no joke to the unhappy author.

One July in the late 1920s he was spending a vacation in a deluxe hotel at Antibes, sunning himself on the sands by day and

making the rounds of the smart bars after dark. During an afternoon siesta he was aroused by the delivery of a telegram. The
dreaded dragon of improvement had arrived in Paris and was already on her way to the Riviera. She would be in Antibes in the
morning for another "heart-to-heart" talk.

That evening Hopwood went to the hotel dining room where
he ate a gourmet dinner and then had an after-dinner brandy on the
terrace. He then strolled to the beach as if answering a summons,
stripped off his clothes, and swam out toward the horizon. In the
morning the surf washed his body up to the shore. Among his papers was found an epitaph he had written for himself:

> Living and dying I loved the truth,
> And I'll speak it now, though it seems uncouth;
> I wrote thirty plays and produced them as well,
> So I don't much care if it's heaven or hell.

The American summer colony on the Riviera — including, that
year, Alexander Woollcott, Robert Benchley, Charles McArthur,
F. Scott Fitzgerald, Charles Brackett, and a fellow playwright,
Philip Barry — learned of Hopwood's death and spent an evening
discussing the pros and cons of suicide. Barry romanticized
Hopwood's end as the basis for a metaphysical argument in his play
Hotel Universe.

John D. Williams, a knowledgeable Harvard graduate who
acted as a literary advisor to Charles Frohman, was another of
Nathan's companions. Both men were dandies and shared tastes in
literature and pleasures. On theatreless evenings they would invite
a pair of young actresses to make up a foursome and dine at the
Beaux Arts or Delmonico's. Williams, an indefatigable raconteur,
had a fund of green-room anecdotes and would regale the company
with stories of Frohman's dealings and gossip about the shy Maude
Adams, Mrs. Fiske and her penchant for downing seidel after seidel of beer without visible effect after bringing down the house in
an Ibsen play, and the eccentric behavior of the Barrymores —
Ethel, Lionel, John, and their uncle, John Drew — all of whom
Williams had served as stage manager.

On other free evenings Williams and Nathan would do a round

of the bars, beginning at the Hotel Knickerbocker on Times Square and ending up the tour in a Bowery saloon or some "open-all-night" tavern on the West Side waterfront to drink schooners of beer and devour sandwiches. Nathan limited these stag outings to once a month for, though he enjoyed imbibing—"I drink to make my friends interesting," he commented—he never allowed alcohol to interfere with his work. Williams, exercising less disciplined restraint, suffered constant hangovers and his boozing was to cause playwrights and players much distress.

When Williams founded his own producing company a few years later, he consulted Nathan on the selection of scripts. Following the critic's advice he produced Galsworthy's *Justice*, with John Barrymore. This fine tragedy, concerned with the ruin of a junior law office clerk who, under emotional stress, commits a forgery and is sentenced to penal service, had shocked the British. It so impressed Winston Churchill that he introduced a bill for the reform of prison procedure. Williams equipped the play with less than sturdy scenery. At one performance Barrymore pounded on the door of his cell with such vigor that it flew open and the wardens had to rush on to lock him up again.

Later Nathan urged Williams to present Eugene O'Neill's first full-length play, *Beyond the Horizon*, on Broadway. Doubtful of its commercial prospects, Williams opened it with a series of matinées at the Morosco, inviting the press to attend the initial performance. The reviews the following morning were so enthusiastic that public curiosity was aroused and Williams transferred the play to another theatre for an extended run. Williams was a resourceful director—his staging of *Rain* with Jeanne Engles attained one of the longest engagements in New York theatrical history—but his heavy drinking made him unreliable.

John Barrymore took an instant dislike to Nathan when they met for the first time at a supper party given by the playwright, Zoë Akins, at her atelier on lower Fifth Avenue. He said nothing, contenting himself with looking at Nathan with an expression which was a mixture of a philatelist studying a counterfeit Peruvian stamp through a microscope and of a small boy beholding his first giraffe. Their next—and only other—personal encounter took place

many years afterwards when, in 1940, Barrymore, his great gifts
squandered in Hollywood, returned to New York for his last
Broadway engagement in a lamentable comedy, *My Dear Children*,
in which he mocked his former self, while his drunken offstage behavior was gloatingly recorded in the newspapers. Nathan was sitting at a bar table in the Monte Carlo Cabaret, awaiting a guest,
when Barrymore staggered through the door and spotted him.
"George," shouted Barrymore in great glee, wrapping an arm affectionately around the astonished critic's neck, "you're just the one
I've been wanting to see." Shakily seating himself, Barrymore then
outlined, between hiccups, his notion for the interpretation of the
role of Macbeth. Despite the actor's sorry condition, Nathan found
his conception brilliant.

    If Barrymore squinted skeptically at Nathan when they were
first introduced, Nathan was skeptical of Barrymore as an artist.
Barrymore's Richard III and Hamlet were acclaimed interpretations of genius and he was hailed as the greatest American actor of
his time. Nathan was only partially in accord with this majority verdict. About Barrymore's Hamlet, he wrote:

> I take it that there is no longer much question that the profi-
> cient modern actor of Hamlet is he who acts the role not with
> his own intelligence but with the intelligence of the audience.
> In plainer words, that Hamlet is, figuratively speaking, no
> longer so much an actor's role as an audience's role and that
> the best actor of that role is he who creates the role less than
> he who mirrors the modern audience's creation of it.
> Barrymore comes to us with this trick and manages it ad-
> mirably. His Hamlet is a calm, cool dramatic critic in the
> robes of the role; it is an analytical and synthetic shadow-
> graph of its audience's reactions; it is — and this is where it
> properly excels — a mere scenario of its emotional implica-
> tions. Yet it is not, for all its undeniably sound plan and saga-
> cious preparation, entirely successful. I am not persuaded
> that Barrymore's critical exact approach to the role, with its
> obvious wealth of study, scrupulously meticulous voice culti-
> vation, and intensive training in gesture, movement and facial
> play, has not deadened to a degree the human warmth that
> might have been projected from a less strainfully perfect pre-

liminary self-instruction and artistic castigation. Barrymore's Hamlet is critically so precise that it is at times histrionically defective.

Barrymore's utterances and acting are not always identical; one detects a self-consciousness of the importance of great occasion, of the austerity and traditions of the role. He goes at the role as a brave and gallant soldier goes into battle; with flags flying in his Sem Benelli heart [Barrymore had just previously played in Benelli's romantic drama of Renaissance Florence, *The Jest*] and with Richard's shining sword raised courageously aloft—but with just a trace of very human timidity and fear holding him in. He is glamorous; he is percipient; he is sound in apprehension; he is eminently praiseworthy—but is not the complete Hamlet.

Barrymore played Hamlet 101 times on Broadway, to break Edwin Booth's record of 100 consecutive performances in New York, and then took the production to London. George Bernard Shaw attended its premiere there and wrote Barrymore a scathing letter, sharply criticizing the drastic cutting of the text. Some believe that the Shavian onslaught and Nathan's qualified estimate of his Hamlet discouraged Barrymore's high ambitions. He abandoned the theatre to star in Hollywood movies for the next fifteen years.

Nathan's attitude toward acting requires some explanation. "When Nathan says that acting is not an art, he is talking arrant rot—who could doubt it after witnessing a performance of the great Duse?" complained Arnold Daly, an actor whom Nathan esteemed above many others. Nathan responded with:

> It seems to me that if this is a satisfactory touché no less satisfactory should be some such like rejoinder as: "When Nathan says that acting is an art, he is talking arrant rot— who could doubt it, after witnessing a performance by Corse Payton." The circumstances that Duse is an artist who happens to be an actress does not make acting an art any more than the circumstance that Villon was an artist who happened to be a burglar or that Paderewski is an artist who happens to be a politician makes burglary and politics arts. Duse is an artist first, and an actress second; one need only look into her

very great share in the creation of the dramas bearing the name of D'Annunzio to reconcile one's self—if not too stubborn, at least in part—to this point of view.

So, also, were Clairon, Rachel and Jane Hading artists apart from histrionism, and so, too, is Sarah Bernhardt: who can fail to detect the creative artist in the *Mémoires* of the first named, for instance, or, in the case of the last named, in the fertile impulses of her essays in sculpture, painting and dramatic literature? It is a curious thing that, in all the pronouncements of acting as an art, the names chosen by the advocates as representative carriers of the aesthetic banner are those of actors and actresses who have most often offered evidence of artistic passion in fields separate and apart from their histronic endeavors. Lemaître, Salvini, Rachel, Talma, Coquelin, Betterton, Garrick, Fanny Kemble, the Bancrofts, Irving, Tree and on down, far down—the line to Ditrichstein, Southern, Marie Tempest, Guitry, Gemier and the brothers Barrymore—all give testimony, in writing, painting, musicianship, poetry and dramatic authorship to aesthetic impulses other than acting.

The implied conceit of the actor who played romantic leading roles often excited Nathan's pen to ridicule. A lady who knew him very well and for many years once remarked that Nathan had never given a good-looking actor a good notice, because, in her opinion, he saw himself in such roles and resented the usurper. Although he praised the playing of William Ferversham and other handsome actors, it is true that he was unfriendly on the whole to the matinée idols of both stage and screen.

For the actor's vanity is not a simple thing, founded like mine and yours upon an easily—nay, almost childish—penetrable donkeyishness but one complex and majestic as the maze of Amenhotep III. It is not so much that the actor views himself as a devastatingly pretty one, a holocaust to drive ladies to drink and servant girls to ruin. There is in this occasionally warrant for him; for surely there was not a chambermaid in all of England who would not have elected a faux pas with George Alexander to one with Lloyd George or Thomas Hardy. Nor is there perhaps in our own country a lady vice crusader or demimondaine who would not fight more tepidly for her honor against John Barrymore or Mr. Chauncey Olcott than against William Gamaliel Harding or Bishop Manning.

Yet for all this measure of justification in the actor's vanity, his chestiness in an ornamental direction takes on an expansion that quite exceeds the bounds of credulity.

He, then, takes the case of Leo Ditrichstein, a stout, elderly actor who sported a toupée in his later life.

The Ditrichstein vehicles have come to be so many dramatizations of a Fatty Arbuckle party, somewhat romanticized by the injection of white gloves, an Inverness coat and a top hat, several allusions to Claridge's, the Riviera, and Paris under the springtime moon, a few gilt chairs, a reference to Pol Roger 1906, and the philosophy that it is better to be poor and in love than to be rich and the president of the Wiesel Insecticide Company.

Last season, however, the M. Ditrichstein announced that he was done with these revelations of himself as the resplendent and invincible Don Juan, and that he would instead appear in a play in which he would portray a fellow excessively homely and unloved. This, his answer to those who had made sport of his egotism. The play in point was the Italian Sabatino Lopez's *The Ugly Ferrante* and, as one knew from the manuscript, it would treat of the love duel between an inordinately unsightly man on the one side and a remarkably handsome man on the other. And the case against Ditrichstein vanity seemed to blow up with a loud report. But wait. The opening night. The fiddlers cease. The lights go down. The curtain goes up. And there, upon the stage, sure enough, is our Ditrichstein made up in an unornamental red wig and horn spectacles. The jury is about to dismiss the charge. But stop. What is this? The actor who plays the remarkably handsome man comes upon the *Bühne*. *O Vanitas est vanitas.* Our Ditrichstein has cunningly cast for the role of the remarkably handsome creature an actor with the face of an Hungarian haberdasher!"

Arnold Daly was a personal acquaintance of Nathan. Daly had a meteoric career. As a young beginner he found employ in the

Frohman office as a runner and clerk and was assigned to be the dresser of the dudish John Drew. Drew, who prided himself on his modish wardrobe, was enraged when he found that his valet was wont to dress up in his clothes to go bar-hopping. When he reprimanded Daly a violent scene ensued. "Here is your damned suit and your shoes," shouted Daly, fueled by a few drinks, as he stripped himself of the purloined finery. "I'm through being your valet. I'm going on the stage and I'll be a better actor than you've ever been." In relating the incident Drew would add generously in his best throw away manner, "And you know, the curious thing about that prophecy is that it came true."

Daly made his first stage appearance on the road in *The Jolly Squire* and his New York debut took place in *Puddin'head Wilson*, a popular dramatization of the Mark Twain novel. This was followed by an engagement in Clyde Fitch's *Barbara Frietschie*, a Frohman production starring Julia Marlowe. An early Shaw enthusiast, he gathered his fortunes and produced matinées of *Candida*, which he directed and in which he played Marchbanks. To the surprise of many, this venture proved successful and, encouraged, he then staged and acted in *You Never Can Tell, Mrs. Warren's Profession, How He Lied To Her Husband*, and *The Man of Destiny*. Daly liked the role of Napoleon so much that he later tried it again in Hermann Bahr's *Josephine*. Nathan liked Daly's script judgment, acting, and productions, being especially impressed by his work in another play by Bahr, *The Master*, a psychological drama about a celebrated physician so dedicated to science that he is indifferent to the human element and whose emotional deficiency is corrected by the advice of his sage Japanese assistant.

This play, unfortunately, was beyond the comprehension of the Broadway audience and afterwards Daly, bankrupt as an actor-manager, played character roles in the productions of others. After he had played in three failures in a row Alexander Woollcott, who disliked Daly intensely, wrote: "Last night Arnold Daly went down for the third and last time." His last appearance was in the Theatre Guild's presentation of Franz Werfel's *Juáres and Maximilian*. Shortly after this, deeply depressed by his failure, he set himself on fire and was burned to death. The next day, Shaw — for whom he had performed pioneering labors in the American theatre — remarked: "Very interesting this death of Daly. Cases of spontaneous combustion are so rare."

♦ ♦ ♦

Had some Greenwich Village fortune-teller in 1908 told Nathan and Mencken that the frivolous, slightly disreputable monthly, *The Smart Set*, would within the decade become the platform of a cultural revolution of which they would be leaders, both men would have asked the prophet the name of the drug in which she indulged. About *The Smart Set* neither contributor had any illusions. What could be made of a magazine scattered with sensational fiction — much of it of dubious grade — poor poetry, and sophomoric epigrams?

Mencken cynically calculated that the majority of *The Smart Set's* readers were fat women lolling in Pullman berths after greasy meals. He also suspected that the magazine had a wide circulation in brothels. He claimed to be indifferent to these odd deductions, rejoicing in having his free say on literature no matter what the audience. Actually *The Smart Set* had a growing readership in university circles, partially because of his literary views.

Nathan, on the other hand, believed that only a tiny percentage of his readers understood what he wrote. There was enough in his articles, he felt, to amuse the mob, but only the fortunate few thoroughly grasped the ideas he was presenting, and he professed to write only for this selective group. R. H. Davis, a Munsey magazine editor for whom he also wrote, once told him: "Never mind where your stuff appears. If it's good the right people will soon see it."

As journalists, Mencken and Nathan scorned no venue, writing for all possible audiences. They were scholarly and authoritative in the university reviews and indulged in what Irving Babbitt, the dry humanist, termed "literary vaudeville" in the popular press. One found them in *The Yale Review* or *The Atlantic Monthly* or *The Nation*; the comic weekly, *Judge*, the movie-fan magazines, Bernard MacFadden's *Liberty*, and the Hearst supplements. *The Smart Set* was at first but another of their many showcases. It brought them together in a friendship that was to be lifelong, but this they accredited to happy chance. They had only a vague interest in the magazine's fortunes and were only slowly and almost unwittingly drawn into its affairs.

Mencken periodically came in from Baltimore, and on these visits would stay at the Algonquin Hotel, whose genial proprietor, Frank Case, was making it a rendezvous for theatrical and literary notables. It faced the Royalton where Nathan resided and on arrival Mencken would telephone him and arrange for lengthy beer-drinking sessions at Luchow's with Huneker or dinner at the Beaux Arts, Sherry's, or Delmonico's over which they would exchange opinions and gossip.

Several newspapers invited Mencken to join their staffs in New York, but he rejected these feelers, claiming he hated Manhattan and would never give up his comfortable residence in Baltimore (which he never did). His "Free Lance" column on the editorial page of *The Baltimore Sun* was bringing him journalistic renown. It was modeled after the column that Eugene Field had introduced in Chicago and the column Ambrose Bierce wrote for the Hearst press, but it was intensely personal in its presentation and parade of prejudices. "The Free Lance" achieved Mencken's avowed policy of "stirring up the animals." Shocked Baltimoreans wrote indignantly to *The Sun*, demanding that this native enfant terrible be stilled. Mencken's comments were denounced from the pulpits and by the mayor himself, but the *Sun* editors stood their ground and luck was on Mencken's side. A Methodist clergyman, chieftain of a crusade to suppress "The Free Lance," was arrested in a YMCA for corrupting the morals of a boy scout. Characteristically, Mencken rescued his enemy from the clutches of the police, securing his release and getting him out of town in a jiffy.

The public Mencken was summed up almost fifty years later by a Washington clergyman, "He loved his drunken pals. He loved to swear in the presence of ladies and archdeacons. To him, every-thing was a racket — God, education, radio, marriage, children." It was this imaginary Mencken who made his first appearance in "The Free Lance."

While Nathan was hammering away at the foundations of the

established theatre in *The Smart Set*, Mencken was waging war on the vapid fiction pouring from the presses: the swashbuckling *Graustark* twaddle of George Barr McCutcheon, the espionage thrillers of E. Phillips Oppenheim, history rewritten as dainty romance by Paul Leicester Ford, O'Henry's short-story trickery, and the heavy humor of Irving Cobb. He admired the artistry of Henry James, but found his Anglomania repulsive and thought James would benefit by a whiff of the Chicago stockyards. To Mencken even Upton Sinclair's novels on labor, despite their socialistic propaganda, were preferable to Edith Wharton's ladylike revelations of high society:

> When one turns to any other literature — to Russian literature, say, or French, German or Scandinavian — one is conscious immediately of a definite attitude to the primary mysteries of existence, to the unsolved and ever-fascinating problems at the bottom of human life, and of a definite preoccupation with some of them, and a definite way of translating their challenge into drama. But it is precisely here that the literature of America is most colorless and inconsequential.

The modern European drama continued to hold Mencken's attention. In preparing his book on Shaw he had begun to read widely in the field, studying contemporary play construction and trying his hand at some short plays. His library contained a formidable collection of Ibseniana and he collaborated with Holgar A. Koppel, the Danish Consul in Baltimore, on fresh English translations of *A Doll's House*, *Little Eyolf*, and *Hedda Gabler*. The first appeared early in 1909 and was quickly followed by the second.

He read the new plays of such playwrights as Hauptmann, Shaw, Wedekind, Pinero, Barrie, and Strindberg as they came out and reviewed their published editions in his book pages. He also listened attentively to Paul Armstrong, a fellow Baltimorean and a popular Broadway playwright, as he rattled off the plots of his trashy melodramas. Armstrong often became so overwhelmed with the dilemmas of his heroines that he would burst into tears. Mencken maintained that had Armstrong lived long enough he would have become a superb movie director. Long before Griffith made *The Birth of a Nation*, Armstrong disclosed to Mencken his plan for a gigantic Civil War screen epic.

Mencken had operated briefly as drama critic for *The Baltimore Sun*, but he found theatregoing a form of torture. He preferred reading plays in his easy chair to "breathing bad air nightly, gaping at prancing imbeciles, sitting cheek to jowl with cads." He had some exceptions to the rule — a burlesque show would occasionally fetch him and he enjoyed Pinero's minor comedy, *Preserving Mr. Panmure*, so much that he often wistfully wished for its revival.

His anti-theatre stance annoyed Nathan, who tried to cure him of his playhouse phobia. As his failures mounted, Nathan, enlisting John D. Williams in the conspiracy, attempted to turn the matter into a joke. He wired Mencken that a new Ibsen had arisen and that on his next New York visit Mencken must break his non-theatre-going vow. The play that Nathan and Williams had selected for the prank was a dreadful specimen of the mother-love melodrama, *The Shadow*, from the Italian of Dario Niccodemi, starring Ethel Barrymore.

When Mencken next checked into the Algonquin Nathan scurried across the street and told him of the plans for the evening. The play was so important that all must don evening clothes. Mencken swore and protested, but to no avail. Williams arrived to urge him into his fancy attire, the while telling him that Niccodemi had written a masterpiece to put Shaw, Galsworthy, and even Hauptmann to shame.

His friends had engaged a stage-box lest Mencken miss some precious mot, subtle exposition, or sustained quality of this gorgeous play. As dreary scene followed dreary scene the theatre-hating Mencken was aghast. "Superb!" "Incomparable!" Nathan and Williams whispered in his ear after each silly exchange. Mencken began to wonder if he had lost his mind. Was what was going on before him not the worst stuff he had ever beheld behind the footlights? Had his sharp critical instinct deserted him? He was not reassured during the intermission as his companions went into ecstasies over Niccodemi's rare genius. Slowly the soggy play dragged itself into its last stages and Mencken could no longer contain himself. "Pure piffle!" he growled as Nathan tried to hush him. "Down-right pish-posh!" he roared, startling the harassed actors who were in the midst of the over-heated climax. Finally, the curtain fell with Nathan and Williams calling out "Bravo! Bravo!" It was only later in a nearby barroom that his friends confessed. "What a dirty trick!" he exclaimed in disgust. "But maybe it has had a salutary measure. That's the last time you ever drag me to a show!"

◆ ◆ ◆

In February, 1911, Col. Mann sold *The Smart Set* for $100,000 to James Adams Thayer, a socially ambitious publisher who hoped that its ownership would aid him in crashing "The Four Hundred" of Fifth Avenue. Both the news and the price of the sale startled not only the staff, but the magazine world.

Thayer was an enterprising operator. He had started as an advertising manager for Frank Munsey and then moved into control of Butterick Publications. With a partner he had bought *Everybody's* magazine for $75,000 and quickly transformed it into a $3 million concern. The appearance of "Frenzied Finance," an exposé of Wall Street business methods, had skyrocketed the advertising rates of *Everybody's* from $150 a page to $4,500 a page.

Thayer was an astute observer of trends. It was the age of Theodore Roosevelt's trust-busting campaigns and the public eagerly devoured revelations of the shameless tactics of the Big Business titans as recounted by the muckrakers. William Jenning Bryan's "Cross of Gold" speech — which had won him the presidential nomination at the Democratic convention in 1896 — had thrilled the lowly as a masterpiece of eloquent oratory and as a manifesto of the "foreward-looking" movement which aimed to limit the powers of wealth and crush too-free enterprise.

Thayer was a shrewd businessman who had become a millionaire by denouncing millionaires, but he longed to hobnob with the idle rich and proposed himself for membership in exclusive clubs. He was aware that the *The Smart Set* could never rival its mass-circulation rivals such as *The Saturday Evening Post*, with its soaring farmbelt readership, but it might turn a profit and serve as a stepping-stone in his social climbing.

His initial move was to alter its slogan from "A Magazine of Cleverness" to "A Magazine for Minds that are not Primitive." No one knew exactly what this meant and Mencken and Nathan adopted a wait-and-see attitude. Thayer, they felt, would be a domineering boss. It was he who would be the editor of any editor he appointed. He first offered the editorship to Mencken who announced his intention of remaining a Baltimore resident, which would make this impossible. Then he approached Nathan who begged off, using his outside work as an excuse. Then he tried to lure Charles Hanson Towne into taking the post, but Towne, too, was wary.

Failing in these maneuvers, Thayer made the following appointments: Norman Boyer, managing editor; Louise Closser Hale (the actress who had contributed novelettes and acted as an editorial reader), associate editor; and Mark Lee Luther, a wealthy New York attorney who dabbled in letters, second associate editor and business manager. James Montgomery Flagg, the popular illustrator, designed some covers which gave *The Smart Set*, under its changed auspices, a new look.

Thayer's business acumen was a boon. He quickly restored the advertising revenue, which had dropped sadly, to a healthy state, but he realized that drastic improvements must be made. Boyer as editor — with Luther as his aide — proved duds. They had no literary judgment for "minds that were not primitive." They were evidently unaware that a new movement in American letters was astir and were distrustful of fledging authors, publishing instead the work of tired old-timers who were too passé even for *The Saturday Evening Post*.

The "Ashcan" school was bringing realism to American painting and in 1913 the Armory Show (an exhibit of the canvases of Picasso, Rouault, and Duchamp, whose "Nude Descending a Staircase" roused the most controversy) opened American eyes to Cubist and Futurist art. Theodore Roosevelt dismissed it as "lunatic."

In Chicago, Harriet Monroe founded her magazine, *Poetry*, to which the Imagist and free verse poets, among them Amy Lowell and Ezra Pound, contributed. In St. Louis, Missouri, William Marion Reedy was editing *The Mirror*, an outspoken weekly of opinion which preached Henry George's Single Tax and Liberalism and in which first appeared the poetry and prose of Sara Teasdale, Orrick Jones, Zoë Akins, Charles J. Finger, George O'Neil, and Edgar Lee Masters' *Spoon River Anthology*.

To evaluate these fresh currents in literature and the arts a fresh critical outlook was required. They could not be judged by the obsolete standards of the Browning Society or such tradition-bound professors as Paul Elmer More, then editor of *The Nation*, and Irving Babbitt of Harvard, who were seemingly opposed to all that happened since the French Revolution.

Huneker aside, Nathan and Mencken had scant regard for any of the other American critics save Percival Pollock. Pollock reviewed books and plays in *Town Topics*, formerly the sister publication of *The Smart Set*. In his columns in that society gossip magazine he fought a futile battle against the entrenched philistinism dominating American life and letters, deploring the frantic dollar chase. "The cart-tail orators prate forever of the Young Nation; is that youth to expend itself in the pursuit of Mammon?" he indignantly inquired. "No, if we would really hold our youth within us, we must let it echo the lyric note in life, and let lucre go." He was truly a prophet wailing in the wilderness of the back pages of Colonel Mann's shake-down sheet.

However, the message he preached in his provocative book on the artistic renaissance taking place in the German-speaking lands, *Masks and Minstrels of New Germany*, was far-reaching. Although the book, published in 1911, had small sales, it was avidly read by Americans who were curious about art trends abroad, providing them with the latest news of what was happening in the field in Central Europe. It told of the young writers and artists of Germany and Austria — and of a few from the Slavic borders of the Austro-Hungarian empire — who were rejuvenating the culture of their countries with startling innovations. Through a shock treatment they were liberating literature and art from the suffocating bourgeois structures that had opposed it during the late nineteenth century; indeed, since the days of Goethe and Heine.

Rainer Maria Rilke, Stefan Georg, and Hugo von Hofmannsthal were restoring German poetry to its earlier grandeur. Naturalism was by now passé, but its outstanding German exponent, Gerhart Hauptmann moving with the times, had turned to poetic drama in *The Sunken Bell* and *And Pippa Dances*, the latter a symbolic tragedy in verse which he came to regard as his finest play.

The theatrical revolt of green Germany was being conducted, as it were, from below-stairs — in the smoky cellar cafés of Munich, Berlin, and Vienna. In these subterranean incubators new ideas were being hatched, and aesthetic activities flourished. This was the "Überbrett'l" movement, modeled after the Parisian *chansonniers* — Le Chat Noir, La Boîte à Fursy, and others in Montmartre and the Latin Quarter. The "Überbrett'l"'s founders were the witty lyric poet and novelist, Otto Julius Bierbaum, and the aristocratic dilettante, Ernst von Wolzogen. Its purpose was to provide civilized entertainment in miniature music-hall style and it catered to students, bohemians and — to employ Thayer's phrase — "minds that were not primitive." On its programs fledgling poets recited their verses; budding diseuses (artists entertaining with monologues) and pantomimists were given their moment in the spotlight and sketches and short plays such as Paul Schlesinger's *The Improvement Society*, full of the most obvious hits at the Kaiser, were performed. Sharo political satire, forbidden in the public theatres, blossomed in these underground nightclubs. Sometimes censorship intervened. Frank Wedekind, the Expressionist dramatist, received a jail sentence for candid criticism of the government delivered in a Munich cabaret.

The "Überbrett'l," though itself transitory, had fruitful results, playing its part in the evolution of the German theatre. Max Reinhardt started his directorial career in one of these intimate cabarets, Schall und Rauch, which, to avoid police interference, maintained a membership policy. On the cramped confines of its tiny stage he presented short plays by Maeterlinck and Strindberg and Oscar Wilde's *Salome* — while it was still under official ban — and engaged two unknowns — Gertrud Eysoldt (who swam into instant favor on some Danish gutter songs) and Emanuel Reicher—as performers. Both were to become ornaments of the German stage. The latter-day school of Viennese operas may also be traced to the movement. Many melodies of Oskar Straus, Victor Hollaender, and Bogumil Zepler, composed for the "Überbrett'l," survive. It was this type of theatre in which, a generation later, Berthold Brecht began as a troubadour, flaunting his anarchistic airs in the face of the philistines. In his plays, too, he adopted the informality of the "Überbrett'l" manner.

In his book, Pollock discussed the rising writers of German letters: Thomas Mann, who at twenty-two had written a masterly novel, *Buddenbrooks*, and who gave further evidence of his genius in his novelettes, *Death in Venice* and *Tonio Krüger*; the Viennese disciple of de Maupassant, Schnitzler; the Bavarian humorist, Ludwig Thoma; the Austrian humorist, Roda-Roda, with his jolly tales of the ridiculous side of life in the imperial army; the Czech Gustav Meyrinck and his fantastic novel of the Prague ghetto, *The Golem*; and the playwrights of the day, Otto Erich Hartleben, Max Halbe, Ernst Hardt, Otto Ernst, and Ludwig Fulda.

Officially, as Pollock observed, a stolid, arrogant militarism reigned in Germany and Austria, and their reactionary guardians of law and order, hostile to the new arts, viewed anything in the least novel with grave distrust. Kaiser Wilhelm II, for example, ordered his army officers not to dance the immoral tango. When Gerhardt Hauptmann was proposed for the Nobel Prize, the Kaiser made his displeasure known. The Nobel Prize was awarded to the Kaiser's candidate, Paul Heyse, a conservative poet of the old school, and it was only the following year that Hauptmann was honored in Stockholm.

The press was tightly muzzled and reflections on the Kaiser, his staff, and his intimates were likely to bring charges of *lèse majesté* and land the offender behind the bars, as happened to Wedekind. The satirical magazines, using humor as a weapon, were more effective in their aim. In *Jugend*, in *Pan*, and in *Simplicissimus*, young malcontents were having their say. The saucy style of these periodicals with their sly digs at those in power were to be reflected in the work of Nathan and Mencken when they became magazine editors.

Poor Pollock did not live to see the full impact of his book on aspiring American writers. Stricken with severe head-pains, he went to Baltimore to check into the Johns Hopkins Hospital for examination. It was discovered that he was suffering from a brain tumor and immediate surgical intervention was deemed necessary. As it was impossible to reach any of Pollock's family, Mencken took the responsibility of granting permission for the emergency operation. But Pollock, beyond aid, died under the knife. Mencken and Ambrose Bierce, who happened to be in Baltimore, were the only mourners at his drab funeral in a crematory chapel and Mencken undertook the depressing chore of shipping Pollock's ashes to his widow.

♦ ♦ ♦

For some time Mencken had been in correspondence with Willard Huntingdon Wright, literary editor of *The Los Angeles Times*. Wright, born in Virginia in 1888, benefited from a far-flung education. Something of a prodigy, he had entered college at fifteen and attended, in turn, three universities in as many years. The last was Harvard, which he left before graduating, characteristically boasting that the professors had no more to teach him. He then spent a year in Paris with his older brother, Macdonald Wright, a Futurist painter, frequenting the ateliers and cafés and adding to his knowledge of modern art. His family having moved to California during his absence, he settled there on his return and at nineteen joined the staff of *The Los Angeles Times*, being promoted to its literary editorship before he was twenty.

On his book page he reviewed Mencken's *Philosophy of Nietzsche* with whoops of glee and a show of erudition, for Wright posed as a superman — self-made — and toyed with translations of his German master. Mencken wrote to thank him for his knowledgeable and sympathetic notice and an exchange of letters followed. Mencken kept urging Wright to come East where, Mencken assured him, he would find a comfortable berth, as there was a crying need for better critics.

Wright acted on this advice as soon as he had terminated his commitment to *The Los Angeles Times*. He arrived in New York in

1911 and was warmly greeted by Mencken who introduced him to Nathan, Dreiser, and Thayer and secured him the post at *Town Topics* left vacant by Pollard's death.

His arrival in New York coincided with the resignation from *The Smart Set* staff of Louise Closser Hale, a well-known actress of literary ambitions, who was employed as sub-editor and occasionally wrote for the magazine. On learning of Miss Hale's departure, Mencken advised Wright to apply for the vacant post. Wright did so at once and was appointed sub-editor of *The Smart Set*, while retaining his duties on *Town Topics*.

Wright made his writing debut at *The Smart Set* with a cantakerous essay on the dismal state of culture in his former hometown, "Los Angeles — the Chemically Pure." In that sunlit, expanding metropolis, he complained, puritanism was entrenched. The yokels that it drew from the farmlands had infested it with Middle West morality, obscuring its picturesque and charming past. The licenses of its famous restaurants had been revoked for infringements of the new anti-alcohol rules and the brothels of Sonoratown had been closed down so that the profane laughter of the bawdy houses' fragile señoritas no longer rang out to mingle with the chimes of the Church of Our Lady of the Angels across the square.

Retired hicks, lured by the balmy climate, outnumbered the civilized natives and governed municipal affairs. They ruled Los Angeles as they would rule a small, backward village. Quaker censorship forbade the more advanced plays, but Wright saw hope in the younger generation which, he predicted, would eventually dispel the oppressive provincial spirit. There was a drama league, and a Little Theatre was under way. Brieux, Wedekind, Strindberg, Schnitzler, and Ibsen had long since been stomached by the potential insurrectionists. Within two years the city would become the motion picture capitol of the world, but this Wright did not foresee. The article caused circulation to jump, which impressed Thayer. The slashing style of attack and underlying ideas of the piece were obviously inspired by the Mencken manner.

Wright, an unruly egotist, was obsessed with making a splash as

a picturesque personality on the New York scene. His odd, obstreperous behavior may have been induced by his addiction to
drugs, for which he was later hospitalized. He seems to have taken
Ibsen's aphorism — "Never be such a fool as to doubt yourself" —
as his principle, but with no sense of the ridiculous to check him,
he was often foolishly reckless. When someone told him that he
looked like Wilhelm II, he dyed his hair, sprouted the ferocious up-
turned mustachios that the Kaiser sported, and spread the rumor
that he was morganatically related to the Hohenzollerns. In this ab-
surd manifestation of "the will-to-power," he was attempting to
surpass Mencken's connection to Bismarck.

Wright's book, *Misinforming a Nation*, is a minutely documented record of the errors and omissions in the 1909 edition of
the *Encyclopaedia Britannica*. To his credit, his rigorous exposé was
effective. In the next edition of the *Encyclopaedia* all the modern authors, artists, and men of science who were slighted or neglected in
the *Britannica*'s 1909 survey received extended biographies and
more intelligent consideration. Wright's volume on modern art was
a valuable contribution too, but his irascible nature and mad affec-
tations thwarted the realization of his high ambitions.

Mencken, amused by Wright's eccentricities, generously accepted him — though with some sardonic asides — at Wright's own
evaluation, praising his industry and scholarship. Nathan, a far
more shrewd judge of character, was less impressed and maintained
a polite, friendly reserve. This showy newcomer was not to his lik-
ing. He saw at once that Wright was unstable, quick-tempered, and
quarrelsome and he suspected that he was treacherous as well.

Dreiser did not hesitate to express his dislike and distrust of the
climber from California. "He has dropped a little tube into your
well and is trying to siphon you out," he warned Mencken, who
paid no heed. When Wright called on the novelist in his Greenwich Village flat Dreiser found his glib and boastful chatter intolerable and ordered him out of the house. But Wright's arrogant
behavior succeeded more often than it failed — at least for a time.
Luck seemed to be with him.

Publisher Thayer, more gullible than Dreiser, appraised

Wright at his own high estimate of himself. Because of the circulation jump brought about by Wright's scathing comments on Los Angeles, he saw Wright as the magazine's savior. Thayer himself had accumulated a fortune by his muckraking of high finance. Now, he calculated, was the profitable moment to dramatically revise American magazine policies. Sensationalism was always a safe bet. The more he listened to Wright the more persuaded he was and within two months Wright had not only jockeyed himself into the editor's chair at *The Smart Set* but had also been promised an absolutely free hand. Nathan and Mencken had refused the top post more than once, partially because they foresaw Thayer's constant interference. But Wright, convinced by his will-to-power complex that he had mastered his master, had no such misgivings. Wright took office as editor-in-chief in February 1913, with the demotion of Norman Boyer.

In his first issue, he outlined his objectives on the page usually occupied by Thayer.

> I believe that this is a day of enlightenment on the part of magazine readers. Men and women have grown tired of effeminacy and the falsities of current fiction, essays and poetry. A widespread critical awakening has come, and with it a demand for better literary material. The demand for pious uplift, for stultification, and for the fictional avoidance of the facts of life has diminished. The reader of today demands the truth.

He continued by voicing his opinion that American writers would be capable of meeting European writers on an equal footing if they only had an outlet. That outlet he proposed to establish. With these sentiments — if not with their sententious tone — Nathan and Mencken concurred, and they welcomed the ascendancy of Wright.

For some time the two critics had been collaborating on the fashioning of a mouthpiece for their ex-cathedra views on art, literature, love, marriage, and politics in a column they introduced into *The Smart Set* pages. "Major Owen Hatteras" was the pseudonym they had concocted for this purpose. Hatteras was a suspiciously outspoken military gentleman and the bizarre opinions he set down would have shocked his fellow officers. Though he was transparently an invention of the magazine's book and theatre critics, with his accent on "the civilized minority," many *Smart Set* readers believed he was an actual person and entered into correspondence with him. The more he indulged in the game of startling the bourgoisie the more his mail mounted. The critics hoped that he would become a national byword like Finley Peter Dunne's imaginary Chicago saloon-keep, Mr. Dooley. The reported remarks of "Mr. Dooley" on national affairs delighted millions of Americans and his cracker-barrel philosophizing was even praised by Henry James. "Major Hatteras" had a long life before him, but he never attained as wide a recognition. His creators invited Wright to join them in expanding Hatteras and the Wright-Nathan-Mencken trinity was formed.

To celebrate Wright's rise to command at *The Smart Set*, Mencken invited his triumphant disciple and Nathan to spend a weekend in Baltimore. He was proud of the *Gemütlichkeit* of his provincial hometown — so much more civilized, he felt, than noisy New York, where a throbbing *Totentanz* seemed perpetually in progress — and he wanted his worldly guests to sample its sane ways and mellow charm.

He booked them into Baltimore's best hotel and escorted them to Cator's second-hand bookstore, from which he had been stocking his library since boyhood. He took them to his favorite restaurant — the Rennet Cellar — to dine on the house speciality, baby turkey smothered in oyster sauce, and was elated when they called for second helpings. On the stroke of eight he marched them into the back room of Hildebrandt's music shop where a group of amateur musicians — most of them medical men or journalists by profession — foregathered on Saturday evenings to play Beethoven, Brahms, Schubert, and Haydn, with Mencken presiding at the piano, and to engage in gargantuan beer-drinking during the concert's intervals.

In general all went well, but there were a few trying moments. Wright gave a display of bad manners by bawling out a waiter at the Rennet, and Nathan's *savoir-faire* was ruffled when a boorish member of the Saturday Night Club cornered him to make whispered inquiries about the affairs of Broadway actresses. The evening concluded with a round of the Baltimore bars which was abruptly interrupted by the midnight liquor curfew. The visitors muttered that such nonsense would not be tolerated in New York and grumblingly retired to their hotel.

Nathan told Wright of the magazine that he and Mencken had long hoped to inaugurate: a review of the arts filled with fearless comment and brilliant writing, a periodical designed to the diversion of "the happy few" which would make no concession to mob opinion. Its prototype was *The Blue Review*, a wish-dream described by H. G. Wells in his novel *The New Machiavelli*. Wright, intrigued, declared that he would transform *The Smart Set* into *The Blue Review*.

Wright—as Mencken had correctly prophesied—caused a sensational stir. The magazine was subjected to a violent and stimulating shake-up that brought it eager new readers—it became a favorite on the college campuses—and made its publisher tremble for its safety from the censors.

Prior to his take-over Wright had done much reconnaissance work and spread his lines of communication far and wide. He obtained stories and plays from the continental avant-garde: D'Annunzio, Schnitzler, Wedekind, Strindberg, Andreyev, Artzibahsev, and Brieux. As a preliminary move he had enlisted Ezra Pound, the Iowa-born poet who resided in London, to scout for him in the British Isles. Pound sent him reams of his own experimental verse and contributions by Robert Bridges, W. B. Yeats, George Moore, D. H. Lawrence, Frank Harris, Max Beerbohm, and W. L. George, as well as Joseph Conrad's one-act play, *One More Day*.

But Wright had no intention of making his magazine solely a depository for famous foreign names. Nor did he want to transform it into a platform for his personal opinions, a habit of independent editors. He threw open its pages to aspiring American writers of all sorts, many of whom were struggling for a hearing.

Barry Benefield submitted a story, "Daughters of Joy," accompanying it with the information that it had been rejected everywhere. "It couldn't have a better recommendation," replied Wright who published it immediately, though its "moral tone" worried Thayer. George Bronson Howard, the playwright, sent in his novelette *The Parasite*, a graphic exposé of Broadway mores in which his fellow dramatist, Wilson Mizner, was savagely caricatured. Howard and Mizner had been rivals for the same lady in the Klondike during the 1898 gold rush. Howard had married the disputed beauty, but he had never forgiven Mizner. Other editors, aware that *The Parasite* was an act of revenge, foresaw a libel suit and refused it. Wright was a sounder judge. He knew that Mizner's contempt was deeper than his resentment and that the witty playboy would smile the attack away — as he did.

Albert Payson Terhune, afterward renowned for his dog stories, was another Wright protégé, obliging with a collection of racy anecdotes about the metropolitan *demimonde*, recounted by his central character, the smooth-talking, know-it-all Raegan. The Raegan revelations delighted readers. John Reed, later to record his witnessing of the Russian Revolution in *Ten Days that Shook the World*, was then a free-lancing, radical journalist, fresh out of Harvard and living in Greenwich Village. Reed found time, between marching in protest parades and agitating for strikes, to try his hand at fiction and Wright purchased and published several of these attempts.

Another eccentric regular was the mysterious Moslem, Achemd Abdullah. He boasted a Russian mother, an Afghan general for a father, an Oxford education, and service in both the British colonial army and the Turkish cavalry. He wrote imitation de Maupassant and tall tales of the African jungle and the fabled Orient for *The Smart Set*. Nathan suspected that Abdullah had never been East of Staten Island, but was amused by his exotic mythomania.

Wright also attracted a number of American poets. Some had been inspired by the European imagists and symbolists and others — like the expatriate Pound — were trying to fashion forms of their own. Their work was utterly incomprehensible to the mass-circulation magazine editors, but Wright lent them a welcome ear, publishing the verse of Sara Teasdale, Harriet Monroe (who had founded the monthly, *Poetry*, printed in Chicago and the official organ of the movement), Joyce Kilmer (who wrote "Trees" and who was to die prematurely in an army training camp in 1917), Louis Untermeyer, Lizette Woodworth Reese (a native of Baltimore and a Mencken favorite), and Edgar Lee Masters (whose grim American-Gothic view of small-town tragedies, *Spoon River Anthology*, ventured into realistic lyricism). In addition, the magazine now printed light, humorous verse. Wright's editing was at once a demonstration of his catholic taste and his knack for showmanship. He succeeded in surprising his readers with every issue.

He soon had a surprise of another nature for his two colleagues. One afternoon he invited Nathan and Mencken to cocktails at his Lexington Avenue apartment. There he broke the startling news of his latest coup. He had convinced Thayer — in the interests of *The Smart Set* — to finance a trip abroad for the three of them. Their duties would be to meet authors, hunt for material, and write about the gaiety of foreign capitals for the magazine. Their articles on Europe's lighter side might later be incorporated into a guide book for the civilized tourist.

His guests were amazed with this unexpected proposal and accepted at once. Each mapped out a different schedule for the expedition. Wright would be obliged to spend time with Thayer who would be easing his liver and nerves at some dull spa. Mencken wanted to visit Italy and tour Germany with a Baltimore newspaper colleague as his companion, while Nathan would make his annual spring inspection of the European theatres and then recuperate with a relaxing stay in Freudenstadt in the tranquil heart of the Black Forest. Their various wanderings would conclude with a reunion in Paris, it was decided.

Nathan was the most travelled of the three. An indefatigable globe-trotter, he had been almost everywhere. He had made it his habit to spend two or three months each year in Europe, usually in the late spring and early summer as the New York theatre season at that time began in late July and its opening summoned him home.

Not only did he know Europe well, but he had visited North Africa, South Africa, Egypt, the capitals of the Near East, the Orient, and South America. One year he travelled through Greece and Turkey with his brother, Fritz. Another spring he took in Scandinavia and another he went to Russia. His excursion into Russia was especially fruitful and he became one of the first American critics to write of the Moscow Art Theater and the rise of three extraordinary Russian directors who were to alter theatrical presentation the world over: the playwright-philosopher-producer, Nicholai Evreinoff, who conducted The Crooked Mirror cabaret in St. Petersburg; the brilliant Vsevolod Meyerhold, who began as an actor in Stanislavsky's company and who was revolutionizing the native stage in the Imperial theatres; and Alexander Tairov, who had just opened his Kamerny Theater in Moscow where he was staging plays of a high intellectual order and employing cubist decor. Later, under Soviet rule, Tairov was to introduce the work of O'Neill to Russian audiences.

"I am not a travelogue," Nathan once remarked when someone inquired about a trip he had made to Egypt, but in his books he reprinted notes on his travels which had first appeared in *The Smart Set*. In a humorous essay on memories of far-off places that are apt to linger, he exclaimed, "What yokel souls, after all, the most of us have," and then documented his claim.

> Take me, for example, I have travelled and lived the world over since boyhood and what of all the grandeur and beauty of foreign lands remains most persistently (and honestly) in my mind? That the shoeshines in Berlin are the glossiest I have ever seen; that a sharp pebble got into my shoe while I was looking at the Sphinx and cut my foot; that I lost my hat in Shanghai and couldn't get another to fit me; that I fell off a tally-ho on the way to the Derby and bruised my knee; that I kissed a French girl in the tunnel near Paris on the way from Calais and got my face slapped; that I was arrested in Florence for trying to steal a small tombstone from a graveyard; that I once discovered an excellent glass of Culmbacher in Constantinople; that the worst stomach-ache I ever had was during a stay in the Engadine...; that a girl in Tokyo took me for a Japanese; that the worst whiskey I ever drank was some I got in Edinburgh...; that I had a devil of a time getting a tooth pulled in Tunis...

Recollections of a more wistful tenor are recorded in a brief backward glance he entitled "There Lies Glamor; There Lay Romance":

> The Malecon at two o'clock of a late spring morning with its tiera of amber lights, the harbor of Havana playing a soft lullaby, against the sea-wall, and Morro Castle blinking like a patient owl across the waters; the garden of the Hôtel de France et Angleterre at Fontainebleau in the twilight, with the cannons of the French artillery in the late summer maneuvers echoing dully in the outlying forest; Hampton Court on a lazy afternoon in the late autumn of the year, deserted, still, with the leaves falling across the withered flower-beds and, up from the Thames, the sound of a lonely paddle; midwinter dawn in the Siegesalle of Berlin; the steps of the Tcheragan Serai in Constantinople on a moonlit night trembling in the mirror of the Bosporus; the palm-bordered road out of Hamilton, Bermuda, on a rainy day in May, with the sea dripping from the great leaves; the hurricane deck of a ship gliding noiselessly through the blue, star-shot cyclorama of a Caribbean night, with the intermittent click of poker chips from the smoking-room and the orchestra below playing the waltz from "Sari"; the Kartner Ring of Vienna just after eleven of a November evening, with its elaborately costumed police, and the hackmen bawling for fares, and the young girls selling Kaiserblumen, and the crowds in dominoes of a dozen colors on their way to the flower ball, and cavalrymen kissing their sweethearts in the middle of the street, the path of pines that winds up the hill on the far side of Lake Mogegan, its carpet of moss still damp from the retreat of April, an hour from Times Square....

Nathan could tickle the wanderlust fancy with his descriptions of the faraway. In later years, he elected the Berlin of Kaiser Wilhelm's reign and Havana as his preferred cities. For *The Smart Set* guide to European pleasures he chose to write on Berlin and Paris. His chronicle of Parisian joys, filled with youthful romanticism, atmospheric flair, and affectionate recollections, took for its swelling theme the gross Americanization of the City of Light (this in 1913):

"True, alas, it is, that gone is the Paris of Paris' glory — gone that Paris that called to Louise with its luring melody of a zithered soul," he wrote. The *Moulin de la Galette* and the *Bal Bullier* are but capons of their former selves, he complains. The revue theatres have been Broadwayized and tea-rooms operated by American old maids have poked their noses into the Left Bank avenues. *The Saturday Evening Post* is on sale at corner kiosks, ice cream has been installed at the *Brasserie Zimmer*, the gypsy orchestra at Maxim's is composed of Germans, and its toy balloons are made by the Elite Novelty Co. of New Jersey, U.S.A.

But these sad tidings are counter-balanced by a lyric admiration for the true Paris, the Paris of the Parisians. Nathan in a dream mood sings of its succulent cuisine, its romance and wit, its lovely girls, and the beauty of its scenery.

After his holiday near Freudenstadt, limbered up by walks in the Black Forest and his lungs refreshed by unpolluted air, Nathan headed for Paris to keep his appointment with Mencken and Wright. They gathered in a tiny flat near the Opéra that Wright was renting. He had rented a grand piano which took up most of the miniature drawingroom and the three spent an evening in cramped quarters, talking, drinking, singing, and taking turns at the keyboard. For *The Smart Set* guide Mencken had written the foreword and Munich, and Wright had covered London and Vienna. As usual, however, Wright had overdone his accounts so that they were more suited for *The Police Gazette*, and Mencken was obliged to edit the material, rewriting the beginning and end of the London piece and toning down the malicious innuendos with which the incorrigible Wright had spiced his inside information on Viennese nightlife. The articles duly appeared in the magazine and later — with illustrations by Thomas H. Benton — in book form as *Europe After 8:15*. Unfortunately, the book was published in August 1914, an unnecessary, out-of-date Baedeker. In the 1920s, however, it fetched a high price as a literary curiosity and a souvenir of a vanished civilization.

During the conferences in Paris Wright moaned and groaned about the ghastly session he had been forced to put in at Carlsbad with Thayer. Not only was the regime of mudbaths-by-day and dinner jackets-by-night extremely trying for an uninhibited bohemian, but the publisher had shown an increasing distrust of Wright's editorial conduct. After a depressing evening of listening to these complaints Nathan remarked to Mencken that Wright's days on *The Smart Set* were obviously drawing to a close.

Shortly after the trio returned to New York relations between the publisher and his editor grew more tense. Thayer's club cronies and some of his advertisers objected to the trend the magazine had taken. Its verse, they argued, was incomprehensible, its stories often bordered on the obscene and its opinions and general attitude ran contrary to the prevailing American idealism. The outspoken "Major Hatteras" had been muted, but even so the periodical was running off in the wrong direction. Nor were the club millionaires and the conventional businessmen alone in noticing the startling change. Nathan felt that Wright was "mussing up the magazine with pornographic stuff" and Mencken warned the reckless editor to "tone things down — at least for the present." "Don't be foolhardy!" he cautioned. But Wright was deaf to the advice of his perturbed colleagues, who endorsed his anti-Puritan stand but shook their heads over his headstrong measures. With firm faith in his "carte blanche" contract, he accelerated his tactics and succeeded in offending and frightening his publisher almost daily.

Thayer had had enough and secretly decided that Wright must go. But how could he rid himself of this egomanical bully without an ugly scandal? If he dismissed him, a long and expensive legal battle would ensue and, worse, Mencken and Nathan might resign in protest.

When he put the question to Nathan the critic was so evasive that Thayer, impatient, boarded the night train for Baltimore to hold a forced conference with Mencken who was ultimately responsible for the hiring of Wright. He rousted Mencken out of bed at first light, enumerated his problems with Wright, and demanded to know if Mencken and Nathan would stay on if he simply fired Wright.

"I am no breaker of contracts," replied Mencken, hinting that Wright's contract had still several months to run. "No, I won't resign and I am certain that George won't."

Reassured, Thayer hurried back to New York on the noon express to await Wright's next move. He did not have long to wait.

Wright was eager to launch Nathan's dream project, *The Blue Review*. Now was the moment to spring it on Thayer, who had once expressed vague interest in it. Without consulting the publisher, Wright prepared a dummy issue and sent it to the printers. When the dummy—and the printers' bill—reached Thayer's desk, Wright found that he had played his last card. The infuriated Thayer accused him of embezzlement—though the printing bill was only $50—and ordered him to quit the premises within twenty-four hours.

Suits and counter-suits were threatened, but at last Wright was prevailed upon to accept a cash settlement for the remaining months of his contract. Following Thayer's early morning visit to Baltimore, Mencken wrote to Wright (who suspected that his mentor had betrayed him) saying that the situation was obviously hopeless and there was no further reason to have a row every month. Mencken, with his usual generosity, apologized for letting his protégé in for the terrible year and at once found him other employment. Franklin Adams (who wrote a literary column under the byline F.P.A.) was leaving *The Evening Mail* for *The New York Tribune*. On Mencken's recommendation Wright was engaged to replace Adams and remained in that post until a wartime scandal deposed him.

PART FOUR

1914 dawned gloomily at *The Smart Set*. With Wright gone, the magazine, in Mencken's opinion, had become as "righteous as a decrepit and converted madam." In the March issue Thayer sounded a dismal call for retreat. His editorial began by quoting the high praise that *The Boston Transcript* had bestowed for the policy his magazine was about to abolish.

"During the past year *The Smart Set* has been gathering laurels unto itself as a unique magazine for those who desire to keep abreast or ahead of modern literary currents," had commented the upscale periodical. "Gathering laurels is one thing; publishing a successful magazine is another," Thayer replied in his announcement, going on to apologize for past transgressions and assuring readers who had been offended by the frankness and somber tone of certain stories that they would now have a good round measure of romantic and humorous relief.

Nathan and Mencken were thoroughly disgusted by Thayer's public apology and they were disturbed by his avowed determination to surrender, followed by his placing the editorial reins in the helpless hands of Martin Lee Luther, a man of few ideas and dubious judgment. In fact, Thayer had become Editor himself. The two worried critics conferred and agreed to sever their connections with the magazine when their contracts came up for renewal in the autumn.

Through the deceptively tranquil spring and early summer of 1914 *The Smart Set* jogged along at a listless trot, unable to recapture the prudish readers frightened away by Wright's bombshells and steadily losing the sophisticated subscribers who now found the monthly indistinguishable from the other popular entertainment periodicals and even less lively. Major Hatteras, with his caustic reflections on the passing vogues, was retired and only in the book and theatre pages was there anything of the former impudence and sparkle.

Nathan, pondering future outlets for his writing, sailed for Europe and was on the Continent when war was declared. Though the popular prediction was that the war could not possibly last more than six weeks, travel bureaus were besieged by tourists anxious to get home at any price. After considerable delay, Nathan secured passage on an overcrowded liner and arrived in New York to find *The Smart Set* office in a state of panic. Thayer had been playing the stock market and suffered heavy losses when the war news caused a sudden plunge on Wall Street, while the magazine, damaged by failing advertising and circulation, was hopelessly in debt.

Beset on all sides, Thayer met with Colonel Eugene R. Crowe of the Perkins-Goodwin Company, supplier of the magazine's paper and its outstanding creditor, offering Crowe receivership of *The Smart Set* in exchange for a release of the $6,000 owed and for Crowe's taking on the magazine's other obligations.

Crowe had recently formed a partnership with a resourceful publisher, Eltinge Warner, who soon after graduating from Princeton, had taken over the dead-weight monthly, *Field and Stream*, and transformed the hunting-shooting-fishing publication into a bestseller. "What you need is an editor," Warner advised. As he scanned the list of contributors, he added, "I think I've got the man for you."

The previous summer Warner, returning from a European holiday, had sailed aboard the new liner *Imperator.* One windy afternoon Warner, taking a constitutional on the promenade deck, passed a fellow passenger in a smart topcoat that exactly matched his own. The two strollers stopped in their tracks, eyed each other, and smiled. The traveler in the topcoat was George Jean Nathan. Over introductory drinks in the bar it was discovered that he and Warner had the same London tailor who had told them the same lie, assuring both his American clients that he had created the latest thing in sea-going apparel for their exclusive use. Warner invited Nathan to dine with him and his wife that evening and the publisher and Mrs. Warner were charmed by the bright young critic, finding him an ideal shipboard companion. Nathan had blandly mentioned his connection with *The Smart Set*, but Warner had never seen a copy of the magazine until its management was dumped into his lap.

After his chat with Crowe, Warner hurried to the Royalton to offer Nathan the editorship of *The Smart Set*. The critic had received this invitation more than once before. He had always declined it, but now he reconsidered the proposition. The tiresome Thayer was at last out of the way and his observation of the mistakes made by former editors might guide him. Still, he was wary of shouldering the responsibility alone.

"Very well, I'll give it a try, but only if Mencken comes in with me," he stipulated.

"Who in hell is Mencken?" the puzzled Warner inquired.

"You'll find out," promised Nathan.

Mencken favored the dual editorship, but he had stipulations of his own. Under no condition would he abandon Baltimore to move to New York. He had earlier refused an offer to join the staff of *The New York Times* because it would necessitate just such a move. He could, he explained, read and report on manuscripts in his Hollins Street home and then come to town for a few days each month to confer with Nathan, who would be in command of the office.

Colonel Crowe was bewildered by these unorthodox suggestions. Two editors and one of them in absentia most of the time? It sounded, on the face of it, like a deliberate attempt to court acrimonious disputes, hopeless confusion, and financial ruin. However, he invited them to weekend with him at his New Jersey country club and they managed to win him over to their point of view. It was decided that Warner would assume the magazine's business side, overseeing circulation, advertising, and bookkeeping. Nathan and Mencken would have absolute editorial power.

Their system of dual editorship was as simple as it was unprecedented. Nathan would give all incoming manuscripts an initial inspection, weeding out those he found unfit and returning them to their authors. Although he had many prejudices, most of them were shared by his colleague. Contributions that survived his first glance were mailed by express post to Baltimore where Mencken went through them, sending back his selection for Nathan's final verdict. Every manuscript needed, therefore, the approval of both editors, while a single "no" was sufficient for a rejection. The October 1914 issue inaugurated the Nathan-Mencken regime, which was to continue for the next ten years.

Warner reduced the magazine's overhead to a minimum. All members of the former staff were dismissed and the office was moved from the spacious, luxurious quarters in the Knox building to cramped rooms renting for $35 a month. The co-editors' only assistant was a hard-working, resourceful stenographer, Miss Sada Golde, who quickly adapted herself to the vagaries of her employers.

In the first issue under their leadership the dual editors assured the readers that *The Smart Set* would contain "nothing to 'improve' your mind, but plenty to tickle you." Under the masthead they printed the proclamation that "one civilized reader was worth a thousand boneheads." A house ad promised the return of the outspoken Colonel Hatteras, a monthly exhibition of national absurdities, and forthcoming novelettes by both editors. Among the contents of the inaugural issue were stories by Alexis Tolstoy, Albert Payson Terhune, the French playwright Eugène Brieux, and Edna St. Vincent Millay, just graduated from Vassar.

While the energic Warner set out to restore the magazine to financial stability, stalking advertising contracts and settling old debts, the two editors alerted friendly rivals — William Marion Reedy, who had published Edgar Lee Masters, Carl Sandburg, Sara Teasdale, Orrick Jones, Zoë Akins, and Fannie Hurst in his St. Louis *Mirror*; T. R. Smith of *The Century*; Ray Long of *The Red Book*; and Ellery Sedgwick of *The Atlantic Monthly* — that *The Smart Set* was on the hunt for young talents who might be deprived of other outlets. The word was obligingly passed along and the pile of incoming manuscripts grew. In his book column Mencken urged beginners to defy the puritanic traditions that held American literature in bondage, but he seemed to be howling in the wilderness. The brave new editors were often reduced to composing a large measure of the magazine's contents themselves under a repertory of aliases.

Their meager budget was a serious handicap, putting the work of the European authors they admired out of reach. Joseph Conrad, pleased by an accolade from Mencken, ordered his American representative to offer one of his stories to *The Smart Set* — for $600. Hearing the price, Mencken leaped from his desk and told the agent to inform Conrad that he could have *The Smart Set* for $600. Later Nathan purchased Conrad's one-act play, *One More Day*, for the magazine for a nominal sum.

James Joyce made his American debut in the magazine when Ernest Boyd, the Irish critic who had been British consul in Baltimore, sent the editors two stories from *Dubliners* which they bought and published. They wanted more Joyce, but as the publisher, Ben Huebsch, was to bring out the collection in book form, no more was available. Two years afterwards, Joyce, living out the war in Zurich, submitted his novel, *Portrait of the Artist as a Young Man*. They were greatly impressed, but it was too long to meet the magazine's requirements. Reluctant to let it go, they debated the possibility of using excerpts from it. Finally they decided that any editing would damage its balance and with grave regrets mailed it back to Zurich, imploring Joyce to let them see more of his work.

Another of their favorites was Lord Dunsany, the Irish nobleman who wrote plays for the Abbey Theater of Dublin and had published two volumes of Poe-esque fables in England. Although he was on active duty with the British army in France, when their communications reached him he posted them a batch of fantastic tales. They bought them all and he became a regular contributor to *The Smart Set*, exposure that founded his American vogue. Soon Dunsany plays were being performed from Greenwich Village to California and he was the preferred dramatist of the Little Theater movement. Even Diamond Jim Brady went down to Grand Street to see his *Gods of the Mountains* when the enterprising Neighborhood Playhouse gave it its premiere.

After the war, Dunsany visited the United States on a lecture tour and the editors invited him to lunch at Delmonico's. They were startled to meet a towering giant in a baggy fur coat who sported a monocle and appeared to be a hunting-shooting-fishing English country squire rather than an Irish poet. Their amazement mounted when he ordered three dozen oysters and proceeded to sprinkle them with sugar. But as the celebrated fantasist gulped down the enormous platter of bivalves he launched into a monologue that held them rapt. His thundering eloquence distracted them from his eccentric behavior and as he described his latest play they listened, fascinated.

Its title was *A Good Bargain*, an ironic retelling of the Faust legend. When his lordship finished, Nathan asked who was to publish the play. "Why, you two, I presume," said Dunsany, waving away protests that *The Smart Set* rates were too low. After lunch Dunsany expressed a desire to see something of the American theatre and Nathan took him to a matinée of Arthur Hopkins' production of Gorky's *Lower Depths*. After one act Dunsany announced that such art was not for him and asked to be taken to a burlesque show.

Frank Harris—whose pro-German sympathies and statements had forced him to quit London for New York when war was declared—also received an invitation to lunch with the editors at Delmonico's. They soon discovered that he was a compulsive monologist. He didn't stop talking from the time they sat down until late afternoon. He told them of his conversations with Thomas Carlyle in the great man's old age and of his hiring a yacht to whisk Oscar Wilde to France when Wilde was out on bail between trials. He also related gossip about Asquith and Churchill and assured Nathan and Mencken that the Germans would win the war. They found him an absorbing raconteur, surpassing even the loquacious Huneker. He consented to write for *The Smart Set* and sent them "How I Discovered Bernard Shaw" (Harris had engaged Shaw to write drama criticism for *The Saturday Review*, which Harris had edited in the 1890s) and gave them the chance to experience his infamous trickery. He had sold the same article to another magazine and the duplicate hit the newsstands on the same day.

In *The Smart Set*'s vault they struck gold, coming on a pile of manuscripts purchased by Wright and written by such eminent Europeans as George Moore, D. H. Lawrence, and Schnitzler.

These bolstered their early issues while they scouted for fresh material. Often, regretfully, they had to settle for what they could get — *The Smart Set* was a grab bag of the first-rate, the second-rate, and the trivial.

In the December 1914 issue they inserted an ad announcing arrangements for the magazine to publish the best new work of Theodore Dreiser, whom Arnold Bennett, Frank Harris, and William J. Locke esteemed as the greatest American novelist. "Mr. Dreiser is not a story-teller for the populace, though his audience is constantly widening," they reminded their readers. "He does not manufacture best-sellers. His appeal, like that of Joseph Conrad, is made to that smaller public which differentiates between genuine literature and empty poppycock. In brief, he addresses himself to the same audience that *The Smart Set* addresses." That issue contained Dreiser's initial experiment at play writing, *The Blue Sphere*, an arresting, original one-act. Thornton Wilder, then a schoolboy in New Hampshire, read it and later said that its technique and ideas inspired his plays *The Happy Journey* and *Pullman Car Hiawatha*.

Dreiser soon expressed his displeasure with the magazine, writing Mencken early in 1915 that he and Nathan seemed to have toned it down to a light, non-disturbing periodical of persiflage and badinage. It was as innocent as *The Ladies Home Journal*, he complained, and too debonair, too Broadway-esque, too full of "josh" and "kid" like a Forty-Second Street curb actor. Everything, apparently, was to be done with a light, aloof touch, which he likened to a soufflé diet. He wanted to feel the cool winds of an Odyssey, advising them to take a tip from Reedy's *Mirror* and *The Masses and International*, two radical periodicals of the day.

Mencken shot back a spirited defense. The light touch was precisely what Nathan and he were striving to maintain — consider the title of their magazine. True, they were frequently compelled to run flimsy novelettes as circulation teasers, but even these were no worse than the bulk of fiction appearing in popular publications with far larger budgets. They were not ideologically opposed to radicals, but few of them could write well. Some of the red-ink boys—Benjamin de Cassedes, Floyd Dell, John Reed, and the poet, Harry Kemp—occasionally did make the grade.

Meanwhile, *The Smart Set* had rid itself of its outstanding debts and was gathering an appreciative public. Nathan had procured a first-rate novelette from Avery Hopwood—whose comedy, *Fair and Warmer*, was a Broadway hit—and a mystery play spoof written by George M. Cohan. In the Cohan burlesque all the characters were disguised detectives trailing one another. But Dreiser remained grumpy and skeptical, sending in caustic comments on the magazine's contents along with the poetry he submitted. He was in the throes of creation and rarely ventured out of his 10th Street digs. There behind pulled shades and by flickering candlelight with his creaky Victrola spinning lugubrious Russian records he was laboring to finish a long novel. It was his habit to write at twelve to fourteen hours at a stretch until exhaustion overtook him. The novel in progress was *The 'Genius'* and its protagonist is an amoral artist (a partial self-portrait) whose over-powering sex drive and promiscuous affairs were described with an exacting realism that brought the censors down upon it in a cause célèbre.

The 'Genius' received a chilly notice from Mencken, who judged it the poorest of Dreiser's novels. He found its flaunting of Greenwich Village aestheticism, its kind words for Christian Science, and what he felt was Dreiser's pseudo-intellectualism intolerable. But some of the other reviews evidenced a moral, rather than literary, disapproval, now displayed under the guise of patriotism. *The Boston Transcript* complained that Dreiser's attitude was utterly pagan and that he seemed to have no thought of himself as a moral influence, while Mrs. Ella W. Peatrie in *The Chicago Tribune* headed her critiques: "Mr. Dreiser chooses a Tom Cat for a Hero" and blamed his German ancestry for his un-American prose epic. In *The Nation*, Stuart Pratt Sherman, a professor of English at the University of Illinois, opened a campaign to demolish Dreiser's "barbaric naturalism" as an affront to Anglo-Saxon gentility.

The 'Genius' sold relatively well in the face of these attacks, but some months later the axe of censorship fell, impoverishing Dreiser for the next decade. Comstock's New York Society for the Suppression of Vice had semi-official status, being chartered by the state to assure the enforcement of the anti-obscenity laws. Sumner, replacing Comstock, was in effect the state's representative. He had already succeeded in banning Horace's odes, *The Decameron*, and the unexpurgated translation of Dumas' *Three Musketeers*, Sumner went through *The 'Genius'*, marking seventy-five passages that he deemed "lewd" and warned its publishers, the John Lane Company, that the book must be immediately withdrawn or he would prosecute.

Dreiser, once more caught in the net of the philistines, howled for help. When first consulted by the worried novelist Mencken thought a few minor cuts in *The 'Genius'* would solve the problem and volunteered to make them himself. But when he examined Sumner's voluminous report — "drawn up with the terrible industry of a Sunday-school boy dredging for pearls of smut in the Old Testament" — he was outraged.

Together with the Welsh novelist, John Cowper Powys, Mencken drafted a protest for writers to sign and submitted it to the Authors' League of America, the officially recognized writers' organization. Although the League was a conservative organization which Dreiser and Mencken had refused to join, the diplomatically worded petition was not an appeal to aid Dreiser alone but to take stand against encroaching censorship.

Certain members of the League — Nicholas Murray Butler and Brander Matthews of Columbia, William Lyon Phelps of Yale, and the poet Joyce Kilmer — refused to be associated with Dreiser even indirectly, but the absence of their names was outweighed by the signatures of the likes of Robert Frost, Percy MacKaye, Ed Howe (whose Atchison, Kansas, monthly magazine had national circulation), Jack London, Amy Lowell, John Reed, Edwin Arlington Robinson, Rex Beach, Rachel Crothers, Max Eastman, Sherwood Anderson, Edgar Lee Masters, David Belasco, Sinclair Lewis, and George Jean Nathan. Eminent British writers — H. G. Wells, Arnold Bennett, and Hugh Walpole — lent their strong support, esteeming Dreiser as America's foremost novelist.

The protest, bearing the names of five hundred highly-respected authors, created much discussion in the press, but the case was lost in a legal muddle and *The 'Genius'* went out of print since its publishers were reluctant to wage an expensive battle to appeal its suppression. Dreiser rescued the plates from the printers, but it wasn't until 1923 that *The 'Genius'* was republished by Horace Liveright in unexpurgated form.

In 1923 Sumner was on another rampage, trying to jail Earl Carroll, the producer of the "Vanities" revues, for displaying photographs of lightly clad chorus girls in the lobby of his theatre. A year later he tried — and failed — to close down Eugene O'Neill's play, *Desire Under the Elms*. He brought the books of André Gide, Arthur Schnitzler, James Branch Cabell, James Joyce and James T. Farrell into the courts on charges of immorality and often obtained verdicts against them. As late as 1946 he secured the banning of Edmund Wilson's novel, *Memoirs of Hecate County*, in his final attack on literature. He survived to the age of ninety-four to witness the collapse of his moral "code" with the breakthrough of the permissive age in the 1960s.

Nathan and Mencken, realizing that any charge by Sumner would bankrupt their magazine, cautiously side-stepped open conflict with him. When Huneker proposed that his novel, *Painted Veils*, about the disorderly private lives of opera divas and Manhattan's artistic bohemia, be published in serial form, they wondered if he had turned practical joker or lost his sense of humor. They thought it superb entertainment, the thing that most revealingly reflected Huneker's Rabelaisian gusto. But it was not merely improper; it was a riot of obscene wit and positively unprintable. "If we ran it, we'd be lucky to get off with forty years in the clink," they told him.

Curiously enough, the most successful novelty of *The Smart Set* was an omission. Between 1914 and 1918 it never printed a single line about the war. Even the work of special favorites had to be rejected to maintain this standard. "'Dusk in War-time' is very tempting," they assured Sara Teasdale, a regular contributor, "but we have made a strict rule."

Soon after the declaration of the European war the United States made known its refusal to become involved. On August 19,

1914, President Wilson issued the following proclamation: "My fellow countrymen: I take the liberty of addressing a few words to you...to urge very earnestly upon you that we must be impartial in thought as well as in action. The United States must be neutral in fact as well as in name." The other principal figure in public life, ex-President Theodore Roosevelt, wrote: "We should remain entirely neutral and nothing but urgent need would warrant breaking our neutrality and taking sides one way or the other." Both the Kaiser and the emissaries of the Belgian king received the same reply when seeking to justify their respective conduct. The President was honored that they should turn to him as "representative of a people truly disinterested," but it would be understood that he could say no more.

Wilson and the American people were to reject this isolationism as the barbaric fury of the war mounted. Richard Harding Davis' graphic reports of the invasion of Belgium struck the initial blow at American indifference and the bombardment of pro-Allied propaganda could not be withstood for long. Probably the deed that made the entry of the US into the War inevitable was the sinking of the *Lusitania* in May 1915. Theodore Roosevelt, executing an abrupt about-face, declared: "It is now inconceivable that we should refrain from action. We owe it not only to humanity but to our national self-respect."

The American press, including the major newspapers of the Eastern seaboard, fell in line. "What a pity that Theodore Roosevelt is not president!" exclaimed *The New York Herald*, James Gordon Bennett's mouthpiece, in huge type. Those urging aid to the embattled motherland were contempuous of Wilson's tepid response to the German submarine domination of the Atlantic. In an impatiently awaited address the President failed to mention either the *Lusitania* or Germany and stated sententiously that there was such a thing as being "too proud to fight."

In such turbulent times impartial thoughts were out of season. *The Smart Set* remained unruffled by mob emotions, but its neutrality did not extend to its editors, both of whom, in varying degrees, were sympathetic to Germany.

Mencken was staunchly pro-German. He made no mention of this in the magazine, but in his "Free Lance" column for *The Baltimore Sun* he declared war on the Allied powers. He sneered at the "pious, beery slobber" about the invasion of Belgium and in 1915 predicted that a German victory was imminent.

The English were his constant target. The Germans had boldly accepted the British challenge, he wrote, and the sinking of the *Lusitania* was the opening of an offensive that would squeeze an iron ring about John Bull's neck so tightly that he would gasp for breath and beg for mercy. Recalling all the crimes of British imperialism, he jeered at the sniveling Britons, running to the Pope to stop a war they were losing. British propaganda agents were swarming everywhere, sounding the buglecall for the defense of the Union Jack, with such hypocritical slogans as "We don't want your money; we don't want your men; all we want is your moral support."

Mencken may have been within his constitutional rights in expressing his opinions, but his truculently expressed views ran counter to the country's thinking and made few converts. The nation was split on the war issue, but public sentiment was anti-war, not anti-British. It was certainly never — save in segments of the German-American communities — pro-German.

Not even as strenuous pamphleteer as Mencken could buck the tide of the times for long. *The Baltimore Sun* proprietors found it increasingly embarrassing to have their "right-thinking" editorials and their support of Wilson contradicted and rudely ridiculed by the infidel "Free Lance," while indignant readers wrote in accusing the columnist of being in the pay of the Wilhelmstrasse. Mencken, having no taste for martyrdom, ceased fire. "I do not believe that mutiny on the quarter-deck would be tolerated," he explained in discontinuing his bellicose dissent. His column disappeared for the duration. However, after the war Mencken again voiced his unaltered views and remarked that a German victory would have secured peace on the continent for a century. In gratitude the ex-Kaiser, exiled to Holland sent greetings, an autographed photograph, and an invitation to come and visit him.

The Baltimore Sun overlords didn't quite know what to do with Mencken after the suspension of his column. Though his views were unpopular, he was a star journalist. Why not send him to Germany as a war correspondent and inform readers that it was only fair to report on both sides of the conflict?

Mencken jumped happily at this bait. During the pre-Christmas shopping rush he stocked up on winter underwear, thick mufflers, and woolly sweaters. In late December 1916, he invited Nathan and Dreiser to a farewell banquet at Luchow's and, under the cloak of a waterfront blackout, boarded a Danish liner, the *Oscar II.* It was a rough voyage as the ship dodged U-boats and the British North Sea patrol.

Once in Berlin he spent a few days listening to the American press corps and officials of the imperial war office. He was then dispatched to cover the battlefront in Lithuania. Attached to the Wehramacht headquarters there, he took his meals with the officers of the command who explained the military situation. All was relatively quiet on this eastern-front post as the Russians, their armies already threatening mutiny, were reluctant to attack. When he heard a rumor that diplomatic relations between Germany and the United States would soon terminate, Mencken, realizing that a war declaration was imminent and haunted by visions of being interned as an enemy alien, hurried back to Berlin. United States Ambassador James Gerard — whose book of memoirs, *My Four Years in Germany*, was to convert hundreds of thousands of Americans to the Allied cause — was preparing to depart.

Through the intervention of Gen. Ludendorff's aides Mencken was accorded red-carpet treatment as an influential spokesman of the Kaiser's cause. Foreign correspondents fresh from the front were obliged to remain in Germany for several weeks before being granted an exit visa, a precaution against leakage of military plans. In Mencken's case this rule was waived. Not only was he permitted to leave the country at once, but a place was reserved for him in the express train carrying the American ambassador and his staff to Switzerland.

From Zurich Mencken made for Madrid, where he obtained

passage aboard a Spanish ship sailing the southern route to Cuba. During the crossing his editors wired him orders to make a stopover in Havana and report on a revolution brewing there. Mencken found that the threatening revolt was of the customary Latin-American variety, the rascals out trying to oust the rascals in. Strict censorship prevailed, but Mencken, always a resourceful reporter, passed his copy to American tourists bound for Florida. His dispatches were telegraphed to *The Baltimore Sun* and *The New York World* from Miami and made the front pages before he returned to the US. He arrived back in Baltimore in early March, a month before Wilson declared war on Germany. This hurried tour abroad had been a stimulating experience, but it was now injudicious to publish his reports on the German side of the conflict.

Nathan's attitude to the Great War was quite different. To him it was a disaster comparable to an earthquake. To object to it was akin to objecting to a raging tornado and he saw pacificists as futilitarians crying out against the storm. War had always been the sport of men and always would be. Those who promised deliverance from mankind's incurable stupidity were either fools or frauds. Reading daily of the mad destruction, of the famine and epidemics it brought in its wake, of crumbling empires and threatening revolutions, he tempered his regret over the disappearance of so much of the world's loveliness with a philosophical resignation.

Mencken's high-spirited tales of his tour of war-torn Europe pointed up the gulf between himself and his best friend. Nothing would have persuaded Nathan to undertake an inspection of battlefields or to wax indignant over the policies of the English or of the French — or of the Germans. He believed, with Burke, that it is impossible to indict any nation.

His own ties to Germany were solely cultural. He relished holiday travel in Germany and Austria and had close friends there as he had in France and England. He cherished the pre-1914 Berlin and erroneously credited the Kaiser for the creation of a capital where new music and drama flourished. Actually, the German emperor loathed and distrusted the very artists Nathan admired. The Kaiser was, in fact, a very symbol of the tyrannical philistine. Gerhardt Hauptmann, whom Nathan considered the foremost living dramatist, was, in the Kaiser's opinion, a dangerous trouble-maker of socialistic tinge and an embryonic traitor. The Imperial Polizei kept watch on the literary cabarets — the cradle of Wedekind, Bierbaum, and later Brecht — and on the satirical comic magazines which Nathan so enjoyed. The Kaiser and his court strongly disapproved of Max Reinhardt and his theatre with its new-fangled treatment of German classics and performances of all the rebellious playwrights of Europe.

Shortly after President Wilson declared war on Germany in April 1917, Congress passed a conscription bill and all men under thirty-five were obliged to register for the draft. This included Nathan, who was thirty-four, and he dutifully obeyed the new law to the jeers of Mencken, who, being thirty-six, was exempt. Over their double desk in *The Smart Set* office Mencken greeted his colleague with smart salutes, and advised him to practice the goose-step in his spare time.

Nathan, with his university degree, considered enrolling for officer training, but when examined by the army medical board for induction it was discovered that his eyesight was too poor for military service and he was permanently disqualified. Later the draft age was extended, and Mencken, an able-bodied bachelor, was placed on call. He was about to depart for a Maryland rookie camp when the armistice rescued him from making the world safe for democracy. In fact, the threat of conscription was the least of the editors' worries, and they made no effort — unlike some other American authors — to avoid the draft.

Wilson had inaugurated a campaign to make the nation war-conscious. His draft bill, an unpopular measure, had passed with only a narrow margin. Despite the raucous calls for war, many citizens had apparently believed that the professional army alone would be sent to fight. "To bring the war home to the American people," the President inaugurated a propaganda bureau, the Committee on Public Information, and appointed George Creel, a "reformer" journalist from Denver, to head its operations.

Creel was an imaginative publicist. He created a motion picture studio for the manufacture of films glorifying General Pershing's forces and depicting, with gruesome realism, Hun atrocities. The Committee's leaflets were handed out by volunteers on street corners, and in art galleries there were photographic displays of the war in action.

With energy and enthusiasm Creel set about the vast and heavily financed task of enlisting the support of the United States. He enlisted a battalion of well-known authors—among them Booth Tarkington, Mary Roberts Rinehart, and Samuel Hopkins Adams—to write on American duties and the Allied cause. He pressed popular magazine illustrators such as Charles Dana Gibson, Howard Chandler Christie, and James Montgomery Flagg to draw recruiting posters, the best remembered of these being the "I Want You" poster on which Uncle Sam points a commanding finger. He called upon stage and screen stars—Mary Pickford, Douglas Fairbanks, Charlie Chaplin—to harangue the multitudes at rallies.

His Committee found 75,000 orators, most of them amateurs, to deliver short pep talks on subjects ranging from the passage of the conscription bill to the sale of Liberty bonds. These four-minute men spoke in schools, churches, movie parlors; at Rotary luncheons and labor union meetings.

Wartime laws against espionage and sedition passed in June 1917, prescribing penalties for speaking, printing, or otherwise expressing contempt for the government, the constitution, the flag, the uniform of the army or navy, using language calculated to aid the enemy cause, or saying or doing anything to discourage the sale of United States bonds. Under these provisions 15,000 persons were soon arrested for disloyal utterances. Objections to conscription were tromped on. William "Big Bill" Heyward of the Industrial Workers of the World—the IWW, jocularly referred to by vaudeville comedians as the "I Won't Work" movement—was sentenced to prison, as were the socialist leaders, Eugene V. Debs and Mrs. Rose Pastor Stokes. The navy warned of possible German invasion along the Atlantic seaboard and the propaganda movies showed such an invasion being followed by Prussian officers ordering mass executions, cutting off the hands of children, and raping beautiful blondes.

Civilians were told to inform the authorities of disloyal remarks and suspicious activities, an appeal to patriotic obligations that set millions to snooping on their neighbors. Rumors appeared as headlines in the newspapers. One of these, asserting that armed uprisings were being plotted in Milwaukee, St. Louis, Cincinnati, and other German-American centers, was thoroughly investigated. So, too, were ill-founded reports that German agents were poisoning city reservoirs, sabotaging productions at the munition factories, and spreading deadly germs in hospital wards.

German opera was banished from the stage of the New York Metropolitan Opera and German music was eliminated from concert programs. Fritz Kreisler, who as a youth had served an obligatory stretch in the Austrian army, was forbidden to play his violin in a New Jersey concert hall by order of the mayor. Dr. Karl Muck, nearly eighty, the veteran conductor of the Boston Symphony Orchestra, was arrested and interned as a dangerous enemy alien. Pretzels disappeared from the lunch counters in Cincinnati saloons and sauerkraut appeared as "liberty cabbage" on restaurant menus; dachshunds, experiencing sudden unpopularity (the Kaiser had been photographed on his yacht with three pets of the breed), were restored to respectability by being renamed "liberty pups."

Nathan and Mencken looked on the spectacle of American patriotism in full eruption with amused contempt, but refrained from commenting until the war was over and the defense-of-the-realm regulations had been abolished. An object lesson was to be found in the imprudent behavior of Nathan and Mencken's former editor, William Wright. Wright, then a columnist at *The Evening Mail*, discovered that his stenographer was spying on him. Her doubts about his loyalty had been fanned by his constant quotations from German authors and she was rifling his files and making carbon copies of his correspondence. Enraged, he at once set a trap to force a showdown. Summoning her to his desk, he dictated a letter filled with sinister innuendoes and mentioned a chat with the recalled German ambassador, Count von Bernstorff. No sooner had the stenographer transcribed his suspicious rambling to her pad than she leapt up and — evidence in hand — rushed out into the street to find the nearest policeman. Wright followed and they were both taken to a neighborhood station house. Wright succeeded in clearing himself during the subsequent questioning — his explanation of his self-protective experiment was accepted. But the story got out and cost him his job on *The Evening Mail*. And Wright's burlesque letter had been addressed to a Washington correspondent; he, too, was taken into custody and grilled by secret service agents.

Nathan and Mencken were appalled by Wright's rash action and severed relations with him. "I regard the whole affair as intolerably idiotic," wrote Mencken to a confidant. "To put such burdens on innocent friends in these crazy days is an unforgivable offense. A man so silly is a public menace."

Everyone, made jumpy by the national hysteria, was of Mencken's opinion and Wright, finding all doors closed to him, left New York to eke out a living doing hackwork for newspapers in the West. Depressed, he resorted to drugs and was soon in a hopeless state, only re-emerging on the literary scene in the mid-1920s. Desperate for money, Wright began to write detective fiction under the name S. S. Van Dine: *The Bishop Murder Case, The Canary Murder Case, The Green Murder Case*. The suave sleuth of Wright's detective novels, Philo Vance, was a well-barbered and well-tailored aristocrat-type who never resorted to false whiskers and was given to aesthetic discourses on Oriental art. (Vance was a sort of a glorified self-portrait, Wright as he wished the public to see him.) These detective novels became bestsellers and the sale of film rights made Wright quite wealthy.

The Creel bureau, beset with fear of treason among the literati, drew up a list of suspect authors. Both Nathan and Mencken were on this list, as their employer, Eltinge Warner, learned at a Washington conference for publishers. Warner, who was above even official reproach, was a supporter of Creel and a member of his Committee. Convinced of their non-subversiveness, he gravely promised to keep his dangerous editors under his personal surveillance and thus protected them from raids on their residences and other harassment.

The circulation of *The Smart Set* staggered, wobbled, and sank into an alarming decline. Increased postal rates, war taxes, and a paper shortage weighed so heavily on the publication that it appeared doomed. The drop in readership was attributed in part to its editors' stubborn refusal to mention the war, but they refused to budge from their stand. Better to go down with flying colors than to surrender to the decrees of the mob.

To obtain needed cash for *The Smart Set*, they proposed that Crowe and Warner finance a pulp magazine that would tickle and trick the boobs. It would exploit the present rage for all things French and it would be called *La Parisienne*. The title, a shrewd Nathan notion, would hint of lascivious Gallic pleasures and at a nonexistent alliance with the notoriously naughty *La Vie Parisienne*.

La Vie Parisienne had been founded by Marcelin (the pseudonym of writer-illustrator Emile Marcelin-Isadore Planet) during the Second Empire, taking its name from the famous Offenbach operetta. Such artists as Doré, Forain, and Toulouse-Lautrec, and such authors as Baudelaire and de Maupassant had been among its contributors. The war had infused it with new life. In war-ravaged France there was no dugout or château behind the lines that did not have pages from *La Vie* pasted on its walls. The delicately suggestive drawings of provocative damsels by Raphael Kirchner were favorite pin-ups of poilus, British Tommys, and American doughboys. Many members of the U.S. Expeditionary Forces signed up for lifetime subscriptions.

The American censors would never tolerate the smirking nudes and abandoned frivolity of *La Vie Parisienne*. What would the clergy have had to say about such devilry, especially when "our boys were dying for Christian principles in France"? *La Parisienne* would be a toned-down, bootleg version of its Parisian model, knowing how far to go before landing everyone connected with it in jail. It would fetch the boobs with suggestive promises; within its pages it would be, technically, "pure."

Many stories too trashy for *The Smart Set* were simply converted into fraudulent French fiction with the names of their characters Gallicized and their settings moved to France. Nathan took charge of this scene-shifting, giving their lowly dramatis personae titles; filling in the backgrounds with descriptions of high life in stately châteaux, in Paris, and on the Riviera; and generally bestowing the "French" touch expected by the clientele to which the periodical catered. Once, despite his vigilance, he was summoned by the Society for the Suppression of Vice to answer for some alleged immorality that had crept into a story. He blandly talked away the charge and was bothered no more.

La Parisienne was an immediate hit, bringing its creators a four thousand dollar profit on each issue. But editing it, rewriting its contents, and keeping it censor-proof were dreary tasks and once it was established as a newsstand favorite, the editors sold their shares in it to their delighted backers who placed its operations in less literary hands.

A year later they were struck by another get-rich-quick idea. Colonel Mann had appropriated the twin swirling "S"s, the trademark of *The Smart Set*, for his soft-core porno pulp, *Snappy Stories*. Nathan and Mencken issued another boob-catcher on similar lines, *Saucy Stories*, filled with leftover junk that had come to their desks. *Saucy Stories* was swiftly launched on little capital and before long its circulation had grown to 120,000 copies monthly. Again the editors found that running a cheap magazine was more exhausting than running a magazine of quality and Crowe and Warner bought up their holdings for $20,000.

The last of the Nathan-Mencken potboilers — they referred inelegantly to these lucrative publications as their "louse" magazines — came after the armistice. It was *The Black Mask*, which was exclusively devoted to detective fiction, a concept then startling novel and one that remains profitable to this day. *The Black Mask*, ancestor of *The Ellery Queen Magazine* and Alfred Hitchcock's monthlies, was their most prosperous venture in the pulp field. To even their surprise, its circulation swiftly skyrocketed to a quarter of a million and when, after it was firmly established, they sold their shares in it to Crowe, they received a sum in excess of $50,000. This released them permanently from bothersome hack labors and they cited it as proof of their theory that it was a simple matter to get rich quick in America. "No one ever went broke underestimating the public intelligence," quipped Mencken as he watched the suckers snap at bait. Even their old nemesis, Woodrow Wilson, was a *Black Mask* fan, they were confidentially informed.

Although pulp writers needed no guidance, contributors to *The Smart Set* were in a different class. A pamphlet was issued summarizing the objectives of the magazine and the Nathan-Mencken code:

> The aim of *The Smart Set*, in general, is to interest and amuse the more civilized and sophisticated sort of reader — the man or woman who has lived in large cities, and read good books, and seen good plays, and heard good music, and is tired of politicians, reformers and the newspapers. It is not what is known as a popular magazine: it hasn't a circulation of 1,000,000 a month, and it never will have. This fact frees it from the necessity to take a hand in the uplift, or to pretend that it is made sad by the sorrows of the world. It assumes that its typical reader, having a quarter in his pocket to spend on a magazine without either gaudy pictures in it or 'inspirational' rubbish, is quite satisfied with both the world and himself, and that even if he isn't, there are times when he doesn't want to worry over schemes of improvement. It is at such times that *The Smart Set* tries to reach him. It offers him, on a small scale, the kind of intelligent entertainment that such a play as Shaw's *Caesar and Cleopatra* offers him on a large scale, or Straus' *Der Rosenkavalier* on a still larger scale....
>
> Some authors seem to have a notion that *The Smart Set* wants only society stories. Nothing could be more ridiculous. The magazine addresses itself, not merely to what is called (by the newspapers) society people, but to all persons who are well-fed, educated, worldly-wise, and of good taste. Naturally enough, these persons are more interested in their own class than they are in the struggles and aspirations of garment workers, pickpockets, Pullman porters, pothouse politicians and missionaries to the heathen, and so the people of stories are usually well-fed and worldly-wise, too, but we like to think that our readers put human interest and artistic value above more milieu and point of view, and we'd print a new Mulvaney story, if we could get it, as gladly as we'd print a new Henry James story.

We have printed detective stories, domestic comedies, stories of international society, stories of the super *vin-rouge* Bohemia; we have even printed a novelette with an undertaker as its hero. But spare us the Eternal Triangle! It begins to crinkle and lose its shape.

We desire, above all things, good workmanship. We send back many stories that, with interesting ideas in them, are crudely written. We believe our readers have a sense of style, that they see the difference between a short story by Lord Dunsany or Lilith Brenda and an ordinary story. We use essays too, and never have enough of them. But they must avoid the usual labored whimsicality and triteness of thought and plow up some new ground. Here style is two-thirds of the battle.

In a more airy mood they printed a "Suggestions to Our Visitors" leaflet, a parody of the house rules of some exclusive club. It contained the following important information:

The editorial chambers are open daily, except Saturdays, Sundays and Bank Holidays, from 10:30 AM to 11:15 AM.

Interpreters speaking all modern European languages are in daily attendance, and are at the disposal of visitors, without fee.

Visitors whose boots are not equipped with rubber heels are requested to avoid stepping from the rugs to the parquetry.

No fist fights.

A woman secretary is in attendance at all interviews between the Editors, or either of them, and lady authors. Hence it will be unnecessary for such visitors to provide themselves with either duennas or police whistles.

Visitors are kindly requested to refrain from expectorating out of the windows.

Cuspidors are provided for our Southern and Western friends.

Photographs of the Editors are on sale at the *Portier*'s desk. The objects of art on display in the editorial galleries are not for sale.

The editors might just as well have omitted the last declaration as it is unlikely that anyone would have coveted the outlandish junk with which they saw fit to decorate their chambers. In the entrance hall was posted the French Government's official warning about the dangers of over-indulging in absinthe, a proclamation swiped from some Paris bar-room. In the waitingroom hung a hideous Victorian tapestry depicting a rescuing Newfoundland hound holding a baby in its mouth. An Atlantic City souvenir banner, posters of losing presidential candidates, and blown-up photographs of demi-nude Ziegfeld beauties filled the walls. A red-plush-and-gold-gilt throne, which Mencken had acquired when Dutch Sadie, a Baltimore madam, closed her brothel and auctioned off her furniture, held the place of honor. Beside it was an ornate spittoon, a relic of an old-time saloon. Another startling piece of funiture was a marble slab, leftover from some tombstone sculptor, on which was spread a free lunch for poets—a repast of dill pickles, cheese, pretzels, and a cold ham on ice. The ensemble gave the quarters the look of a third-rate theatrical booking agency. Its honky-tonk tone expressed the editors' disdain for the stuffy dignity affected by rival magazine offices.

Harry Kemp, a Village literary light who ran away with the first Mrs. Upton Sinclair and who later wrote indiscretely of his lovers and his experiences as a hobo in his autobiography, *Tramping on Life*, was cautioned against gorging himself at the free-lunch counter. When he continued to nibble on the pretzels and cheese Mencken went to a cupboard, took out a shotgun, and chased him downstairs. On one occasion Kemp, a careless dresser, was obliged to accompany Nathan to a publisher's reception.

"You won't want to walk down Fifth Avenue with me, George," Kemp informed the critic. "I have no hat."

"That's all right," said Nathan. "You're more presentable without a hat than you would be with the sort of hat you'd have if you had a hat."

The humorless Dreiser was the butt of many of their practical jokes.

"Why not try a society story?" they urged him, swallowing their grins. "Something very swell and tony. Get out of the tenements and dirty undershirt atmosphere for a change. It'll do you good."

Oblivious to any facetiousness, Dreiser agreed that he might try his hand at such a story and about two days later his elephantine effort arrived. It was set in Cincinnati on the occasion of a great ball given by the leader of the city's elite. There were "no less than dozens of butlers" and the heroine, an heiress of the *beau monde*, swept down the grand staircase in "very trig green satin." Other ladies present were also in "trig green satin" and the climax of the "trig" affair came when the hostess confronted the fashionable multi-millionaire, Mr. Diamondberg, and accused him in the middle of the ballroom of having swindled her husband out of a street-car franchise.

When the editors stopped laughing and mailed the story back to Dreiser — not quite certain whether he, in turn, was making fun of them — he complained that they had wasted his valuable time and energy.

Intent on dispelling his moodiness, Nathan and Mencken paid calls on him in his West 10th Street apartment. There Dreiser would sit for hours rolling and unrolling his handkerchief as he listened to mournful Russian music emitted from a squeaky phonograph. Dreiser was extremely susceptible to the arty fads of Greenwich Village and was well acquainted with their purveyors. He was fascinated by the theories of Charles Fort, a writer who held that all science was fiction. When Dreiser signed a contract with the up-and-coming publisher, Horace Liveright, to reissue his early books and publish his new ones, he tried to insist that Liveright add Fort's works to his list. Liveright, though otherwise indulgent with the famous novelist, stood his ground. Dreiser was full of wide-eyed wonder for Isadora Duncan who, back from Europe due to the war, was preparing to dance Beethoven's Ninth draped in a red banner to celebrate the Russian revolution. Nathan and Mencken would stuff Dreiser's mail-box with small American flags accompanied by scrawls issuing Black Hand threats, letters ostensibly written by Woodrow Wilson urging Dreiser to come at once to the White House for a confidential talk, and the like.

Dreiser, after their rejection of his society story and their noisy surprise descents on his home, viewed all their suggestions with suspicion. Knowing how badly he needed money they collaborated with an acquaintance connected with the movies in an effort to bring him easy funds and permit him to write in comfort. For $2,000, all Dreiser would have to do was to pose before the camera, seated at his writing desk. A movie dealt with a novelist and the idea was to show a well-known author at work by way of introduction. He was not to figure in the story and after a few short shots his work would be done and the money his. Pleased with themselves, since the project involved no invasion of his dignity, they hurried to 10th Street to break the news. Firmly convinced that they were up to another prank, Dreiser cursed them roundly and refused them the honor of personal contact with him until further notice.

Not even their idol, James Huneker, was immune from their practical jokes. In his autobiography, *Steeplejack*, Huneker had written glowing praise of Theodore Roosevelt, after the ex-president had invited him to luncheon at his Oyster Bay residence. Roosevelt with his professional optimism and rambunctious public image was not among the heroes of *The Smart Set* editors. Worse, they felt, Huneker had joined the enemy, by accepting membership in the National Institute of Arts and Letters, an organization of authors who were trying to hold the old respectability line against the rising insurgents such as Dreiser, Cabell, and, indeed, Huneker himself. When the war ended the members of the avant-garde received recognition — most of it scandalous enough to make their names household words. Yet Huneker — "Lord Jim," as Nathan affectionately dubbed him — was to have a last laugh at the expense of his rebellious disciples. In 1919, with only two more years to live, Huneker incorporated in his last and probably most enduring book everything then considered unmentionable, from syphilis to lesbianism. Titled *Painted Veils*, it was cast as a novel, but an improper novel in both senses. Relating the career of an American opera diva from her girlhood seduction by a black revivalist preacher through her amorous adventures in pre-war Europe and on to her conquest of Manhattan's plutocratic society, it was a riot of obscene wit. Its

theme was the unveiling of all the heroine's secrets and her exposure as the singing whore of modern Babylon. As a novel it was as
meandering as *Tristram Shandy*, its narrative frequently interrupted
by gossip about the famous of the worlds of music and letters and
by audacious soliloquies on women and art. Horace Liveright cautiously published it in a deluxe, limited edition for subscribers, for
had it been offered on the open market it would have been at once
suppressed.

The "Répétition Générale" department, which they conducted
jointly, was a forum for a monthly airing of their prejudices. In
turn, their influence and attitudes were mocked. Berton Braley's
parody jingle, "Three-Minus One," was widely reprinted to be recited joyfully by their detractors.

> There were three that sailed away one night
> Far from the madding throng;
> And two of the three were always right
> And every one else was wrong.
> But they took another along, these two,
> To bear them company,
> For he was the only One to ever know
> Why the other two should be;
> And they sailed away, these three —
> Mencken
> Nathan
> And God.

> And the two talked of the aims of Art.
> Which they alone understood;
> And they quite agreed from the very start
> That nothing was any good
> Except some novels that Dreiser wrote
> And some plays from Germany,
> When God objected — they rocked the boat
> And dropped Him into the sea.
> "For you have no critical facultee",
> Said Mencken
> And Nathan
> To God.

> The two came cheerfully sailing home
> Over the surging tide

And trod once more on their native loam
Wholly self-satisfied;
And the little group that calls them great
Welcomed them fawningly.
Though why the rest of us tolerate
This precious pair must be
Something nobody else can see
But Mencken
Nathan
And God!

The resentment that the independent pair had aroused with their sardonic reevaluation of accepted thinking and standards and their brash irreverence toward public figures ran deep. When Mencken's *A Book of Prefaces*, a collection of studies of Conrad, Dreiser, and Huneker, together with a chapter on "Puritanism as a Literary Force," was published, the old guard retaliated with a vengence. Its foremost spokesman, Stuart Pratt Sherman, reviewed the volume with all the venom at his command. Sherman had fought in the front ranks to suppress *The 'Genius'*, accusing Dreiser of "Teutonic naturalism."

Sherman found Mencken's preferences distasteful and unrefined. He objected to Mencken's penchant for Conrad's Slavic pessimism, Huneker's continental joie de vivre, and Dreiser's ash-can realism. As an intended final blow he pointed out that Huneker and Dreiser — like Mencken and his publisher Alfred A. Knopf — had German names.

Sherman's heavy-handed WASP critiques failed to retard the spreading influence of the controversial editors. They made themselves almost bulletproof by their stubborn refusal to wax indignant over even the most grossly unfair attacks. "A man in the brick-throwing business must expect to be hit occasionally," sighed Nathan on reading Sherman's warning that Anglo-Saxonism was being threatened by alien doctrines, while Mencken invented a stock reply to the army of cranks that constantly wrote him. Each post brought him hate mail and each was cordially answered. No matter what opinion was expressed it received the same reply: "You may be right."

The controversy that raged over *The Smart Set* was, of course, superb publicity, the vehemence of its detractors serving as unpaid advertising. It was forever being assailed by patrioteers, by right-thinkers, by the literati, by professors, by reformers, from the pulpit, and in newspaper editorials. Before long there was scarcely a literate person in the United States who had not heard of the editors. The hullabaloo delighted them — they had fulfilled their ambition to "stir up the animals." Mob approval they abhorred and acceptance of their attitude would have caused them to retreat. "Those whom the gods would destroy they first make popular," said Nathan to his co-editor. They had not become popular, but they had become notorious.

Curiosity about the two of them grew with every assault. The attacks, though furious, were often contradictory. They were accused, for example, of being both agents of the Kaiser and the Bolsheviks. To satisfy the inquisitive they prepared a pamphlet titled *Pistols for Two* in which they pretended to unravel their secrets. It was published by Knopf and was credited to their favorite creation, Owen Hatteras, whom, readers were informed, was now a major in the American Expeditionary Forces and had been decorated for bravery somewhere in France.

A foreword explained that biography, like psychology, often fails because it mistakes complexity for illumination. "Its aim is to present a complete picture of a man; its effect is usually to make an impenetrable mystery of him. In trying to account for him in every detail, to give an unbroken coherence to all his acts and ideas, it makes of him a wax dummy, as smooth as glass but as unalive as a dill pickle."

"It is by no such process of exhaustion that we get our notions of the people we really know. We see them, not as complete images, but as processions of flashing points," explained the major, going on to prove his theory by citing the general misconceptions held about some magazine editors who differed from the public knowledge of them. Following this introduction were studies — of a candid-camera nature — of the *Smart Set* twain. Mencken portrayed Nathan in a series of brief anecdotes and Nathan obliged with a similar biography of his associate.

The Mencken vision of Nathan, though semi-fictional, pro-
vides a look at the critic as he was in 1917:

> He is a man of middle height, straight, slim, dark, with eyes
> like the middle of August, black hair which he brushes back *à
> la française*, and a rather sullen mouth.
>
> His boyhood ambition was to be an African explorer in a
> pith helmet, with plenty of room on the chest for medals to
> be bestowed upon him by the beauteous Crown Princess of
> Luxembourg.
>
> He smokes from the moment his man turns off the mati-
> nal showerbath until his man turns it on again at bedtime.
>
> He lives in a bachelor apartment, nearly one-third of
> which is occupied by an ice-box containing refreshing bever-
> ages. On the walls of his apartment are pictures of numerous
> toothsome creatures.
>
> He dresses like the late Ward McAllister and wears daily
> a boutonniere of blue corn flowers.
>
> He dislikes women over twenty-one, actors, cold
> weather, mayonnaise dressing, people who are always happy,
> hard chairs, invitations to dinner, invitations to serve on
> committees in however worthy a cause, railroad trips, rye
> whiskey, chicken, daylight, men who do not wear waistcoats,
> the sight of a woman eating, the sound of a woman singing,
> small napkins, Maeterlinck, Verhaeren, Tagore, Dickens,
> Bataille, fried oysters, German soubrettes, tradesmen, ports,
> married women who think of leaving their husbands, profes-
> sional anarchists of all kinds, professional music lovers, ven-
> tilation, men who tell how much money they have made, men
> who affect sudden friendships and call him Georgie, women
> who affect sudden friendships and then call him Mr. Nathan,
> writing letters, receiving letters, talking over the telephone
> and wearing a hat....
>
> He never reads the political news in the papers....
>
> Like the late McKinley, he smokes but half a cigar. Like
> Mark Twain he enjoys the more indelicate varieties of humor.
> Like Beethoven, he uses neither morphine nor cocaine. Like
> Sitting Bull and General Joffe, he has never read the Consti-
> tution of the United States.

An anarchist in criticism, he is in secret a very diligent student of Lessing, Schlegel, Hazlitt and Brandes.

He would rather have Lord Dunsany in *The Smart Set* once than William Dean Howells a hundred times. . . .

He believes politically in the autocracy of the elect, for the elect, and by the elect and is in favor of universal military service, imperialism, and birth-control.

He frequently spends an entire afternoon polishing up a sentence in one of his compositions. And he often stops writing for a couple of days, or as long as it takes him to hit upon an appropriate adjective or phrase.

He knows nothing of country life, and cannot tell a wheat field from a potato patch. He regards camping out as the most terrible diversion ever invented by man.

He cannot operate a motor car, or cook, or wind a dynamo, or fix a clock, or guess the answer to a riddle, or milk a cow. . . .

He believes that Shaw's *Caesar and Cleopatra* is the best modern English play, Brieux's *Les Hannetons* the best modern French play and Dunsany's *Gods of the Mountain* the best Irish play.

He believes that twelve per cent of all reformers and up-lifters are asses, and that the rest of them are thieves.

Nathan's parallel portrait of Mencken followed these lines:

In philosophy he is a strict mechanist of the Loeb-Haeckel school. In psychology he leans toward Adler. He questions pragmatism, but admits its workableness. He is an advocate of absolute free speech in all things — and exhibits the utmost intolerance in combatting those who oppose it.

He rejects the whole of Christianity, including especially its ethic, and does not believe that the soul is immortal. His moral code is from the Chinese and has but one item: keep your engagements. He pays all bills immediately, never steals what he can buy, and is never late for an appointment. He has missed but one train in his life.

He believes with Nathan, that the three best stories printed in *The Smart Set* under their editorial direction have been "The Exiles' Club" by Dunsany; "Ashes to Ashes" by James Gardner Sanderson; and "The End of Ilsa Mentieth" by Liilith Benda. He believes, with Nathan, that the best epigram has been that sent in by an anonymous contributor: "When love dies there is no funeral. The corpse remains in the house."

He is, at bottom, a sentimentalist. True, he has no use for such things as babies, love stories (however good), or the Champs-Elysée in the springtime, yet he succumbs to Julia Sanderson singing "They Wouldn't Believe Me," to a cemetery in the early green of May, to the lachrymose waltz from *Eva*, which he plays upon the piano in melancholious pianissimo, and any poem about a dog (however bad).

Many of the editors' admirers, and all of their enemies, accepted *Pistols for Two* at face value. It became the source book for information about their private lives, habits, preferences, and prejudices and formed their public images.

A wartime paper shortage forced the printing of *The Smart Set* on yellow pulp sheets that were so full of wood that the editors suggested that Warner would make more money if he went into the toothpick trade. In addition, authors were succumbing to the blare of fife and drum and there were so few stories to meet the magazine's no-war policy that the editors were driven to writing some themselves. Among Nathan's fictional contributions were "Nothing to Declare," "But I Love Her," "The Soul Song," and "The Triple Expense," which appeared under the pseudonyms of George Naret, Rupert Cross, and William Drayham. Mencken sometimes used the last of those. Nathan's fiction is somewhat akin to that of the British satirist, Saki, tart and often cold and cynical. The style is an imitation of two American authors then active: Julian Street and Charles Belmont Davis.

The war, though thousands of miles away, was making inroads into American life. Meatless days, wheatless days, coalless days, and boozeless days were instituted. The Wilson administration took over the railroads as an emergency measure with catastrophic results. Women replaced men as street-car conductors as the draft broadened. Mail delivery slowed and correspondence with friends and colleagues was erratic, partly due to the official inspection of all communications to and from Europe. The war was the subject of every conversation and such militant slogans as "Doing Your Bit" and "Over the Top" were used, often quite irrelevantly, in advertising copy. Broadway musicals joined the patriotic drive with a 1917 Ziegfeld Follies tableau including Uncle Sam and the chorus singing "Can't You Hear Your Country Calling?," a *pièce d'occasion* by Victor Herbert, while George M. Cohan's "Over There" became the United States army's marching song. Irving Berlin, having been drafted and promoted to the rank of sergeant, wrote a soldier show at Camp Yaphank which included "Oh, How I Hate to Get Up in the Morning," and which, imported to the New Theater on Central Park West, brought $82,000 into the camp coffers.

Nathan, indifferent to the hubbub, plunged into the work that was to found his permanent reputation, *Another Book on the Theatre*. Ben Huebsch, a perceptive and erudite publisher, egged him on, assuring him that it was time that his work appeared between covers.

The self-deprecating title of Nathan's initial book was deceptive. It was, as it proclaimed, another book on the theatre, but it was quite unlike any other book on the subject. Many of its ideas had been aired in magazine and newspaper articles, but the young critic, aware of the deadliness of reprinting reviews, reorganized the material, arranging it in a fresh and attractive form. *Another Book on the Theatre* was something bright and something new.

Though informal in presentation, *Another Book on the Theatre* was not only serious but revolutionary, urging defiance of conformity and of decayed rules and precepts. It has a youthful bluster, and in form and content it has a Nietzchean touch, both in its preaching of the gay science of the arts and in its lightning illuminations of wide territories.

The standard methods of dramatic criticism are demolished by use of amusing examples and some hallowed theatrical reputations are blown sky-high. Reading it now, eighty years later, its springtime vigor retains freshness. Its opening salvo sounds its abiding principle:

> In the American theatre, "the play's the thing" in the follow-

ing proportions: 1. The "star", 2. The press-agent, 3. The scenery, 4. The lighting effects, 5. The modiste or tailor, 6. The play (provided that it is not a good play).

The star system was dismissed as a substitute for acting; acting as a substitute for drama; and the drama as a substitute for movies. He found American farce to be chained to middle-class superstitions about bourgeois decorum, lacking in the deliberate and healthy vulgarity of farce in France, England, and Germany. Granville Barker, the English dramatist-director who was staging *Euripides* outdoors in a New York baseball stadium (where billboards of Campbell's soup and Olus underwear peeked across the top of the bleachers to non-Grecian effect), was denounced as an artistic mountebank.

"I am a progressive and our theatre, as you know, isn't," declares the preface, going on to give a list of Nathan's views: that the late Clyde Fitch was a laughably overestimated fellow; that David Belasco had not thus far written one good play; that musical comedy should be a frank appeal and stimulant to the sex urge; and that there is no such thing as dramatic technique (on which Professor Brander Matthews and Professor George Pierce Baker were instructing their pupils).

As the matters that are serious to one generation are ever comic to the next, he proposes to continue in this vein until the theatre has progressed to the point where it can presnt Maude Adams, the symbol of blushing, coy maidenhood, in a play in which she is "ruined"; a play in which a character showing symptoms of cardiac malaise in the first act does not die in the last; and a play in which a seduced "baggage" does not sentimentally observe, in narrating her sad story, that she was tossed aside like a broken flower.

In an essay entitled "The Unimportance of Being Earnest," he claims that all the truly great men and real artists have, consciously or unconsciously, a strong streak of the fake. "Was P. T. Barnum, probably America's greatest amusement artist, a sincere man?" he rhetorically demands. "Is Brand Whitlock, probably America's most clear-sighted public official, a sincere man? Isn't Gordon

Craig laughing at us and isn't Reinhardt dead-serious — and isn't Craig three times the artist Reinhardt is?"

The sales of *Another Book on the Theatre* were modest but it reached the right people, introducing Nathan to European readers and having an impact on American dramatic criticism. Receiving a copy delayed by the war-time post, Gordon Craig responded with enthusiasm. "I read it through and enjoyed and marked much of it," he wrote, inaugurating a correspondence that was to last until Nathan's death. "I like so much the amazing Americanisms."

Craig's book, *On the Art of the Theatre*, became the bible of the theatrical avant-garde. Nathan described Max Reinhardt as Craig's Paul; in St. Petersburg, Meyerhold, Evreinov, and the Russian symbolists discussed his proposed reforms and Bakst and Benois sought to apply his theories of scenic design in their decor for the Diaghilev ballets.

Like most prophets Craig was feared rather than honored in his native land. An extremist — his creed was the "All or Nothing" of Ibsen's *Brand* — he was distrusted by the London managers who saw him as an impractical visionary and rejected the proposal that he be given a theatre and financing to train his own company. In any case, he was scarcely in step with the English theatre of the era. He judged Beerbohm Tree's Shakespeare productions as cumbersomely ornate and rated Granville Barker as a mechanical and uninspired *metteur en scène*. With the London theatre doors closed to him, he exiled himself in Italy where he conducted a theatre school in Florence and published a magazine, *The Mask*, in which he preached his doctrines and kept an eagle eye on the modern movement in the performing arts.

Despite their mutual admiration Craig and Nathan never met, Nathan's plans to visit Craig in Italy continually falling through. Once Nathan fell ill in Paris, and on another occasion he was obliged to cut short a European trip to arrange the sale of *The Smart Set* and the launching of *The American Mercury*. The two only encountered one another in letters but Nathan saw in Craig a kindred spirit.

"I have never known a franker correspondent," commented

Nathan. Accused of fraud and pretence, he is as completely honest a man as I have ever known. To my mind he is the one wholly sincere man in the world of modern theatre."

Nathan's book pleased Huneker: "A writer more malicious, more brilliant and better informed would be hard to find," Huneker wrote Mencken. "Paris is where that young man ought to be. There he would be appreciated. Here he only bruises his brain against the eternal box office."

The "eternal box office" took umbrage. *The Smart Set*, independent of theatrical advertising, was immune to the blackmailing threats of the managers. Several Broadway producers, stung by Nathan's criticisms, protested to the magazine's publisher. But, rather than apologizing, Warner called Nathan to his office to congratualte him on his might.

Newspaper reviewers were in a more precarious position since their editors had to worry about the possible loss of advertising revenue, and so tended to side with the managers. Samuel Hoffenstein, as has been related, was dismissed as critic for *The Evening Sun* on a complaint from Belasco.

Not every magazine editor stood by their critics as firmly as Warner stood by Nathan. Frank Crownenshield of *Vanity Fair* obeyed Ziegfeld's command to fire Dorothy Parker after she had caustically summarized the mannerisms of Billie Burke (Mrs. Ziegfeld) in W. Somerset Maugham's comedy, *Caesar's Wife*.

Warner may have ignored complaints about Nathan, but that did not stop them. Belasco, infuriated by a review, noted that Nathan's uncle, S. F. Nixon, was a member of the Theater Syndicate, and hinted that this was responsible for the critic's scathing accounts of Belasco's independent productions. Nathan, in point of fact, was opposed to the syndicate's monopoly and had often so written. The syndicate's president, A. L. Erlanger, had cost him several assignments. When he dubbed Hall Caine's *Margaret Schiller*, produced at the New Amsterdam Theater by the Messrs. Klaw and Erlanger, "a cheap melodrama" and predicted its doom, Erlanger called in his secretary and dictated an angry letter. "Hall Caine is one of the greatest writers living and who is Nathan to say that he isn't?" he sputtered. "Nathan ought to stop criticizing and go to sweeping up the streets!" The producer refused to admit him to his theatres and caused the Philadelphia *North American* and *The Cleveland Leader* to drop his syndicated column. Erlanger also persuaded the proprietor of the magazine *Puck* to discontinue Nathan's weekly reviews.

"There are managers and there are managers," Nathan wrote. "It never has been and it probably never will be necessary for the Bradys, the Ameses, the Williamses, the Hopkins, the Cohans and Harrises and the Tylers to go officially into the critic-barring business.

Another Book on the Theatre was the first of forty-two books, twenty-seven on the theatre and drama and fifteen on other subjects, by Nathan. From 1915 on, he came out with a new book annually (in some years, two). The last, *The Theatre in the Fifties*, appeared in 1953.

On his part, Mencken had found a convivial companion in Phil Goodman, a jovial, extrovert advertising agent and ad-copy writer who had come from Philadelphia to New York in search of booty. Goodman, a hearty drinker and gargantuan eater, tipped the scales at three hundred pounds. His clothes were as loud as his talk and his table manners were such that St. John Ervine claimed there were few uglier sights than Goodman devouring a plate of spaghetti. Of German-Jewish origins, he relished German literature, German cuisine and Pilsen beer, and enjoyed shocking with his outspoken, unconventional opinions, trying to top Mencken at his own game.

Mencken invited Nathan to meet Goodman in roister-doister at a luncheon. Goodman, an expansive personality, at once took over, recounting his latest get-rich-quick scheme. He was quitting advertising and turning publisher. He already had signed a contract with a drugstore chain to market his books. They would sell cheaply, have national circulation, reach a wide audience, and reap large profits. As yet he had no books.

Impressed with Goodman's assurance, Nathan suggested a trial balloon. He had tossed off a trifling manuscript, a sort of joke book. Its title was *Bottoms Up*, and was too airy in tone for Huebsch.

Goodman leapt at the idea and *Bottoms Up* was the first book he issued. Mencken, too, had a contribution. He gave Goodman both his *Damn, A Book of Calumnity* and *In Defense of Women* to publish.

Goodman, it developed, was not a proficient publisher, but during the 1920s he found a lucrative niche as a Broadway producer, having two phenomenal hits. The first was Don Marquis' *The Old Soak*, about a saloon frequenter exiled from its haunts by Prohibition. The second great Goodman success was the musical comedy, *Poppy*, in which W. C. Fields had his first straight acting role after years of comic juggling and appearances in revue skits.

Goodman's experiment as a publisher having gone up in smoke, Mencken returned to Knopf and took Nathan with him. This developed into a rewarding association for all three. Later Knopf was to finance and manage the business affairs of their magazine, *The American Mercury*, and to issue most of their books for the next three decades.

New publishers sprang up to serve the new literature. Ben Huebsch, a pioneer in the field, brought out Nathan, Sherwood Anderson, James Joyce's *Portrait of the Artist as a Young Man*, and the poems of D. H. Lawrence. The English-born Mitchell Kennerley followed this lead and before 1914 published translations of Schnitzler, the poetry of Vachel Lindsay and Edna St. Vincent Millay, Zoë Akins' comedy, and the critical writing of Van Wyck Brooks. Thomas Seltzer, an able translator himself, specialized in continental fiction and Seltzer's nephews, Charles and Albert Boni, proprietors of a Washington Square bookshop where the Greenwich Village intelligentsia gathered, had a press of their own.

In 1916 the Bonis entered into partnership with a breezy toy/gadget salesman from Philadelphia, Horace Liveright, and founded the Modern Library, a collection of cheap, leather-bound reprints of Ibsen, Wilde, Gorky, Kipling, Nietzsche, Maeterlinck, and Strindberg. The Modern Library was an instant success with young intellectuals. On its profits Boni-Liveright Inc. moved uptown and was soon known as a publishing house with a startling new look. T. R. Smith, editor of *The Century* and an intimate of

Nathan and Mencken, was appointed literary advisor and arranged for the American publication of George Moore, Sigmund Freud, and Rose Macaulay, while the bustling Liveright signed up Dreiser, O'Neill, and later Hemingway, Sherwood Anderson and William Faulkner.

After graduating from Columbia, Alfred A. Knopf had served his apprenticeship as a drummer and scout for Doubleday. These duties had taken him to England, where he had made the acquaintance of Conrad, Kipling, Galsworthy, and other notables. He especially admired Conrad and was instrumental in boosting the sales of Conrad novels at Doubleday. He had read Mencken's glowing tributes to Conrad and on a business trip to Baltimore introduced himself to the critic. Mencken liked Knopf and listened attentively to his theories, but was a bit skeptical about his practical abilities.

In 1915 Knopf became a publisher himself. He operated with a miniature but efficient staff in a $45-a-month office on West 42nd Street. His father, Samuel Knopf, acted as business manager, and he hired a clever young assistant, Blanche Wolfe (who later became his wife), to help him in the search for manuscripts and handling of authors. Knopf issued the most attractively printed, designed, and bound new books on the market, and his selections revealed high literary standards. He reissued Gogol, Garshin, and Lermontov; republished W. H. Hudson's *Green Mansions* with a preface by Galsworthy; and had an intuitive instinct for budding talents: Carl Van Vechten, the music critic of *The New York Times*, whose witty light fiction — *Peter Whiffle*, *The Blind Bow Boy*, and *The Tattooed Countess* — was in perfect tune with the *Zeitgeist* of the twenties; Willa Cather; Elinor Wylie; Clarence Day; Conrad Aiken; Ezra Pound; and T. S. Elliot were writers to appear on the roster of the new house, and European literature was soon to be represented on the Knopf lists by Thomas Mann, Oswald Spengler, André Gide, and Knut Hamsun.

The Knopfs adopted the figure of a leaping, aristocratic borzoi as their trademark. This led Samuel Knopf, in hopes of increasing sales, to have an electric sign set up in Columbus Circle. It depicted the graceful dog in action, accompanied by the command "Read

Borzoi Books." It proved only that people who read signs don't read books.

Mr. George Jean Nathan Presents was the first of the critic's books to bear the borzoi device, appearing in 1917. In a chapter entitled "Legend's End" the grandest and boldest of Broadway bluffers, David Belasco, who posed as such a lofty artist that he wore a clerical collar, is mercilessly mocked:

> I admire Mr. Belasco as a showman — he is probably the best and certainly the most successful in the Anglo-Saxon dramatic theatre. Indeed, if ever I write a bad play, I promise him the first refusal of it. I admire him for having gauged the American esthetik as probably no other showman since Adam Forepaugh and Barnum have gauged it. And I admire him, further, for having done several really good things really well. But, though he has been ever to me an urbane host and though ever he has subtly flattered my sense of humor by hesitating to bid me inspect his 'studio' or his first-edition E. Phillips Oppenheims or his collection of Byzantine soup ladles, I cannot but believe, albeit unmannerly, that he has by his many counterfeits worked a vast and thorough ill to the American playhouse and its drama. And I cannot but further believe that his legend is ending to the brightening of a new and more understanding dawn in the native theatre.

Probably the most prophetic essay in Nathan's 1917 book is one on a black Harlem troupe's acting of *Othello*, an example of his sympathy and foresight. Nathan had a deep interest in the Negro arts long before they became popular in the twenties and had contemplated editing a magazine devoted to the black experience by black authors; they planned a periodical of sociological and literary value. Nathan was always intent on surprising his readers.

"That Shakespeare in the Teutonic is a more tuneful fellow than in the English is pretty generally agreed," he begins. This in itself is a remarkable presumption for it is unlikely midway in the war that anyone — save Mencken and Max Reinhardt — would have been in agreement with the statement. He continues:

> But that Shakespeare for his finest effect, his most superb beauty, must look to the super-Pullman-porter or elevator

chauffeur is surely a nosegay to stagger the vanity, confound the complacency and lance the pride of the White man.

Yet in a performance of *Othello* given by our mezzotint brothers at the York Theater in commemoration of the Shakespearan trecentenary, the fact was established with a vitality that first baffled, then put to rout, the plump resistance of sovereign snickers and sardonic elevations of the nose. Under the direction of Mr. R. Voelckel and with a company headed by Mr. Edward Sterling Wright...the familiar tragedy was read with a singular impressiveness and an ear-haunting tonal quality. I have, in my day, heard Othello from many tongues in many lands, but never, unless my ears deceive me, have I heard a reading now more liquid and silver, now more full-throated and golden, than this reading of the Moor's fable....Here was the music of the prose voiced not in the dry semi-cackle of the Haymarket and up St. James's way, nor the sometimes monotonous ventriloquy of the Volksbuhnen, nor the messy twang of Longacre Square. There was...something of the violin, the alto-saxphone, something of the muffled drum, the harp, something even of the sacring bell, the octavin keyed in B flat, the grand piano, the mescal.

Mr. George Jean Nathan Presents came out in August 1917, and between then and the appearance of his next book, *The Popular Theatre*, in September 1918, the world felt the first tremors of a major upheaval to come.

In Russia the Kerensky Revolution of February 1917, which had deposed the Czar, set up a democratic regime, and swore to fight the war to a finish, fell to the Bolshevik Revolution of October. The new leaders, Lenin and Trotsky, sued for a separate peace with the Central Powers. This was signed at Brest Litovsk on March 2, 1918, and Germany, liberated from attack in the East, made a final grasp for victory, opening its 1918 spring offensive which carried its armies to the gates of Paris. On Good Friday the French capital was bombarded at long range by the monster cannon, Big Bertha, seventy miles away. A shell crushed the roof of the Madeleine Church in the city's center and hundreds of civilians were killed. The news was received with great outrage in the

United States. Another conscription bill was immediately passed, ordering all men up to age forty-five to register for future draft calls. Nathan and Mencken were both reexamined for military service. Nathan was again rejected for defective eyesight and frail health, but Mencken was placed in the reserves to be summoned at the year's end.

In Europe the Allied commanders, spurred by the enemy advances, outlined a major counter-offensive for the spring of 1919 in which fresh American troops were to play a large part and Berlin was to be taken. The Allied ministers and generals had overestimated the foe. Though Paris was in danger of capture twice during the summer of 1918, the German army, having reached the end of their spirit and resources, had nothing more to fight with. Wilson had already prepared his Fourteen Points for Peace — which would be disputed and mauled at the conference table — and negotiations for a halting of hostilities were being secretly conducted after the summer's terrible slaughter and the turning of the war tide in the early autumn. Rumors that the war was over spread and a "false" armistice was celebrated on November 7. On November 11 the armistice was officially proclaimed.

In the last months of the war an influenza epidemic broke out in Europe. In London it claimed more deaths than the Black Plague of 1665–66 depicted by Defoe. In September it invaded the Atlantic seaboard, raging in Boston, New York, Philadelphia, Baltimore, and Washington and then surged westward. One fourth of the nation was infected by this pandemic, nineteen out of every thousand fatally, the medical establishment unable to check its progress. It killed half as many soldiers in army camps as fell in battle overseas, the death toll in the United States rising to nearly 700,000 people. In early 1919, it subsided as suddenly as it had begun.

Nathan's beloved younger brother Fritz was one of the victims. After he and their mother had moved to Philadelphia, Fritz had become a manager for the Nixon Theater chain. Nathan attended the funeral and, on returning to New York, fell ill himself. Exhausted and bewildered, he lay prostrate in his darkened Royalton flat. He had been stricken by a less virulent case than his brother, but

Mencken, arriving from Baltimore where coffins were piled high in the railroad station, found him running an alarming fever and in an inconsolable state. He summoned doctors and a nurse.

During Nathan's slow convalescence Mencken tried to cheer his shaken comrade with good news: Wilson had dissolved the wartime censorship board a few days after the armistice. Conscription was to be abolished and there would be no more draft calls. Gordon Craig had granted permission to use his estimate of Nathan criticism in advertising copy and Knopf, who had just issued *The Popular Theatre*, had rushed to a job printer on Eighth Avenue and ordered 100,000 copies of the Craig encomium to be distributed. The new book would outsell any book on the theatre published in the US.

With such encouraging reports Nathan's health and morale improved and within two weeks he was on his feet again. On Nathan's first outing, Mencken took him to dinner at Roger's on Sixth Avenue and over the clatter they discussed playwriting, coming to the conclusion that writing a play was child's play as compared to writing a book.

"Let's write one to prove it," exclaimed Mencken.

"Very well," replied Nathan, "but where is your character?"

Mencken had been re-reading Edgar Saltus' *Imperial Purple* and Heliogabalus came to his mind. By the time dinner was over they had plotted the play and six weeks later it was finished.

"Writing it turned out to be absurdly easy — in fact, a sort of holiday from criticism — and I ceased to respect dramatists from that time," Mencken related.

Heliogabalus has been described by Huneker as "a hell-broth of wit, humor, fantasy and downright idol-smashing, one of the most brilliant farces I've read since Gilbert's or Shaw's." Set in 221 A.D. at the court of the Roman emperor, it concerns the troubles Heliogabalus encounters when he falls in love with a Galatian maiden who, with the aid of Simon of Cappadocia, would puritanize his palace and convert him to Christianity. In the end the proselytizing pair fail to win the emperor to the new, gloomy faith and his happily pagan courtiers go back to their old wicked ways. Knopf published the text in a limited edition which was sold out before publication.

A short play by Nathan alone, *The Eternal Mystery*, was seen in a one-time production in a program of one-act pieces at the New York Princess Theater in 1913. It portrays a dying agnostic who, in his last moments, after a violent denial of God and all religion in the name of the Darwin and Huxley revelations, is converted to Christianity by beholding on the wall of his sickroom the sign of the cross. The cross is only the shadow of his young son's kite in the sharp sunshine outside, but despite such a rational explanation the enigmatic tone of the play leaves it open to differing interpretations. It poses, but makes no attempt to answer, the eternal question.

The Eternal Mystery was denounced as blasphemous at its premiere and was instantly withdrawn, causing William A. Brady, the Broadway producer, to resign from the Princess Theater's board. It was successfully performed at the Little Theater of Philadelphia and at the Pitt Theater of Pittsburgh without incurring any protests, but in Detroit it was again charged with impiety and withdrawn. Nathan was dismayed at this repeated reaction and forbade its further performance anywhere in the United States except Chicago, which he judged to be a rational and evenly balanced community, then hatching a school of promising young writers.

By the close of 1918 Nathan, fully recovered, was back at his desk in *The Smart Set* office each morning and each evening found him promptly just before curtain-time in his aisle fauteuil at the theatre. Neither he nor his schedule had altered, but it seemed that everything else had. This change showed up both in the manuscripts that came to him and in the plays he saw. The pre-war American styles of literature and stagecraft had vanished, never to return — a change for which he was in part responsible.

Rather than taking an interest in Wilson's "New Freedom," it was the new freedom in the arts that held Nathan's attention. It was to sweep him and his indefatigable associate into the national spotlight. America, awakening from the nightmare of the war, was eager for fresh adventures, and the younger generation was seeking spokesmen. The Nathan-Mencken reign in letters and daring ideas was about to begin.

During the tumult of World War I the American stage had experienced a gradual change, a gentle rocking of the boat. It came not from within but from without. The smugly ensconced Broadway managers, with their empires of road houses across the country, saw no reason to alter their profitable policies. They were assured—figures don't lie—that they were supplying what the public wanted: sentimental slobbergobble, strong "think" melodramas reinforcing accepted views, fashionable drawing-room fluff from London, bedroom farces bowdlerized from the French, and musical comedies and operettas in which the lovers were separated at the close of the first part and reunited for the finale. However, two progressive young men with higher ideals, sounder taste and greater daring were challenging this stand-pat attitude: Arthur Hopkins and Winthrop Ames.

Hopkins, a friend of Nathan from Cleveland, began as a booking agent. Harry Lauder, the Scottish singer-comedian; the ex-cowboy sage, Will Rogers, and the ballroom dance exponents, the Castles, were among his clients. In 1912 Hopkins inaugurated his producing career by presenting Eleanor Gates' fantasy, *The Poor Little Rich Girl*, staging it himself. Nathan wrote an appreciative foreword to the published play, a preface to Hopkins' book, *How's Your Second Act?*, and hailed Hopkins as "the foremost American producer":

> The producing theory of Hopkins is, generally speaking, very simply to invest naturalism with as much the quality of beauty as is reasonably to be imagined a part of it. A rose may fall from the window of a Pullman and light upon a New Jersey dunghill—a Cossack marching off to war may carry in a locket the picture of his baby girl—through the skylight of the tenement one may glimpse the stars.
>
> He is no "Master," no "Wizard." He is just a young fellow with a dream, who fails twice where he succeeds once, but who feels and knows that to succeed even once, bravely, finely and without compromise, is worth failing fifty times for.

Hopkins, in point of fact, seldom failed artistically in these early years. Having studied the work of European producers abroad, he emulated their versatility and selected scripts of all sorts. In 1914 he co-produced—with Cohan and Harris—Elmer Rice's first play, *On Trial*, which introduced the "flashback" technique at once gobbled up by the movies.

He staged Henning Berger's Scandinavian tragedy, *The Deluge*, which brought to the fore a remarkable young actress, Pauline Lord. Clare Kummer's charming airy farces, *Good Gracious, Annabelle* and *A Successful Calamity*, both with William Gillette; Alla Nazimova in Ibsen's *Wild Duck*; a dramatization of Longfellow's *Evangeline*; and Mrs. Fiske in Philip Moeller's biographical drama of the strong-minded, cigar-smoking, trouser-wearing French lady novelist, George Sand, were among his war-year contributions, as was Rita Wellman's artfully devised study of a mixed marriage, *The Gentile Wife*, which Nathan considered a notable first play.

It was under Hopkin's tutelage that John Barrymore grew in stature. Barrymore had first broken into serious drama in John Williams' production of Galsworthy's *Justice*. Hopkins cast him in Tolstoy's *Living Corpse*, retitled *Redemption*, and then, after extended voice study, cast him as Richard III, with Barrymore playing a sly, suavely malicious Crookback. Later he cast John and Lionel Barrymore together in Benelli's romance of Renaissance Florence, *The Jest*, embellished by decor by Robert Edmond Jones. In the twenties Hopkins would produce Barrymore's famous *Hamlet*.

Winthrop Ames, of old, well-to-do New England stock, leased the Castle Square Theater of Boston after graduating from Harvard and directed a resident company there for several repertory seasons. In 1909 he was appointed manager of the New Theater (later known as The Century)—a magnificent edifice of opera-house size on Central Park West. Its construction was financed by a society of millionaires who donated fortunes to improve theatre standards culturally. The theatre opened with a giant spectacle: *Antony and Cleopatra*, with E. H. Southern and Julia Marlowe, the leading Shakespeareans of the period. But at the play's premiere it was belatedly discovered that the vast theatre's acoustics were defective.

For two seasons it maintained a permanent company in a repertory that mingled the classics with new plays of superior quality: *The Bluebird* of Maeterlinck, Pinero's *Thunderbolt*, Galsworthy's *Strife*, and Edward Sheldon's *The Nigger*. But after that the high-minded millionaires admitted defeat and the New Theater was leased to George Tyler for a spectacular staging of Robert Hichens's dramatization of his popular novel about sacred and profane love engaged in a struggle against the background of the Sahara, *The Garden of Allah*. There seemed to be a jinx on the playhouse, for on the opening night the sandstorm effect went berserk and the desert cyclone swept into the auditorium to assail the audience.

In 1923 Max Reinhardt and the scenic artist, Norman Bel Geddes, transformed the New Theater — then known as the Century — into a Gothic cathedral for the mammoth pantomimic pageant, *The Miracle*, which proved an enormous success, running for over a year. In 1929, after commercial management, in particular the Shuberts, had tried musical comedy and motion pictures in the glamorous house, it was torn down as a hopeless white elephant.

After the millionaires stopped squandering money on Central Park West, Ames formed his own production company, built the Little and Booth Theaters in the heart of the Broadway district, and distinguished himself by presenting Schnitzler's *Affairs of Anatol* with John Barrymore and Doris Keane; Arnold Bennett's *The Great Adventure*; Laurette Taylor in *Pierre the Prodigal*, a pantomime; Shaw's *Philanderer* with Barrymore; *Prunella* by Lawrence Houseman and Granville Barker; several of the best of Galsworthy's later plays; and three Gilbert and Sullivan operettas. All were impeccably staged.

There were stirrings that denoted change on off-Broadway, too. In 1915 the Misses Alice and Irene Lewisohn built and endowed the Neighborhood Playhouse (at 466 Grand Street) in the Henry Street settlement. There a professional troupe acted specimens of the modern drama: plays by Lord Dunsany and Shaw; Percy Mackaye's *This Fine Pretty World*, a regional drama about the Kentucky mountaineers; the Hindu classic, *The Little Clay Cart*, all intriguing novelties, and an annual satirical revue, *The Grand Street Follies*, which commented tartly on the Broadway scene and its performers.

Also in 1915, Edward Goodman, Robert Edmond Jones, Lawrence Langner, Albert and Charles Boni (the publishers), and Philip Moeller formed the Washington Square Players. They found performing space in the tiny Bandbox theatre on East 57th Street and on weekend evenings, operating on a minimum budget, they presented one-act plays by Chekhov, Maeterlinck, John Reed, Alice Gerstenberg (who employed the inner monologue in her *Overtones*, a device that O'Neill appropriated for *Strange Interlude*), Lawrence Langner, Zoë Akins, Susan Glaspell, and Zona Gale. In its acting fold were several young beginners with prominent Broadway futures: Roland Young, Glenn Hunter, José Ruben, Helen Westley, Frank Conroy, and a novice actress, Katharine Cornell. The Washington Square Players made ends meet and later moved to the larger Comedy Theater to experiment with full-length plays. Before the war was over this company blossomed into the Theater Guild, which was to bring the very best of European drama to Broadway itself.

The Little Theater movement, alive in many American cities, was another factor of change. The acting and direction were often amateur, the scenery and costuming makeshift, but it presented plays that appealed to those disgusted with the vacuity of the commercial stage. To the intellectual and the would-be intellectual, Broadway provided the equivalent of cheap fiction for the empty-minded. Just as established publishers were hostile to the new literature so the New York managers—with a few honorable exceptions—firmly opposed the new drama. Strindberg, Andreyev, Maeterlinck, and Wedekind, like Ibsen before them, made their American entrances by the back door.

A group of Greenwich Village artists and writers—all of them eager for a revolt in the arts and most of them fiery political radicals—gathered in garrets and saloons to confer on various "world improvement" schemes. In this band were John Reed, Louise Bryant (whom he later married and who accompanied him to Russia in 1917 to report on the Bolshevik takeover), Floyd Dell (on the staff of *The Masses* and the author of *Love in Greenwich Village*), George Cram Cook, and his wife, Susan Glaspell.

Miss Glaspell had written a comedy, *Suppressed Desires*, spoofing the misapplication of Freudian theories, news of psychoanalysis having reached the Village to become the latest fad. When the Washington Square Players, principally occupied with importing modern foreign drama, rejected her play, she and her husband decided to start their own theatrical movement which would center on the introduction of new American playwrights.

The Cooks and their Village associates spent the summers in Provincetown, Rhode Island, a tranquil fishing settlement on the tip of Cape Cod. Their presence transformed the quiet town, reminiscent of whaling days, into an art colony during the hot weather months. After *Suppressed Desires* premiered in the parlor of a resident couple, the Cooks found an abandoned fish house on the end of a dilapidated pier, the property of their friend, Mary Heaton Vorse, and set about making it over into a theatre.

They built a 2-by-4 stage in what they baptized the Wharf Theater. Wartime restrictions on wood prevented them from installing benches, and the playgoers had to bring their own chairs. Between the floor boards the bay's waters could be heard and seen, filling the house with a strong salt tang at high tide. At the back of the performing platform were two large doors. These, when suiting the stage action, were swung open to disclose an authentic seascape setting: night sky, passing ships, twinkling harbor lights, and the beacon of a nearby lighthouse.

A visitor to Provincetown in the summer of 1916 was Eugene O'Neill. Tall, lanky, athletic, with jet black hair, black mustache, and glowering dark eyes, he was usually clad in navy sweater, slacks, and sandals. At twenty-seven he was still uncertain what road, if any, to take in life. Melancholy and introspective by nature, influenced by his reading of pessimistic authors, he often thought the race was not worth the candle and he had attempted suicide.

He was the son of the dashing, romantic actor, James O'Neill, known throughout the nation from his touring in *The Count of Monte Christo*, and Nathan's mother's old school friend, Ella

Quinlan. By 1908 James O'Neill had played Dumas' Edmond Dantès over five thousand times. He had long grown tired of it, but it inevitably filled the house.

The young O'Neill had been born in a Broadway hotel and as a child had been taken by his parents on the extensive, cross-country tours. He spent his boyhood in Catholic boarding schools and entered Princeton at nineteen, but he dropped out after his freshman year. Two years later, a girl with whom he lived announced that she was pregnant. He hastily married her in a registry office and never saw her again, fleeing family obligations by signing on as crew member aboard a Norwegian steel bark bound for Buenos Aires with a cargo of lumber. He had loafed about the waterfront of the Argentine capital and then shipped as a seaman on another voyage to Liverpool. His ambition at that time was, he confessed, to be Jack London, he-man sailor. Another adventure had taken him to Honduras to prospect—in vain—for gold.

In 1912 he was back at his father's New London summer home and had secured a job as a reporter and columnist on a local newspaper. Heavy drinking had wrecked his delicate health and the family doctor diagnosed incipient tuberculosis. As his father had grown miserly with increasing financial failures, his son spent six months in the state hospital. There he had tried his hand at writing short plays. A volume of early essays, *Thirst and Other Plays*, was published in Boston in 1914 by Richard C. Badger with James O'Neill footing the printing costs.

The book served to earn him admission to Professor George Baker's post-graduate course in drama at Harvard. Several of the Baker pupils attained subsequent success on Broadway—Edward Sheldon, Philip Barry, Sidney Howard, S. N. Behrman, and George Abbott. O'Neill's construction of plays may have benefited from the lectures, but he was rather scornful of Baker's methods, suspecting them of being merely a preparation for commercial playwriting, especially as the Baker idols seemed to be Pinero and Henry Arthur Jones rather than Ibsen and Strindberg. His distrust deepened when Augustus Thomas, the manufacturer of box-office melodramas, was invited to work with the class. O'Neill felt he knew the commercial theatre only too well. He had grown up in it.

He discontinued his studies under Baker to haunt the New York waterfront saloons, including Jimmy the Priest's where, on a small monthly allowance from his father, he took up residence — at $3 a month — to rub elbows with sailors, Wobblies (members of the IWW), anarchists, prostitutes, pimps, and assorted riff-raff.

O'Neill knew many of the Bohemian Provincetown crowd from the Village. He liked and admired John Reed and was in love with Louise Bryant. But he was not a mixer. He preferred frequenting the Harbor bars, listening to the yarns of the sailors and the Portuguese fishermen, and sometimes getting roaring drunk. He lived in a tumbledown shack on the doors of which he had painted up a warning "Go to Hell!"

Some of the art colony members thought this isolation a pose, but he was painfully shy. When George Cook learned that O'Neill had a play in his baggage, he asked for a look at it. The play, *Bound East for Cardiff*, was a one-act depicting the death of a sailor aboard an Atlantic cargo vessel. Professor Baker had seen little in it, but Cook summoned his company and friends to hear it read in the parlor of his house. O'Neill sat in the dining room while the play was read to Harry Kemp, his wife, Mary Pyne, John Reed, and Louise Bryant. All were enthusiastic and crowded about the author to extend congratulations and to offer to stage it at once.

Bound East for Cardiff was put into rehearsal the next morning and two weeks later had its premiere at the Wharf Theater. John Reed played one of the seamen, Harry Kemp another, and O'Neill, stand-offish attitude thawing under their eager interest, collaborated on the production and appeared in the one-line role of the Mate.

In the autumn the Provincetown players returned to the Village and had their first New York season in an improvised theatre on MacDougal Street and *Bound East for Cardiff* was presented again, with its author reprising his role. Another O'Neill playlet, *Before Breakfast*, a monologue in which a nagging wife berates her offstage husband so bitterly that he cuts his throat while shaving, was also performed. O'Neill's hand reached out for the shaving bowl at one point and he rendered the deathrattle of the expiring husband at curtain-fall.

Stirred from lethargy by the performance of his work, O'Neill wrote at fever pitch during the winter of 1916–17, in Village quarters provided by a generous landlord. *The Moon of the Caribbees, Ile, In the Zone,* and *The Long Voyage Home,* all inspired by his sailor days, sprang from his pen in a sudden spurt of energy. Frank Shay, who had taken over the Washington Square Book Shop from the Bonis, urged him to submit these sea plays to *The Seven Arts* magazine which Waldo Frank, James Oppenheim, and Van Wyck Brooks edited and to which Robert Frost, Amy Lowell, Theodore Dreiser, and Sherwood Anderson contributed. But when *The Seven Arts* editors rejected them, O'Neill sent them to *The Smart Set.* In his cover letter, he explained that he was not offering them for publication as they were not the sort of thing the magazine usually published, but he wanted opinions on their worth. O'Neill, like most striving authors, was a faithful *Smart Set* reader and looked to Mencken and Nathan for validation.

Mencken replied promptly, writing that he liked the plays and was passing them on to Nathan. Soon came a letter from Nathan, concurring with his colleague's estimate, and accepting the one-acts for publication. O'Neill had not included *In the Zone* as it had already been performed by the Washington Square players and was requested for a tour on a vaudeville circuit. He thought it theatrically tricky and below his best writing. But *Ile, The Moon of the Caribbees,* and *The Long Voyage Home* appeared in *The Smart Set* during 1918. O'Neill regarded this as his first real recognition as a playwright. *The Seven Arts* had published his story "Tomorrow," and his plays being acted by the Provincetowners, but in *The Smart Set* he reached a wider audience with the approval of its editors, known for their exacting standards.

More letters were exchanged and O'Neill was invited to drop by *The Smart Set* office as the editors were curious to have a look at him. The curiosity being mutual, he presented himself one afternoon. After introducing him to Mencken, Nathan questioned him about his plays and projects.

A few weeks later they met again in Nathan's Royalton flat and afterwards Nathan wrote his guest that he was gratified to find him as proficient at drinking cocktails as he was at concocting dramas.

O'Neill had half-expected Nathan to be aloof and coldly discerning, enveloped in the armor of a caustic intelligence. Instead, he found Nathan warm, friendly, and human, as hinted at by the good-will and easy humor of his letters.

Certain similarities bound the novice dramatist and the established critic. Both were by nature secretive, cautious in personal relationships, and reluctant to expose their deeper feelings. Both—though Nathan had the veneer of the social dandy—were reserved and self-centered. Neither was quick to make new friends, but an accord developed rapidly between them due to their respect for one another's work. They were allied, too, as leaders in the revolt against Puritan culture.

Although the playwright was pleased and reassured when Nathan approved a new script, when he disapproved O'Neill would respond indignantly, accusing him of misunderstanding his purpose and defending with vigor whatever he had written. Later he sometimes admitted that he had been wrong, but absolutely refused to listen to advice.

It was not Nathan's practice to insist. He would state his opinion and when the two met they might further thrash out their differences. Nathan agreed with Wilde that the only thing to do with good advice was to pass it along as he knew men resent over-guidance.

In the 1930s O'Neill informed his editor, Saxe Commins, who was preparing a selected volume of his plays, that he was rejecting the proposition that Nathan contribute the preface. While he was grateful, of course, for the campaigns that Nathan had waged on his behalf, he had by no means ever considered Nathan as critic of his work, he wrote. Nathan, he felt, had no understanding of its inner spiritual trends. He argued that the critic, by his own frank admission, had too many blind spots; that he was antipathetic to plays with religious feeling and to plays involving any tinge of social revolution; that he despised *Lazarus Laughed*; totally misunderstood the intention of *Dynamo*; thought *The Hairy Ape* was radical propaganda; and read his own conceptions of life into the plays, to their author's irritated amusement.

In 1918, O'Neill completed his first full-length play, *Beyond the Horizon*. It is a tragedy of two New England farm brothers and their missed opportunities. The unimaginative brother goes to sea to no purpose; the second, a romantic dreamer and potential poet who would have profited by seeing the world, remains at home, failing as both a farmer and a husband and dying in bitter despair.

When Nathan received the script of *Beyond the Horizon*, he promptly, judged it to be an important American play and dispatched it to his close friend, John D. Williams, the producer, insisting on an immediate decision. Williams, similarly impressed, read it and bought an option on it the following day, but, preoccupied with other matters, he let the manuscript linger on his desk. Many months passed until Richard Bennett, then appearing under Williams' management in Elmer Rice's *For the Defense*, picked up the play while waiting for an appointment with his manager. When the tardy Williams arrived Bennett begged Williams to put it on for some trial matinées and, his request granted, he rounded up a cast, including Louise Closser Hale and Edward Arnold. Like Bennett, they were playing in Broadway theatres in the evenings, but were at liberty on certain afternoons.

Beyond the Horizon had its premiere at the Morosco Theater on a February afternoon in 1920 with the reviewers of the leading New York dailies in attendance. (Another guest was the author's father, James O'Neill, who, seated in a stage box, rejoiced that his wayward son had at last achieved Broadway.) Heywood Broun of *The New York Tribune* contended that the play, with its honest realism and tragic power, sounded the death knell for plays of popular trickery, and Woollcott of *The New York Times* hailed O'Neill as one of our foremost playwrights, writing that there was greatness in the drama. The matinées drew such large audiences that the play moved to the Little Theater for a long engagement and at the season's end O'Neill was awarded the Pulitzer Prize.

Later the same year the Provincetown Players produced O'Neill's *Emperor Jones* in the MacDougall Street Theater with the remarkable black actor, Charles Gilpin, as the ex-Pullman porter turned jungle monarch. With the success of these two plays O'Neill's reputation was established.

In 1921 O'Neill rewrote *Chris Christopherson* after it had failed (with the rising young actress, Lynn Fontanne, as its heroine) in an Atlantic City tryout, retitling it *Anna Christie*. Nathan had doubts about the play's finish, in which the former prostitute Anna, daughter of the Swedish tugboat captain, and the Irish sailor, Matt Burke, are reconciled after he has learned of her past.

Nathan first sent the script to the Selwyns who rejected it as a risky venture because of its grim realism and gloomy waterfront setting. He then took it to Arthur Hopkins and convinced that producer to desert his preference for European drama for an American play of genuine quality. Hopkins was quickly won over and cast an actress in whom he had great faith, Pauline Lord, as the wistful, forlorn Anna. It was the great dramatic hit of the season, winning O'Neill a second Pulitzer Prize and a handsome sum for the motion picture rights.

In the following years O'Neill required no introduction to Broadway managers. In collaboration with Kenneth MacGowan and Robert Edmond Jones he produced some of his own plays at the Greenwich Village theatres (*All God's Chillun Got Wings, Desire Under the Elms*, and *The Great God Brown*, the last two subsequently brought uptown for long engagements) as well as plays of other dramatists, such as *The Spook Sonata* by Strindberg. Later O'Neill trusted the staging of his work to the Theatre Guild. Nevertheless, Nathan's influential reviews were often extremely helpful, as well as his advance praise of *Marco Millions* and *Strange Interlude*, which appeared in *The American Mercury* when the magazine was the bible of American intellectuals.

Nathan discovered another major talent in the stories of F. Scott Fitzgerald. Fitzgerald was then only twenty-four and utterly unknown. He had cut short his education at Princeton to enlist when America entered the war, but, though commissioned as a lieutenant and feverishly anxious for action, he was never sent overseas, spending the duration drilling conscripts in army camps. While stationed at Fort Taylor in Alabama he attended a country club dance and met a beautiful Montgomery belle, Zelda Sayre. One glance at her and he was wildly in love. He wanted desperately to marry her, but she — and her parents — thought it best to let marriage wait until after the war when he had a secure job and could support her. On being demobilized he hurried to New York to make his fortune. By day he wrote advertising copy for a meagre salary and by night he wrote fiction in a top-floor room of a boarding house on Morningside Heights. His first sale of fiction was to Nathan, receiving $30 for a short story's appearance in *The Smart Set*.

Mencken's *Smart Set* review of Fitzgerald's first book, *This Side of Paradise*, which came out in March 1920, alerted his readers to sit up and take notice. Here, he proclaimed, was a new novelist of infinite promise and diverting originality.

Millions who had never read — and would never read — a word by Fitzgerald read about him in the newspapers as he aired his views on his contemporaries, writing trends, and the future of the flapper. When the reporters neglected him for a week he stood on his head in the Biltmore Hotel lobby. It worked.

Nathan was amused by the sight of his protégé splashing happily in the waves of publicity and he was enchanted by Fitzgerald's bride. Zelda's exhibitionistic feats were also reported in the press as she rode to appointments on the roofs of taxis, disrobed in Grand Central Station, and downed drinks like a trooper. All this was held to be but wholesome deviltry, a manifestation of her rebellious spirit, her compulsion to be a pace-setter and out-dare any other contenders for notoriety. That her alarming antics were symptomatic of incipient insanity seems to have occurred to no one at the time.

The Fitzgeralds, the most famous young couple on the New York scene, were expected to live up to their non-conformist reputation. Spurred on by the example of his wife, Fitzgerald tried to top her exploits, dancing in the aisle with an usher when the band struck up "I'm Just Wild About Harry" at the Negro revue, *Shuffle Along* and tearing off his shirt at the premiere of George White's *Scandals*. He was badly beaten by a bouncer he challenged in a cabaret. Sometimes these enfants terribles performed in unison, laughing loudly together at serious moments of a play or playing tag with each other through the Broadway traffic.

The obstreperous newlyweds were often the guests of Nathan at theatre openings and would finish the evening in his company at a table on the Ziegfeld roof to watch *The Midnight Frolic* in which W. C. Fields, Eddie Cantor, and Will Rogers clowned amid the bevy of glorified beauties. Other outings would terminate at the Montmartre Supper Club where college kids and theatrical and movie celebrities danced to the music of Paul Whiteman's orchestra. When they stayed at home there were cocktail parties that lasted from twilight until dawn.

Early one afternoon, Fitzgerald, Edmund Wilson, Donald Ogden Stewart, and Edna St. Vincent Millay, all the worse for liquor, descended on Nathan's study at the Royalton and applied matches to the rubber bindings on the pillows of the sofa. On another occasion Scott and Zelda, both quite tipsy, paid a surprise visit and, with Nathan's fencing foils from the wall, began a duel, slashing an oil painting in their combat. But Nathan, like their other friends, tolerated the mischief-making pair, admitting that he was "A Prisoner of Zelda."

A dinner party at which John D. Williams, producer, entertained the Fitzgeralds and Nathan at his home off Union Square nearly ended in night court. During the meal Zelda disappeared, making off to take a shower in the Union Square fountain. Noticing her long absence, Williams and Fitzgerald rushed out into the square to find Zelda stark naked and very damp, in the custody of a police posse. Arguing with the aggravated cops, Fitzgerald was arrested as an accomplice to the charge of indecent exposure. At this point Williams informed the arresting officers that their prisoners were the Fitzgeralds and the officers, supposing Fitzgerald to be a popular Irish comedian of the same name, released the disturbers of the peace and begged for autographs.

Scott being anxious to get on with his next novel, the Fitzgeralds took a country house near Westport, Connecticut. Nathan was often a guest as were many distracting, drunken acquaintances made in Manhattan. The raucous weekend drinking sessions continued far into the night but Nathan, who bored quickly, would turn in at a reasonable hour. One party lasted so long and raised such noise that he was unable to get to sleep. Rising at dawn, when the festivities in the drawing-room were still at their height, he went down to the cellar in hopes of finding some peace and quiet. As˜he rummaged about he came on Zelda's notebooks and began reading them. They were so interesting and clever that he thought they might be material for *The Smart Set*. Next day at luncheon, as the Fitzgeralds nursed hangovers he made Zelda an offer. Before she could reply Scott jumped up and bluntly rejected the proposition. Zelda's diaries, he declared, had given him many ideas for his fiction and he intended to use parts of them in future stories. This he did — in *The Jelly Bean* and *The Ice Palace*.

Nathan carried on a constant correspondence with Zelda. "Dear Blonde," read one of his notes, "why call me a polygamist when my passion for you is at once so obvious and so single." Zelda preserved these mock love letters, which led a Fitzgerald biographer to hint that Fitzgerald grew jealous of Nathan's open declarations, fearing his wife might yield to the critic's professed ardor. It is more likely that Fitzgerald tired of the joke, being its butt. In any case, Nathan objected to the biographer questioning the innocence of his flirtation with Zelda and the pseudo billets-doux failed to sever the friendship of the two men.

By temperament, Fitzgerald was a hero-worshipper and in 1920 he paid generous and sometimes hysterical homage to Mencken and Dreiser. He threw himself at the feet of Edith Wharton when she visited the Scribners office. In Paris he wasted an afternoon sitting on a bench outside Anatole France's Villa Saïd residence hoping to catch a glimpse of the master. At a dinner arranged by Sylvia Beach where he met James Joyce he threatened to jump out of the window to commemorate the event. Later came his blind idoltry of Ernest Hemingway as both an author and a person, an adoration that survived some cruel snubs. The unfinished novel on which he was at work at the time of his death, *The Last Tycoon*, contains in the character of Monroe Stahr a glorification of Irving Thalberg, the movie studio boss whose acumen provided MGM with box-office hits, a Hollywood genius.

Fitzgerald was dazzled by Nathan, in whom he saw something he longed to be: the debonair, assured sophisticate, perfectly attuned to his hedonistic philosophy, who maintained an enviable lifestyle. Amazingly youthful in appearance, handsome, fastidious in dress and manner, a success with women, a critic of rising importance and reputation, and a brilliant talker whose conversation was tinged with playful, worldly-wise cynicism, Nathan was the personification of the Fitzgerald ideal, 1920 model.

Fitzgerald could, as his friends witnessed, give a credible imitation of Nathan sitting at table and he could mimic the critic's mannerisms. He could record what Nathan said and the tone of his voice in saying it, but what went on in Nathan's mind he could not reproduce. As one of his intimates observed: "Fitz cannot depict how Nathan thinks or how anyone thinks except himself and possibly Zelda. He finds after writing about a character for a while it becomes just himself again." The heroes — or principals — of all Fitzgerald novels are basically versions of himself. *The Beautiful and the Damned* is a novel about the futile marriage of a young jazz-age young couple being carried by drink, dissipation, and listless drifting to their destruction. Nathan was too tempting a character to be excluded and many of his traits appear in the person of Maury Noble.

In describing this figure Fitzgerald reduces Nathan, fourteen years his senior, to a college chum of Patch. Noble is Patch's best friend, "the only man of all his acquaintances whom he admires and, to a bigger extent than he likes to admit to himself, envies." In appearance Noble is like nothing so much as a large, slender and imposing cat. Behind his attractive indolence, his irrelevance and his easy mockery lies a surprising and relentless maturity of purpose. His intentions, as he stayed in college, has been to use three years in travel, three in utter leisure and then to become immensely rich as quickly as possible. He is at leisure when first seen and the last we hear of him he is about to marry a Philadelphia heiress, snubbing Anthony who, in a drunken stupor, tries to borrow money from him just as he is making his escape in a taxi.

The close companionship of Fitzgerald and Nathan is affectionately portrayed in an early scene in which Anthony, finding himself at loose ends on a winter Saturday afternoon, stops at Noble's residence, a bachelor apartment hotel on 44th Street (The Royalton), and is overjoyed to find that his friend is at home. The telephone girl has positive instructions that no call be passed to him before the caller has given his name. She has a list of people to whom he is never in and another list of those to whom he is always at home. This was in fact a tactic of Nathan. Anthony is on the second list, and his spirits soar faster than the ascending elevator at the prospect of seeing his friend.

Noble attends the Gloria-Anthony wedding breakfast to inquire: "What is a gentleman, anyway? ... An American who can fool an English butler into thinking he's one." Noble later expounds his theory that the Bible was written by ironic ancient skeptics who, yearning for literary immortality, compiled a great book that will last forever to mock the credulity of mankind.

Maxwell Perkins took exception to the latter passage, fearing that many readers would take offense at the irreverent treatment of the Bible. As both Zelda and Mencken had praised the monologue, Fitzgerald rose to its defense. He would not be intimidated by the Scribner company or public prejudices and cited Voltaire, Samuel Butler, Shaw, and Mark Twain, all of whom had similarly questioned the literal interpretation of the Scriptures. Noble's opinions on the origins of the Bible as a sample of his growing pessimism appear in the published book, which he dedicated to Shane Leslis, Nathan, and Perkins.

Though their editorial responsibilities obliged them to correspond with and meet authors of every stripe, Nathan and Mencken shunned the literary cliques that were springing up in the post-war sunshine. Greenwich Village, then wallowing in Dadaism, unpunctuated verse and prose, and wild programs for political and aesthetic reforms, was alien to them. The Village, in their view, was a depressing refuge for hicks and cranks, full of spluttering firebrands, pseudo-poets, hopeless canvas daubers, and opinionated flappers escaped from the cornbelt.

"The Baptist virgin from the Middle West arrived in Sheridan Square has no thought save to get rid of her flannel underwear and flood her recesses with Chianti," Mencken recorded. "But in a few weeks she is making batiks, learning rhythmic dancing, writing a novel, or rehearsing for one of Harry Kemp's plays."

A constant companion of *The Smart Set* editors in these years was another editor of like cosmopolitanism: T. R. Smith of *The Century*. Smith, then in his forties, had had long practical training in the book trade. On manuscript hunts abroad he had befriended many European authors of eminence with whom he kept up a correspondence. They furnished him with the latest literary news and he placed their works. George Moore, Max Beerbohm, and James Huneker contributed regularly to *The Century* and under Smith's control it developed into a sophisticated monthly.

In 1921 he joined the Boni-Liveright firm as editor-in-chief and it was largely due to his managements and intuition that the house quickly gained a reputation for audacity and discovery. He noted the growing curiosity about psychoanalysis and opened negotiations whereby Boni-Liveright became the American publishers of Freud and Stekel. He persuaded Isadora Duncan to write her autobiography and it became a best-seller after her tragic death — she was strangled by her scarf which caught in the wheel of a speeding car on the Riveria. Remembering the success of books about Napoleon, he snatched up the English-language rights of Emil Ludwig's Napoleon biography before it appeared in Germany. He lengthened the Modern Library list with reprints of Blake, Swinburne, Gissing, D. H. Lawrence, Dunsany, Henry James, Frank Norris, and Stephen Crane and engaged John Galsworthy, Floyd Dell, Arthur Symons, and W. B. Yeats to write introductions to these new editions. When word reached him from Paris that a young American journalist was writing superb short stories in a new-fangled style he signed the unknown at once, publishing the first volume of Ernest Hemingway in the United States.

Smith knew that good authors needed money as well as tactful handling. He advised Liveright to subsidize Sherwood Anderson while he was at work on *Dark Laughter* in New Orleans, a move that led Anderson to abandon his first publisher, Ben Huebsch, for the new house. Anderson returned the favor by recommending a fellow New Orleans resident, and Smith thus brought out William Faulkner's first novel, *Soldier's Pay*. It was Smith, too, who urged Liveright to bring out a definitive edition of George Moore and to publish Huneker's *Painted Veils*, unexpurgated, in a limited edition for subscribers at $10 a copy, a stratagem that bypassed any attack by the lurking censors and grossed $13,000.

In addition to his shrewdness in acquisitions, he was a highly respected editor. George Moore stipulated that no one else was to edit his copy and even the cantakerous Dreiser permitted Smith to cut what he deemed superfluous from the bulging manuscript of *An American Tragedy.*

On sight Smith might have been mistaken for a benevolent college president. Of stubby stature, he wore a pince-nez to which was attached a broad, black ribbon after the manner of Chesterton. He was a genial mixer away from the editorial chambers, a deep drinker with a keen eye for feminine beauty. Sex was one of his favorite subjects and he compiled a weighty tome of erotic verse which included translations of Oriental love poets. On his nightly round of parties and in the speakeasies he frequented he extended invitations to all the pretty women he met to come and ornament the cocktail receptions he hosted after hours in the Liveright building, a brownstone town house on East 48th Street. These festivities were soon famous as the best parties in New York.

Nathan and Mencken relished Smith's company and his general attitude to work and play. One evening "Schmidt" (as they called him) invited them to cocktails at his apartment where they found with him a stranger who was introduced as one Lewis. The fellow was known to neither of them save as the author of a negligible serial that had appeared in *The Saturday Evening Post* and as the author of a play called *Hobohemia* which Nathan had characterized as being "epizootic."

This momentous meeting has been humorously preserved by Nathan. In his *Intimate Notebooks* he writes:

> Rarely had we taken off our hats and coats and before Smith had an opportunity even to fish out his deluxe corkscrew from behind his deluxe sets of the works of the more esoteric Oriental and Polack amorists, when the tall, skinny, paprika-headed stranger simultaneously coiled one long arm around Mencken's neck and the other around mine, well nigh strangling us and putting resistance out of the question, and — yelling at the top of his lungs — began "So you guys are crit-

ics, are you? Well, let me tell you something. I'm the best writer in this here gottdamn country and if you, Georgie, and you, Hank, don't know it now, you'll know it gottdamn soon. Say, I've just finished a book that'll be published in a week or two and it's the gottdamn best book of its kind that this here gottdamn country has had and don't you guys forget it. I worked a year on the gottdamn thing and it's so far ahead of most of the men you two think are good that I'll be gottdamned if it doesn't make me sick to think about it! Just wait. You've got a treat coming, Georgie and Hank, and don't you boys make no mistake about that."

Projected from Smith's flat by the self-endorsing uproar — it kept up for fully half an hour longer — Mencken and I jumped into a taxicab, directed the driver to speed us posthaste to a tavern where we might in some peace recover our equilibrium and our ear-drums, and looked at each other. "Of all the idiots I've ever laid eyes on, that fellow is the worst!" groaned Mencken, gasping for breath. Regaining my own breath some moments later, all that I could add was that if any such numskull could ever write anything worth reading, maybe there was something in Christian Science too.

Three days later he received the following letter from Mencken who had returned to Baltimore.

Dear George; Grab hold of a bar-rail, steady yourself and prepare yourself for a terrible shock. I've just read the advance sheets of the book of that *Lump* we met at Schmidt's and, by God, he has done the job! It's a genuinely excellent piece of work. Get it as soon as you can and take a look. I begin to believe that perhaps there isn't a God after all. There is no justice in this world. Yours in XT., M.

The book was *Main Street* and brought its self-endorsing author recognition as the most observant and penetrating recorder of middle-class American life. *The Smart Set* editors, agreeing about his talent, quickly revised their original dismissal of him as a boor and a bore. He did not curtail his bumpkin behavior on becoming famous but they simply accepted it and joked about it as part and parcel of his "rough diamond" personality. He burlesqued Main Street, but Main Street was in his veins.

They submitted to many Lewis outbursts after befriending him. Once Nathan was present when "The Red Menace," as they dubbed him, paralyzed a barroom by standing on a chair and reeling off an interminable discourse on the necessity of good fellowship among businessmen. This overpowering address was later incorporated into his next novel, *Babbitt*, which gave the English language a new word.

On another occasion he summoned Nathan and Mencken to his side when he lay ill with a temperature of 102 in a New York hotel. As soon as they entered he leapt from his sickbed, his white, old-fashioned nightgown flapping about him, to launch into an evangelical salvation spiel. With tears in his eyes and his voice cracking with pious exaltation, he entreated them as wretched sinners to see the holy light, mend their worldly ways and "come to Jesus." His preaching done, he sank back, pulled the covers over his head, and fell asleep. His guests tiptoed away, fearing that his fever was of the brain. Soon after, the hell-fire sermon he had delivered was found in another of his novels, *Elmer Gantry*, a sardonic portrait of a devious Protestant clergyman and a savage attack on organized religion. Some of his irrate readers threatened to lynch him for his mockery of their faith.

Lewis had been living in London for some months, working on *Arrowsmith*, the story of a self-sacrificing doctor, when Nathan arrived there on one of his annual spring visits. At a luncheon party Nathan found himself seated next to Philip Guedella. As soon as introductions were made, Guedella said to him, "You are an American and I have a message for you. If your country doesn't recall Sinclair Lewis, there will be war between England and the United States." Abroad — as at home — Lewis had been making stupefying scenes.

At literary gatherings he would address the assembled in vaudeville dialects, reproving British critics for not responding more enthusiastically to his novels as well as those of his American confreres. He delighted in mimicking the eminent British authors he had met. For his imitation of Bernard Shaw he purchased false whiskers and had photographs taken of his performance. These snapshots he showed to Shaw, who was not amused.

When *Arrowsmith* was awarded the Pulitzer Prize Lewis, on Mencken's advice, refused it because he had not received one for *Main Street*, objecting that the committee was insufficiently qualified to judge. In 1930 he received the Nobel Prize for literature, the first American to be so honored, and his friends questioned him about his forthcoming speech of acceptance.

"What am I going to say?" he roared, waving his arms in the air and knocking down two lamps. "Well, you guys listen! 'Your Gracious Majesty and Officers of the Coldstream Guards: it is a great pleasure, let me tell you, for a little feller from Sauk Centre to meet you big Swedes. I feel proud and honored, believe me, boys, and when I get back home and tell the folks of the swell reception you've given me, they're going to be not only proud of me but of you too. After all, we're all brothers in Kiwanis, whether we're Swedes, Americans or Bohunks, and our hearts are in the right place. So what do you all say to going out, King, and having a little drink?"

This was idle boasting. Despite his threats, his conduct in Stockholm at the Nobel Prize ceremonies was exemplary. Indeed, it was so formal and proper that the King and some of his courtiers, having read of the eccentric American comportment in his novels, inquired if he were not partially of British extraction.

◆ ◆ ◆

The Sumner-inspired "Clean Books Bill," which demanded the immediate suppression of *Women in Love* by D. H. Lawrence, *Casanova's Homecoming* by Schnitzler, the anonymous *Young Girl's Diary* (with a preface by Freud), and Petronius' *Satyricon*, went before the New York State Assembly with only feeble opposition from the press. *The New York Times* meekly commented that the suppression of Petronius would be a loss to human knowledge "whatever may be thought of Lawrence and Schnitzler."

The measure failed to pass due to the courage of the publisher, Horace Liveright, who went to Albany with his lawyers to prevent a curtailing of literary expression. His rivals refused even to endorse his action. It was a speech by a young state senator, James J. Walker, later the dapper mayor of New York City, that turned the tide. Walker remarked that he had never heard of a woman who was ruined by a book. The majority of the assembly laughed and voted down the bill to the rage of the would-be censors who vowed to continue their campaign.

Magazine editors, too, thought it wisest to avoid baiting the smut-sniffers who were now in full cry, swearing to "protect young minds from pernicious ideas." *The Little Review* was prosecuted for publishing chapters from James Joyce's *Ulysses* and no publishing house dared bring out the book which is today required reading in many universities.

W. Somerset Maugham's short story about the encounter of a San Francisco prostitute and a sex-obsessed Protestant minister who meet on a Pacific island outpost, "Miss Thompson," was rejected by the big-circulation magazines and came to *The Smart Set* at a marked down price: $300. The editors grabbed it at once and its appearance boosted their magazine's circulation. Maugham had not seen the material for a play in his story, but he granted John Colton permission to try a dramatization. The Colton adaptation, *Rain*, opened the following season to become one of the most famous plays of the 1920s.

A new department began to appear in *The Smart Set*. It contained the conversations of its editors on various topics as set down by the imaginary Major Owen Hatteras. The following is a sample discussion:

ON LITERATURE

Scene: The Lackawanna Ferry-ship at Jersey City.

Time: Four o'clock of a Winter afternoon.

NATHAN: The literatus suffers, but he is not actually alone. Nay, he has company, as murderers have company in the death-house and theologians on their way to hell. He has his conscience, as sharp as no razor ever was, and his memories, as sickly sweet as stale beer. He remembers the girl who wore the black and orange jersey. He remembers the girl who made him promise to stop drinking Aquavit. He remembers the girl who married the Congressman with the toupee and sent him back his faded valentines. He remembers what he owes, what he ate in 1902, what it felt like to be 30 years old, what he learned in college — all that he has endured in this damndest of all worlds. But this is only half of the story. After all, a man's conscience is usually so cowardly that it is afraid even of him, and so it doesn't bother him much — and his memories cloud and clot as the years go plunging by. But day in and day out his body is wasting, and as it wastes it hurts; the disintegration of colloids is painful. What man of forty can go into a room alone without feeling a dull ache somewhere? . . .

MENCKEN: . . . When I go into my lonely writing chamber and sit down to compose I feel every twinge and alarm of every one of those kidney cells. The accumulated surgical shock is sometimes downright maddening. I break into a cold sweat. It is as if an infinite multitude of ultramicroscopic pins were being thrust through my gizzard. And in the room of every dead cell, once the carcass has been hauled away by the blood stream, there is scar-tissue — a stiff, unyielding, uncomfortable substance, as irritating as a speck of sand in the eye. As you hint, the effect on the literatus, penned up in his chamber with such tragedies is almost maddening. It is only the dull brute, the stock broker or traffic cop turned author, who does not suffer. . . . I have sat for four days trying to fetch up a single phrase — and had more pains and malaises in that time than a man with the botts. Literary endeavor is the cause of my hypochondria. I remember well one day when I was working on *A Book of Prefaces*. So many aches suddenly appeared. North, East, South and West, that I jumped to the conclusion that I was coming down with lockjaw, with maybe Asiatic cholera as a complication. It was all I could do to keep from leaping to the window and yelling for the coroner. I suffered more in four hours than Debs has suffered in all his time at Atlanta.

NATHAN: And no wonder! A Socialist is ideally fitted for going to jail. All his ideas are ready-made and quite solid, and so he can risk being alone. Socialism is thus a sort of insurance against insanity, like patriotism and religion. A man swallows it, gives up thinking, and is happy.

MENCKEN: What is called business has the same effect. It

dulls the perceptions and so makes for happiness. As you know, I hate it quite as much as you do, but this hatred is largely snobbery: I am, to that extent at least, a genuine literary gent. As a matter of fact, I believe fully that our joint business affairs have been the salvation of both of us. Business engages the mind, but makes no actual demands upon it; it takes infinitely more concentrated mental effort to write even a bad fugue than it takes to start a national bank or swindle the Government. A business man may thus suffer from mental decay for years and never discover it. I could give you examples. But in the case of a literary man, the slightest departure from the normal shows itself at once: one concludes, reading his book, that the fellow is balmy. Hence free verse. Free verse is simply the pathological production of a poet who has gone crazy trying in vain to write poetry — a sort of toxin thrown off by a sprained mind. It has the same chemical and psychological basis as the inchoate words that religious maniacs babble at Methodist revivals. . . .

NATHAN: Say no more. What you endeavor to impart is, after all, quite clear to me. I do not reject the theory as untenable: . . . It is the only truth of which a careful man may say without qualification that it is substantially true. What I believed in 1912 I no longer believe, but someone else *does* believe it — some pathetic ass. Thus every truth with any merit in it whatsoever is kept alive. As one crowd of believers goes out, another comes in.

MENCKEN: Very nobly put. . . . Today you preach a certain body of critical doctrines, the product of gazing nightly at herds of half-naked women in stuffy theatres. By tomorrow you will have begun to doubt these doctrines. But meanwhile they will be filched by the critics of the New York newspapers, translated into bad English, and launched upon the white-goods buyers who sit beside you in the show-houses. Next month or next year they will reach the critics of Pittsburgh and Kansas City; a year later they will conquer the Columbia faculty, and then the Yale faculty. But by that time you yourself will be quite purged of them, and so you will be made ill by the very thought of them. In their place you will have a new set. . . . Put down half of it to the chivalry aforesaid, and the other half to my interest in literature. The love of literature is, I suppose, in itself a form of chivalry; chivalry toward its creator's expressed or suppressed vanities. Give all literature your eye and you'll find that this is so, from Benvenuto Cellini, say, at one extreme, to Robert W. Chambers at the other. In each and every case, the written document is a polite, low bow to the writer — as the writer desires to see himself....

[Harriet Beecher Stowe] want[ed] to be ... a bloodhound. She wanted, in her stupendous vanity, to be a tracker-down, a scooter after fugitives, an instrument of vengeance, which is to say, justice. She was the lady Upton Sinclair of her day. Had she lived in 1907, she would have written Thomas W. Lawson's books. Had she lived in 1912, she would have written *My Little Sister* and the other white-slavery brochures. Had she lived in 1915, she would have written Cleveland Moffett's *Invasion of America*. And were she alive today, she'd be bawling for the Blue Laws.

Though this conversation — like the others — was devised for publication (taken down by their stenographer and then revised) their off-duty banter was in the same tone.

Edmund Wilson, then editing *Vanity Fair*, which had quarters in the same building as *The Smart Set*, recalled a surprise visit to his office. His secretary brought in a card announcing that Nathan, Mencken, and Maeterlinck were in the waiting-room begging audience. Nathan and Mencken were ushered in and began apologizing profusely for the absence of Maeterlinck.

"I told you to keep an eye on him. He probably ran off with a Ziegfeld chorus girl when you weren't looking," remarked Mencken, indignantly reprimanding his friend.

"Always this compulsive pursuit of beauty. What can you expect?" returned Nathan.

Maeterlinck was in New York at that moment and the newspapers were full of him. The Belgian poet-philosopher who lived "withdrawn" in an ancient abbey in Normandy, who looked the brooding dreamer (photographers were not excluded from his romantic residence), and who speculated of the mysteries of existence and the soul fascinated a vast public. His allegorical children's fable, *The Blue Bird*, had held the stage from Moscow to Broadway. In 1911 he had been awarded the Nobel Prize for literature and his American vogue was now at its zenith. His *Life of the Bees* was a best-seller; all the Little Theater groups in the country were playing his pale, portentous fantasies; and his play, *Pelléas and Mélisande*, was the libretto for Debussy's opera. Not adverse to collecting a few dollars, he was in the United State on a lecture tour.

Maeterlinck believed that he had taught himself English by a self-invented system of phonetics and in his initial lecture he rose to demonstrate his linguistic expertise before an audience that packed Carnegie Hall. No one could understand a word he said and an interpreter had to be summoned.

Another Maeterlinck experiment proved more lucrative. Reports of his genius had reached the ears of the illiterate movie moguls and he was invited by Hollywood to compose scenarios. After some months at a high salary he informed his employer, Sam Goldwyn, that he had completed his script and that he would present it to him at the railroad station on the hour of his departure. Goldwyn and his staff of photographers gathered at the Los Angeles depot for the ceremonial farewell. The presentation of the precious screenplay was made as cameras clicked. As the train disappeared Goldwyn impatiently tore open the package and glanced at the scenario. "The hero is a bee!" he exclaimed in exasperation.

The Smart Set pair discussed with Edmund Wilson the extravagant reception being accorded other literary visitors. A whole army of them seemed to be loose in the land and most of them, Mencken grouchily complained, were "gaudy frauds."

Vicente Blasco Ibañez, the Spanish novelist, was being rapturously interviewed wherever he went. He had contracts for his fiction with the Hearst magazines and the motion picture studios were buying the rights to his books. His novel, *The Four Horsemen of the Apocalypse*, with its vivid description of the Battle of the Marne and its savage portraiture of the brutal Huns, had achieved gigantic sales and had done its bit in 1917 in swaying public opinion to the Allied cause before the United States entered the war. Ibañez was a showy fellow and basked like a fat cat in the sunshine of his popularity. He took great pride in his dress but was infuriated when Charles MacArthur, then a reporter in Chicago, after an hour's private audience with him, wrote three columns praising only the brilliance of his shoeshine.

Wilson listened amused to the banter of his colleagues and noted their manner of dual delivery. Mencken would plunge into a fulsome statement of one of his opinions. Then Nathan would chime in with some barded aside, in agreement or disagreement, rounding out the dissertation. They complemented one another so exactly that their discourse, though spontaneous, resembled a sketch.

Their published conversations brought them offers to write for the stage. Ziegfeld proposed that they collaborate on the book for one of his *Follies* and Winthrop Ames suggested that Nathan write a topical revue for his Little Theater.

Knopf was bringing out a Nathan book each year. Following *The Popular Theatre* (1918), came *Comedians All* (1919), *Heliogabalus*, and *The American Credo*, both in collaboration with Mencken (1920), *The Theatre, the Drama, the Girls* (1921) and *The Critic and the Drama* (1922). For these, Nathan revised his published articles for permanent preservation. A chill falls on most first-night notices even a few days after the event. They belong not to the ages but to the day-before-yesterday's newspaper. Nathan had the genuine literary gifts and the shrewd eye of a sound editor. He reorchestrated his material to devise books of contagious gusto. Their pages flash with enduring wit and keen perception.

By now he had a loyal and growing following. *Comedians All* outsold all previous books on the theatre by an American. The daily newspaper reviewers published their verdicts the morning after a premiere, but the discerning minority wanted to know what Nathan thought. So did, increasingly, playwrights and producers. For them, he was a court of appeal. He often differed sharply from his daily colleagues and was capable of saving a play.

In a lengthy essay that appeared in the first of his series of *Prej-*

udices volumes Mencken analyzed the theory and practice of his partner. Nathan, in Mencken's estimate, had added dramatic criticism to what Nietzsche called the gay sciences, making it amusing, stimulating, and even startling:

> He has brought to the business, artfully concealed, a thorough acquaintance with the heavy work of the pioneers, Lessing, Schlegel, Hazlitt and Lewes and an even wider acquaintance, lavishly disposed, with every hook and corner of the theatrical scene across the water. To discharge this extraordinarily copious mass of information he has hauled and battered the English language in new and often astounding forms, and when English has failed he has helped it out with French, German, American Swedish, Russian, Turkish, Latin, Sanskrit, and Old Church Slavic, and with algebraic symbols, chemical formulae, musical notations and the signs of the Zodiac.

But what kept a man of such intelligence and talents, a man now on the threshold of forty, in the theatre, "breathing bad air nightly, gaping at prancing imbeciles, sitting cheek by jowl with cads"? Mencken, groping for an answer, mentioned a secret romanticism — "a lingering residuum of boyish delight in pasteboard and spangles, gaudy colors and soothing sounds, preposterous heroes and appetizing wenches." To this he added another possible explanation: the sense of humor of a zestful spirit to whom life is a spectacle that never grows dull. "For the theatre is not life in miniature, but life enormously magnified, hideously exaggerated and in this the stage show is diversion for a cynic."

Nathan's own *Weltanschauung* appeared first in the pages of *The Smart Set* and reappeared as the foreward to his next book, *The World in False Face*:

> What interests me in life is the surface of life: life's music and color, its charm and ease, its humor and its loveliness. The great problems of the world — social, political, economic, and theological do not concern me in the slightest. I care not who writes the laws of the country so long as I may listen to its songs. I can live every bit as happily under a king, or even a Kaiser, as under a president. One church is as good as another to me; I never enter one anyway, save only to delight in

some particularly beautiful stained-glass window, or in some fine specimen of architecture, or in the whiskers of the Twelve Apostles. If all the Armenians were to be killed to-morrow and if half of Russia were to starve to death the day after, it would not matter to me in the least. What concerns me alone is myself, and the interests of a few close friends. For all I care the rest of the world may go to hell at today's sunset. I was born in America and America is to me, at the time of writing, the most comfortable country to live in — and also, at the time of writing, the very pleasantest — in the world.

This is why, at the time of writing, I am here, and not in France or in England, or elsewhere. But if England became more comfortable and more pleasant than America tomor-row, I'd live in England. And if I lived in England I should be no more interested in the important problems of England than I am now interested in the important problems of Amer-ica. My sole interest lies in writing, and I can write as well in one place as in another, whether it be Barcelona, Spain, or Coon Rapids, Iowa. Give me a quiet room, a pad of paper, eight or nine sharp lead pencils, a handful of thin, mild cig-ars, and enough to eat and drink — all of which, by the grace of God, are happily within my means — and I do not care a tinker's damn whether Germany invades Belgium or Belgium Germany, whether Ireland is free or not free, whether the Stock Exchange is bombed or not bombed, or whether the nations of the earth arm, disarm, or conclude to fight their wars by limiting their armies to biting each other.

On that day, during the world war when the most critical battle was being fought, I sat in my still, sunlit, cozy library composing a chapter on aesthetics for a new book on the drama. And at five o'clock, my day's work done, I shook and drank a half dozen aperitifs.

Such, I appreciate, are not the confessions that men usu-ally make for they are evil and unpopular confessions. My only apology for them is that they are true.

Life, as I see it, is for the fortunate few — life with all its Chinese lanterns, and sudden lonely tunes, and gay sadness. In so far as I have any philosophy at all, it is founded upon that theory. For the Nietzschean 'Be hard!' I have no use, however. It savours too much of the cannon, thong and overly intense purpose. For myself I substitute "Be indifferent." I was born indifferent; and at forty I find myself unchanged in attitude.... Indignation does not make, and never has made, the world any better than has my own objectionable philosophy of contentful laissez-faire.... Rome, the greatest nation in history, was never indignant about anything. Nor has been or is the nation of tomorrow, Japan. The chronic indignation of France is rapidly driving her onto the rocks.

It is this spirit that I seek the theatre as an outlet for my ideas. An idea, on whatever subject, seems to me to be more in key with my attitude toward life if it is predicated upon an art. Art is, in the view of nine-tenths of the human race, bootless, "unpractical." Life, to me, is artificial; and my criticism of drama is based upon the theory that drama is artificial life. There isn't so very much difference in my way of looking at things, between life as it actually is and life as it is shown in the theatre.

Nathan was not convinced that only great art can inspire and produce great criticism, and illustrated the argument by citing how Dryden's *Defense of an Essay on Dramatic Poesy* grew out of a third-rate preface to his brother-in-law's book of fourth-rate plays; how Goethe wrote imperishable criticism from viewing plays by Kozebue, Raupach, and Iffland; how Zola's first critical writing sprang from being forced to sit through trifling exhibitions when he was a drama reviewer; and how Shaw's critical essays were founded upon *Trilby*, *The Girl I left Behind Me*, *The Colleen Bawn*, *The Sorrows of Satan*, the plays that held the London boards in the 1890s, those of Sydney Grundy, Stanley Weyman, Marie Coreeli, Paul Potter, and David Belasco. "A thousand trivialities are placed in the test tubes of aesthetics so that a single piece of sound criticism may endure," he claimed.

The theatre to which I devote my pen with a pestiferous catholicity of taste embraces *Medea* and *The Follies*, Eleanora Duse and Florence Mills. I do not take it very seriously for I am the sort that takes nothing very seriously; nor in the other hand do I take it too lightly, for one who takes nothing very seriously takes nothing too lightly. I take it simply as, night in and night out, it comes before my eyes: a painted toy with something of gold inside it. And so it is that I write of it. I criticize it as a man criticizes his own cocktails and his own God.

At these self-revelations some smiled and others bridled. An American Legion chapter consigned them to the flames as blasphemous and unpatriotic for their irreverent references to the late war. Nathan's heartless dismissal of the world's woes offended the pious and up-lifters, as did the statement, an echo of Stendhal, that life is only for the favored few. During World War II they were denounced anew as a horrible example of the irresponsibility of intellectual leaders of the twenties, who spread poisonous disillusionment among the young with their "sentimental pessimism."

Yet these confessions, couched as they are in a piece of bravura writing, are, in their author's phrase, not to be taken either too seriously or too lightly. Certainly they must not be taken literally. They purport to be the stock-taking of the critic at forty, but they are less an accurate portrait of their composer than they are the public image he wished to project at that time.

In subsequent bursts of self-criticism Nathan qualified certain opinions, his *Weltanschauung* mellowing as the years slipped by.

This glimpse in the mirror had been devised to surprise and vex and it did so. The American literati discussed, disputed, and remembered it. One commentator declared that it was merely evidence that Nathan lacked the imagination to embrace humanity. Another, in defense, cited the critic as the First Apostle of the Self-Centered with the courage to admit it. Alfred Kazin, two decades later, likened it to an undergraduate restating of Oscar Wilde's "art for art's sake" code, though Wilde had borrowed the theory from Theophile Gautier as he had borrowed Gautier's penchant for gaudy attire.

PART FIVE

In his inaugural address, President Harding had proposed "a return to normalcy." By 1922 the nation was settling back more or less contentedly into its former paths. In Europe inflation had reduced Germany and Austria to appalling poverty. Admiral Horthy's counterrevolution had disposed of Bela Kun's Communist dictatorship in Hungary. Famine had led to cannibalism along the Volga following the civil strife in Russia and Herbert Hoover was raising funds for Russian relief. In Italy Mussolini's black-shirted Fascist army marched on Rome, seized power, and stamped out the embers of revolt. But Americans, the nightmare of the war fast fading from memories, were oblivious to the upheavals abroad. The stock market surged upward and prosperity loomed. Prohibition was a dreadful inconvenience to the majority, but the Red menace had evaporated like a bad dream. It seemed unlikely that Lenin and Trotsky, with a starving population on their hands, were plotting an invasion of the United States.

By 1922 the New York theatrical district had undergone an amazing transformation. Prohibition had closed most of the glittering pleasure domes, though the Palais-Royal, where Paul Whiteman's jazz band made loud the night, stood as a reminder of past glories. Gone were the Knickerbocker Hotel with its King Cole bar, Rector's, and Churchill's. All hotels were now officially "dry" and alcoholic beverages were no longer served at another late-night oasis, Jack's, across from the Hippodrome under the Sixth Avenue El. Prohibition agents had raided Resienweber's, the uptown haunt of Columbia students and migratory night-hawks. Plain-clothes detectives had wrecked Jansen's, smashing the furniture and the mirrors with fire-axes and arresting the personnel and customers on learning beer was on tap. The Greenwich Village Inn was an early victim of Prohibition — when its amiable proprietor, Barney Gallant, pleaded guilty to the charge of selling booze, he was sentenced to a term in the Tombs. New York nightlife went underground, into "membership clubs" and up to Harlem, which had just opened as a fashionable playground.

Monumental movie palaces rose to ornament Broadway and the "legitimate" theatres were shoved into the side-streets. The playhouses that still stood on the Great White Way between Times Square and Columbus Circle were often rented out for the premieres of the super-films as a way of endowing the movies with some artistic reputability.

Perhaps the movies, by luring the morons with celluloid versions of the sort of trash the stage had discarded, were ridding the theatre of an undesirable element. This siphoning off of low-brow theatre customers was evidently incomplete for a sufficient number remained to patronize the rubbish of the stage. How otherwise could the success of *Abie's Irish Rose* be explained? It held the New York boards for five years and attained a longer run than any previous play in the history of the American theatre.

Perhaps the movies in clearing the theatre of its peanut gallery spectators were beneficial, but Nathan saw in them a deadly menace to dramatic art. He had mocked the movies in many of his books — *The Popular Theatre* contains a chapter travestying the film scenarios of the period — and in a syndicated article titled "The Hooligan at the Gates" in 1921 he sounded a three-alarm warning:

> More than any force, more than any other ten forces all compact, have the moving pictures in the last half dozen years succeeded brilliantly in reducing further the taste, the sense and the general culture of the American nation.
>
> Like a thundering flood of bilge and scum, the flapdoodle of the films has swept over the country, carrying before it what seeds of perception were sprouting, however faintly, among our lesser people. And today the cinema, ranking the fourth industry in the Republic, proudly views the havoc it has wrought and turns its eyes to new Belgiums.
>
> Controlled in the overwhelming main by the most ignorant social outcasts . . . by hereditary toothpick suckers, soup coloraturos and six-day sock-wearers, controlled in the mass by men of a complete anaesthesia to everything fine and everything earnest and everything dollarless, the moving pic-

tures — the physic of the proletariat — have revealed themselves the most effective carriers of idiocy that the civilized world has known. Here in America, their fortress, they have cheapened a national taste, already cheap, to a point where cheapness can seem to go no further. They have lurked near schoolhouses and seduced the impressionable minds of children. They have crawled up alleys and side-streets and for thirty pieces of copper have sold youth into aesthetic corruption. They have gagged the mouths of almost every newspaper in America with a rich advertising revenue; if there is a newspaper in the land that has the honor and the respectability to call the moving pictures by their right name, I haven't heard of it. They have bought literature and converted it, by their own peculiar and esoteric magic, into rubbish. They have bought imaginative actors and converted them into face-makers and mechanical dolls. They have bought reputable authors and dramatists and have converted them into shamefaced hacks. They have elected as their editors and writers the most obscure and talentless failures of journalism and tawdry periodicals. They have enlisted as their directors, with a few exceptions, an imposing array of ex-stage butlers and chauffeurs, assistant stage managers of turkey troupes, discharged pantaloons and the riff-raff of Broadway street-corners. And presently they sweep their wet tongue across the American theatre.

The article constitutes a view that he amended only slightly in after years. From the late 1890s, when primitive images in motion commenced to bob and flicker on music-hall screens as epilogues to vaudeville shows, the motion pictures were sneered at. The very name given them — "movies" — was an appelation of contempt. Through their nickelodeon stage — "5 reels for 5 cents" — and on to the introduction of eight-reeled features they gained scant encouragement from the educated minority. Shortly before World War I newspaper publishers, bribed by fat advertising contracts, began to notice them in theatrical columns, but it is significant that *The New York Times* had no official film reviewer before 1924.

Intellectuals made a pose of ignoring them. "They are for those with empty lives and empty heads" was the opinion of the Hungarian dramatist, Molnár. "By morons for morons" was Mencken's well-known comment. Sinclair Lewis, when an interviewer in Moscow inquired about the development of the American film, replied with the enigmatic question: "How long is a piece of string?" Authors were quite willing to sell their novels and plays for filming, but balked at closer association. Willa Cather, after the release of an inept, embarrassing film version of her novel, *The Lost Lady*, refused all subsequent movie offers.

In Europe there was relatively less snubbing of the movies. H. G. Wells announced that the cinema was potentially a great art. Bernard Shaw confessed to delight in the screen antics of Douglas Fairbanks and Mary Pickford; William Archer, the veteran drama critic and translator of Ibsen, recommended Robert Flaherty's documentary of Eskimo seal-hunters, *Nanook of the North*; James Agate of *The Manchester Guardian* was enraptured by Charlie Chaplin's *The Kid*, considering it an exquisite blending of comedy and pathos; while in Paris Jean Cocteau published accolades to Buster Keaton and the Western star, William S. Hart, and founded the French film fad. Partly as a result of European approbation, those in high places began to appreciate movies. President Wilson had private showings of new films every afternoon in the White House, and his successor, President Harding, invited Hollywood stars and producers to publicized luncheons in the executive mansion.

King George V and Queen Mary attended the Drury Lane premiere of D. W. Griffith's screen spectacle, *Intolerance*, but this last bit of news did not in the least impress Nathan. Surveying the statistics of royal attendance at the London theatre over a long period, he had concluded that there was a common streak in royal taste. "With Synge, Schnitzler, Galsworthy and Hervieu playing down the block, Buckingham Palace has ever generally selected instead a bedroom farce, a crook melodrama or a leg show. Let us therefore invite our American professors to make dramatic criticism somewhat safe for democracy."

Unlike the poseurs who boasted of never going to the movies and damned them out of hand, Nathan made a study of them, keeping a critical eye trained upon them. Though opposed to the film as a mechanical toy — a popular pastime as witless as a fair-ground merry-go-round — he cited the men who controlled its fortunes as a major drawback to its possible artistic development. "Not one of them under penalty of death could tell you the difference between *The Two Gentlemen from Verona* and *The Gentlemen from Indiana*," he complained.

> The movies will never be worth a hoot until the business end of the enterprise is absolutely and entirely separated from the actual producing department. What few fairly worthwhile pictures we have had were made by producers independent of the Zukors, Mayers, Foxes, and other such financial padrones, by players or director in command of their own destinies: Chaplin's *The Kid*, Fairbanks' *Thief of Bagdad*, Griffith's *Broken Blossoms*. What other comparatively decent pictures have come along from time to time have been the result of continuous fights with the money overlords on the part of directors and players, with the latter triumphing by hook or crook over the former's hostility and objections.
>
> The movies must tell not the drama's stories in the drama's way, but its own stories in its own way. Now and again, it makes such an effort, pointing to what it may conceivably some day accomplish. *The Last Laugh* and *The Thief of Bagdad* are movies stories; the stage could not handle them; the movie can and does."

The strict censorship that prevailed over the screen did not, Nathan maintained, damage the films.

> [The censors] did not interfere with *The Last Laugh*; they not only let *The Big Parade* and *What Price Glory?!* alone, but even allowed them to do and say things that, in the instance of the drama, would have brought the police at a gallop. All they cut out of the Russian picture, *Potemkin*, were a few feet showing a wormy piece of meat and a baby having its head smashed in, both of which were nauseating and unnecessary and rid of which the picture was better than before. And if they made 'Variety' foolish in certain hinterland communities by converting the old fellow's inamorata into his wife, let us remember that they did nothing of the kind in the larger cities and one can't judge the movies by Podunk any more than one can judge literature by Boston.

When someone wrote that the state censorship boards allowed vulgarity and sickly sentimentality, but forbade the slightest trace of realism in the few good movies that came their way, Nathan challenged the statement with evidence to the contrary.

> They forbid nothing of the kind, painful as it is to have to admit it. From the child-birth episode in *Way Down East* to the Zolaesque realism of *Greed*, from the Grand Guignol realism of the decapitation and disemboweled soldier episodes in *Intolerance* and *Hearts of the World* to the realistic amatory and seduction scenes in *The Patriot* and *A Woman of Affairs*, from the realistic concupiscence of *The Merry Widow* to the violent realism of *The Sea Beast* and *China Express*, the liberality of the abused censors has been disturbingly apparent.

The attachment of sound to the film did not impress the critic in the least. He saw in it a retreat and defeat. He regretted the vanished dreamlike fluidity of the silent screen and its lovely women — many of whom proved to have squeaky voices when tested for the Vitaphone. Even the best talkie was inevitably, by its intrinsic nature, only a road version of theatre drama. When they tackled Shakespeare with a talkie of *Romeo and Juliet* he wrote one of his most fulsome reviews on the medium.

> Aside from its million dollar investiture, much of it superfluous and not a little absurd, it is infinitely less singing, moving and exalting than even a third-rate stage presentation of the play. Leslie Howard's Romeo suggests that he has swallowed an air-cooling plant; he contains and displays all the romantic ardor of a painstaking polished milk bottle and in the balcony scene gives the impression of reading his impassionate lines from a book held aloft by his stand-in. Norma Shearer is pictorially satisfactory as Juliet, but purveys the feeling that she is simply reciting, like a school-girl, a well-learned lesson.
>
> When we give ear to a passage of moon-tinted poetry that disembodies its lovers and makes them soar on the wings of beauty into the clouds above and then, in the close-ups of the actor playing Romeo and in the actress playing Juliet, are made painfully conscious of the distensions of the chords in their throats, the agitation of their Adam's apples, the strainings of their neck sinews and the external symptoms of overwork on the part of their accessory thyroid, lacrimal,

Bowamn's, Gay's and other such glands, when, as I say, we suffer this visual obligato, the picture we get is infinitely less one of the poetic romance of two star-crossed lovers than of a couple of charts out of a book on physiology and anatomy talking to each other.

It is curious that as perceptive a prophet as Nathan dismissed the potential of a theatrical form that developed during his career, viewing it with ferocious hostility as an enemy of art and intelligence. Now and again he would cite a sample of film achievement, but his contempt for the men who dominated the movie industry blinded him to what the medium might accomplish.

In the twenties, the American stage was experiencing a radical change and Nathan's smarting slapstick had played its part in driving out the fixed formulas of old. He had taught the new generation of reviewers to laugh at the aged pretentions. None of the men and women engaged to comment on the theatre were as learned or as inventive as he, but they followed his lead, often borrowing his cavalier approach and even helping themselves to his prose.

A. B. Walkley of *The London Times* was known as the Great Allusionist for the inevitable references woven into his reviews. Aristotle was his god and Dickens, Voltaire, the Goncourts, and Benedetto Croce were often quoted to prove some point about the most trifling comedy. Walkley delighted in Nathan's "Americanisms" and the two men became close friends.

Walkley's assistant, Charles Scott-Moncrieff, was being trained to follow in the footsteps of his master. Scott-Moncrieff, a graduate of Edinburgh University, had served as an officer in the King's Own Scottish Borders during the war. He had won a military cross for gallantry in the field and was wounded in the battle of the Somme. On being demobilized in 1917, he joined *The London Times*, becoming Walkley's aide. Walkley, an early admirer of Proust, suggested that his protégé translate *A la Recherche du Temps Perdu*, the first volumes of which had appeared. The result was a masterpiece of which Walkley was the godfather.

William Archer, who had urged Shaw to try playwriting and who had collaborated with Shaw on his first play, *Widowers' Houses*, was another giant of the London scene. He had translated all of Ibsen and was in the front lines of the battle to introduce the Scandinavian dramatist to England. Like Walkley, he was *au courant* of new ideas everywhere. He read Freud's *Interpretation of Dreams* and wrote a book on the subject himself. One of his own dreams made him a fortune, inspiring the play, *The Green Goddess*, in which George Arliss played a crafty, malevolent rajah who holds English travellers as hostages on his vast estate, appeared on both the London and New York stages and was filmed as both a silent and as a talkie.

The younger London reviewers at that time included James Agate of *The Manchester Guardian* and later *The Sunday Times*; the urbane literary critic, Desmond McCarthy of *The New Statesman*; Ivor Brown, a shrewd commentator from Scotland; the Dutch-born J. T. Grein, versed in many languages and literatures, who had founded the Independent Theater (where the plays of Ibsen and Shaw were first seen); and the Ulster playwright, St. John Ervine.

The New York critical corp, Nathan excepted, were scarcely to be compared to their London colleagues. On the Manhattan dailies were Percy Hammond, Woollcott, Heywood Broun, and Burns Mantle (who reported for the new and enormously popular tabloid, *The Daily News*, and chronicled the season in an annual statical volume). In the magazine field were Robert Benchley, writing humorously of the theatre in the comic weekly, *Life*, and Dorothy Parker with her flip wisecracks in *Vanity Fair*. Three others — Frank Tuttle, Charles Brackett, and Lewis Sherwin — quit theatrical journalism to write and direct in Hollywood. There was also an ancient of British birth, J. Ranken Towse of *The Post*, who disapproved of all actors unless they were old, arthritic, and English.

If the New York theatre coverage could not match in erudition the London standards, it had progressed since the dreary William Winter time. The tottering Towse might complain that John Barrymore was not Henry Irving, but he did not, as Winter had, foam with rage at the mention of Ibsen, Hauptmann, Pinero, or Shaw. The Manhattan press gang may have been provincial, but it was purged of the former moral indignation and hostility to fresh ideas from abroad. Most of its practitioners had a sense of humor and wrote in a jaunty journalese.

Shaw claimed that after he had cleared the trail for the new drama in England with his relentless tirades in *The Saturday Review* against the established London theatre, he had looked about him and found so few intelligent plays in the modern manner that he was forced to write some himself as evidence for his cause. Nathan, after performing comparable demolition work on the other side of the Atlantic, began to hunt for new dramatists to replace those he had dispatched.

"Behind every great dramatic critic you will find a great dramatist," he observed. Ibsen was the great dramatist behind the critical writings of Shaw and Archer; it was his championing of Hauptmann that elevated Alfred Kerr of the *Berliner Tagblatt* to fame; and Jules Lemaître of the Paris press gained attention by his sympathetic reception of the new school of French playwrights in the 1890s: Maurice Donnay, Batille, Porto-Riche, and Alfred Capus.

O'Neill may be identified as the great dramatist behind Nathan. But while O'Neill was probably Nathan's major "discovery," he was one of several. Nathan, in a sense, "discovered" the modern European drama for the American stage. When he first wrote of foreign playwrights he was accused of inventing their strange-sounding names. It is significant that prior to 1918 native critics thought that Freska, Evreinov, Ettlinger, Biro, Vajda, Lengyel, and the Capeks were names that Nathan had bestowed on imaginary authors to attract attention.

During the 1920s the works of many of these Europeans were seen in the United States. Broadway productions had multiplied since the war; 196 were seen in New York during the 1921–22 season — comedies, farces, adaptations, musical comedies, dramas, and revivals. In those pre-air conditioning days, the season then usually commenced in late July and the theatre year continued until the following June. It was Nathan's custom to sail to Europe every April for an inspection tour of the stages of London, Paris, and Berlin. Sometimes he would go on to Prague, Vienna, and Munich. After that he would spend a relaxing fortnight at Freudenstadt in the Black Forest. He would be back in New York for the early openings. He delighted in the heat of a Manhattan summer, finding he worked best when the thermometer was high. In cold weather he turned on all the radiators in his quarters so that his apartment became a hothouse.

The younger set of Broadway reviewers, he felt, were given to over-enthusiasm. "The word artist is the most loosely handled word in our language," he wrote. "In the old days an artist was someone like Michelangelo or Shakespeare or Beethoven. Today, an artist is someone like D. W. Griffith, Johnny Weaver or Fannie Brice. There is some doubt about Richard Strauss, it would seem, but none at all about Joe Cook. So far as I can make out the only person writing, painting, singing, composing, dancing, modeling, acting or juggling billiard balls in America who isn't unanimously conceded to be an artist by a jury of Columbuses is Theodore Dreiser. Poor Chaplin, clown extraordinary, a movie comedian of the first rank, and a soul of brilliantly amusing antic, now becomes a mere great artist like the others."

Certain playwrights, Nathan objected, were being ridiculously overestimated in these critics' search of genius. Nathan proceeded to cut them down to size, though praising such gifts as they had. Was America in the midst of a dramatic renaissance, as overexcited reviewers claimed? According to Nathan's wide knowledge and lofty standards it was not. There was increased theatrical activity and staging methods and to an appreciable degree writing had improved, but he doubted that a golden age had dawned.

Nathan judged the first plays of Philip Barry as "negligible efforts" and his other pleasant little comedies of upper-class Americans — *Paris Bound* and *Holiday* — as "several notches below other American comedy writing." Sidney Howard, winner of the Pulitzer Prize for *They Knew What They Wanted* in the season of O'Neill's *Desire Under the Elms*, was dismissed as "a box-office playwright and little else.". Howard looked at life "with a campus brand of realism and, though he wrote some good single scenes, his plays in their entirety had an amateurish mental ring, an aspect of strained youthful bravado like little boys trying manfully to smoke their fathers' cigars."

George S. Kaufman and Marc Connelly were, precisely speaking, "less playwrights than scenewrights." They showed themselves as fresh and witty fellows in *Dulcy* (a farce about a bird-brained wife who speaks in the clichés of the day, a character borrowed from FPA's column) and in their adaptation of Harry Leom Wilson's novel, *Merton of the Movies*, with a film-deluded provincial counterjumper invading Hollywood to be a romantic screen lover and ending up a slapstick favorite.

Some new plays were beginning to show insight into contemporary American life. Booth Tarkington's comedy about an awkward young man, *Clarence* (which Tarkington wrote to give a rising actor, Alfred Lunt, a good part), caught the flavor of native humor. So did Frank Craven's comedies of middle-class newlyweds, *The First Years* and *Too Many Cooks*. Ernest Howard Culbertson's study of a Negro tenement in Washington, D.C. had tragic force.

Nathan urged many young authors to write for the theatre. He suggested that F. Scott Fitzgerald attempt it and Fitzgerald complied by writing some playlets for *The Smart Set* as well as his only full-length play, *The Vegetable*, an expressionistic fantasy about the American dream in which a postman dreams that he has been elected President. Sam H. Harris gave *The Vegetable* a tryout performance at Atlantic City, but its reception was so disappointing that it was not transferred to Broadway.

When S. N. Behrman, a Broadway press agent with a Harvard education, submitted a story to *The Smart Set*, Nathan bought and printed it and wrote its author that it contained an idea for a possible play. After some delay Behrman dramatized his story as *The Second Man*. The Theater Guild produced it with Lynn Fontaine and Alfred Lunt and it founded Behrman's reputation as a confector of mundane comedies.

In 1914 Lewis Sherwin, the drama critic of *The New York Globe*, had brought Maxwell Anderson's work to Nathan's attention. Anderson was then writing poetry and newspaper editorials, and showed ability in both fields. Some of Anderson's verse was published in *The Smart Set* and after the war he wrote his first play, *White Desert*, a tragedy set in the snow-bound badlands of Dakota. It had merit, but failed. Nathan judged Anderson's best play to be *What Price Glory?*, the first realistic drama of American soldiers in World War I.

The play benefited from the collaboration of Lawrence Stallings, who had served in the marines and lost a leg in combat. Stallings also contributed to *The Smart Set*, devoting one ironic essay to the advantages of having a wooden leg. The immediate success of *What Price Glory?* brought Stalling offers to write for the screen. He went to Hollywood and there, drawing on his battlefield experiences, wrote the scenario for the famous war film, *The Big Parade*. On a visit to California in the 1930s, Nathan met Stallings again and advised him to come back to the theatre. Stallings replied that he had said all he had to say and was quite content to call it a day and shut up. He spent his last years editing movie documentaries.

Anderson, though occasionally employed to do screen scripts, remained loyal to the stage and attained, thanks to the boosts of reviewers, formidable, though now evaporated, renown. His industry was startling. He wrote realistic plays of modern life such as *Saturday's Children*, about a young middle-class couple, and *Both Your Houses*, an exposé of political chicanery practiced in Washington. He delivered dramas in the romantic vein: *First Flight*, concerned with the youth of Andrew Jackson, and *Winged Victory*, about the unhappy marriage of a high-born Chinese to a New England sea captain. He dramatized Jim Tully's autobiography of his hobo days, *Beggars of Life*, as *Outside Looking In*. Charles Bickford and James Cagney won attention as ragged vagrants of the road in *Outside Looking In* and soon answered the call of Hollywood.

The ambitious Anderson responded to a higher call. He yearned to be a dramatic poet, so he boldly penned plays in imitation of Marlowe, composing dramas in blank verse on historical subjects: George Washington (*Valley Forge*), Mary Stuart (*Mary of Scotland*), Joan of Arc (*Joan of Lorraine*), the Meyerling tragedy (*The Mask of King*), the Sacco-Vanzetti case (*Winterset*), Anne Boleyn (*Anne of the Thousand Days*), and Socrates (*Barefoot in Athens*).

"Every playwright has a bad Christ play in him; some of them write it," Nathan had warned. Anderson wrote his—*Journey to Jerusalem*. These grandiose what-nots, interspersed with patriotic plays on World War II, were generally accepted with awed respect by the press and public, but Nathan did not join in the cheering.

Another poet-turned-dramatist was Zoë Akins, though after an experimental venture at a blank verse play, *The Magical City*, she limited herself to prose in writing for the stage. Her early comedy, *Papa*, a tale of two easy-virtue daughters who maintained their vain dandy of a father in the luxury to which he was accustomed, was repeatedly mentioned by both Nathan and Mencken as comparable to Schnitzler and Molnár in its cosmopolitan sophistication. They published a playlet of hers, another society comedy, *Did It Really Happen?*, in their magazine and she was soon one of their intimates. In addition to her writing ability, she was a unique personality of the period.

Akins boasted that on her mother's side she was a descendant of the Earl of Pembroke, Shakespeare's friend. She took pride in ancestry and adopted a grand manner, affecting an English accent so exotic that Ethel Barrymore at a first meeting mistook her for a Polish immigrant. The great actress was even more astonished when the young woman told her that she had written a wonderful play for her and that it would be one of her major triumphs.

Miss Barrymore had her doubts, but not long after she received the script of *Déclassée*, a Pinero-type drawing-room drama about a British lady of title who leaves her aristocratic husband when he suspects her of infidelity. Ostracized in her homeland, the lost lady comes to live in New York, selling her jewelry to pay her mounting bills. As a token of her pride, she rejects the marriage proposal of a self-made millionaire. Leaving a soirée at his mansion, she is struck by a skidding taxi and carried back to the house. She expires, sipping champagne, surrounded by weeping admirers. As its author predicted, it became one of Ethel Barrymore's popular vehicles when it opened at the Empire Theater in November, 1919. It ran two seasons on Broadway and then toured the nation.

"*Déclassée* is a distillation of the venerable Pinero juices," wrote

Nathan, "but handled by the Akins girl with force, skill and a sound flavor of romance.... Let this Akins girl remain the independent artist of *Papa*, the artist uncontaminated by the devastating boll-weevils of Broadway, and she will produce work uncommon to our stage. Let her become inflamed with the success of *Déclassée* and pursue the more popular species of writing and she will ruin as engaging a potentiality as the curtain of the American stage has lifted upon."

Broadway stars now wanted her plays and she wrote some to order, such as *The Varying Shore* for Elsie Ferguson and *Daddy's Gone A-Hunting* for Marjorie Rambeau. Shortly after the premiere of *Déclassée* Mencken ran into Zoë Akins in the Algonquin lobby and scarcely recognized her. The bohemian from St. Louis was done up in the latest outré mode. "What's this?" he gasped, blinking at her sparkling attire. "Now that I've found success, haven't I the right to flaunt it?" she laughed. And she relished the flaunting.

Max Reinhardt produced her plays on the Berlin stage and the Boni-Liveright firm brought out a volume of them. At the Algonquin round-table her grand duchess pose was joyfully ridiculed. But when Woollcott uttered an acid complaint about a sophisticate from the Ozarks writing about the British nobility, Ethel Barrymore reproved him, retorting in her booming voice: "Can nothing good come out of Nazareth?"

The Algonquinists put together a satirical revue for a single Sunday night performance. They added a sketch entitled *Zowie! The Curse of an Akins Heart*. Its leading character, impersonated by Woollcott, was a lordly society stomach specialist attending a mundane soirée and speaking highfalutin lines in imitation of *Déclassée* dialogue. Jascha Heifetz, participating, obliged with a violin solo behind the scenes, and there were enough manservants on hand to serve the most extravagant mansion of Akins' imagination. The subtitle read: "A Suppressed Desire, born in the Ozarks, *circa* 1900." The parodied authoress laughed with the rest. She was in good company. O'Neill, James Barrie, and A. A. Milne were also targets of the Algonquin arrows.

Another vehicle she designed for Ethel Barrymore was *A Royal*

Fandango, in which the majestic actress played a coquettish Ruritanian queen, vacationing on the Bay of Biscay and averting her husband's assassination. This time it was Molnár, not Pinero, whose style inspired her and the premiere was ill-timed. A week or two before Molnár's romantic comedy of European royalty, *The Swan*, had come to town and comparisons were inevitable.

Arthur Hopkins produced *A Royal Fandango* and two young actors with screen futures, Spencer Tracy and Edward G. Robinson, were in the cast. Mencken, who claimed an incurable distaste for theatregoing, broke his rule and attended the fashionable first night. Afterwards he and Nathan were guests at Miss Akins' superlative supper party in her luxurious Park Avenue apartment. As the author was in her Spanish phase, its salon resembled the throne room of the Madrid court. Mencken was so pleased with the evening that he broke another rule and wrote a blurb for the press release. "Here is a comedy by Miss Akins in her best manner," ran his endorsement of *A Royal Fandango*. "She is always tremendously amusing and she is always shrewd and pungent." Nathan, while approving of her sense of high style, was disappointed with the play and thereafter accorded his protégée few favorable notices:

> The plays of Zoë Akins are, with two eminently admirable exceptions, servant-girl drama written for ladies and gentlemen. That, at least, is their texture, although usually there is need for the ladies and gentlemen to be either under twenty, in which event the plays may conceivably impress them as at once fresh and poignantly romantic, or over sixty, in which event they will serve wistfully to recall to them their early days of theatregoing.

In a report headed *Shanty Elegance* Nathan lit into *The Furies*, holding it up as "a horrible example of what affectation can do to a real talent":

> Such an amount of tony quackery, pugnacious dandyism and lorgnette pretense has crept into her work that all honesty has taken to its heels and has left in its wake nothing but high-sounding and purpled hallowness. While it is no part of the critic's business to venture beyond the playwright's work into the playwright's personality, there is one such critic who

can't help believe that Miss Akins dramatizes not her elegant characters so much as her own elegant aspirations and ambitions. She seems to be suffering from a suppressed desire to have a butler.

The latest of the great lady's exhibits which might have been an interesting play is found to be so overburdened with airs and affectation that it comes ridiculous. Dramaturgically, this affectation is just as apparent as it is in the matter of externals. Plainly desiring to be a bit deeper than deep and to show all these newfangled playwrights that she can be even more newfangled than they are, she not only duplicates a leaf from O'Neill's *Strange Interlude* and introduces the static aside to convey her characters' unspoken meditations, but concocts a veritable mince by going indiscriminately—and without rhyme or reason—for the Chekov method of indirection, for the Greek chorus, for Maeterlinck symbolism, and for almost everything else but simple, straightforward and honest playwriting.

As for the externals, her bogus *bienséance* persuades her to have her fashionable bachelor's table waited on not only by a butler but a serving maid, to bring the District Attorney of New York City in person and in a very doggy dinner jacket to cross-examine the suspects in a murder case in the widow's drawing-room, to serve champagne with what presumably are the hors d'œuvres, and to play *Tristan* off-stage when what she perhaps vaguely wanted was Brahms' *Intermezzo in E Minor*.

Miss Akins returned the insult by attempting to caricature Nathan in her next play. It was far more Broadway than her gilded society fictions and had a magnetic title: *The Greeks Had a Word for It*. A ribald comedy about three Ziegfeld chorus girls who join forces for their manhunts, it was a huge hit and was sold to the movies—as she soon was. The contrasting of the three showgirls was clever, each having individualizing traits, and it presented a fairly accurate picture of a segment of New York life during Prohibition.

In the prologue, set in a speak-easy, a music critic reviewing colleagues appears. He had Nathan's poise, carriage, and manner of address. Lest the point be missed, a disgruntled musician, falling into conversation with the music critic, quotes from one of his devastating "pannings" of a concert. The quotation is a pastiche of lofty Nathanesque disdain and the intent is unmistakable, but fails as portraiture since the music critic, cornered and accused of being a cadger, a snob, and a phony, is robbed of the smart retorts Nathan might have made in such a situation.

The success of *The Greeks* took Zoë Akins to Hollywood to supply dialogue and scripts for the newfangled talkies. Her screen-play *Morning Glory*, for Katharine Hepburn, was awarded an Oscar, and her adaptation of *Camille* for Garbo was far above the routine film treatment.

The enormous salaries from the movie studios permitted her to indulge her wildest whims. At her Pasadena residence, "Green Fountains," her Catherine the Great complex had full play. She entertained lavishly, and among her favored guests were Prince Vassili Romanov and his beautiful wife, Princess Natasha. The prince's father was the Grand Duke Alexander, grandson of Czar Nicholas I, and his mother was the sister of the last Czar, Nicholas II, executed with his wife and children by the Bolsheviks.

The regal Akins estate had the traditional Hollywood swimming pool, and peacocks strutted on the lawns. Members of the emigré New York literati, like herself wage-slaves in the studios, gravitated to this cultural oasis. Her suppressed yearning to have a butler was at last gratified. So was another of her romantic aspirations: marriage into the British aristocracy.

Hugo Rumbold, a retired officer of the British Grenadier Guards, had dabbled in the arts as a painter, a musician, and a scenic designer, and he had staged operas for Sir Thomas Beecham at Covent Garden. In America he was a café society drifter, addicted to the card table and the bottle. The course of his marriage to Zoë Akins did not always run smoothly, but it only ran for six months. Rumbold stumbled and fell down a flight of stairs after some grand party. He died of his injuries. His widow insisted on a funeral befitting his rank and he lay in state wearing a regal periwig. When the coffin was to be closed the studio prop department demanded that the wig be returned to them and a wrangle ensued.

Though the younger American playwrights were scarcely comparable to the great dramatists of Europe, they possessed, Nathan insisted, speculative minds and a brave independence that their predecessors had lacked. Had any of these newcomers submitted their work to the reigning managers before the war they would have been told to emulate David Belasco and Augustus Thomas, who cuckooed the prevailing platitudes. It was Shaw, Strindberg, and Chekhov whom these youngsters had taken as their models and for much of what they wrote there was now a public. The Little Theater movement, presenting plays of intellectual content in cities across the country, had educated theatergoers with its pioneering.

In New York the Theater Guild, an outgrowth of the semi-amateur Washington Square Players, organized an acting company and specialized in European plays. The Wall Street philanthropist, Otto Kahn, provided it with a theatre — the Garrick, which Jacques Copeau had had his troupe occupy during the war — and loyal subscribers liberated the Guild from dependence on boxoffice considerations. Each new play was guaranteed a six-week run by subscription support and if its reception warranted it was thereafter transferred to another playhouse.

The importation of foreign companies and plays set examples for the more ambitious American playwrights. Expressionism, the post-war rage in Berlin, was reflected in O'Neill's *The Hairy Ape*; in *Beggar on Horseback*, which Kaufman and Connelly adapted from the German play by Paul Apel, *Hans Sonnenstösser's Höllenfahrt*, in Elmer Rice's *The Adding Machine*; and in John Howard Lawson's *Processional*, a sociological satire of the national scene in burlesque-show frame, described as "a jazz symphony" and produced by the Theater Guild, proof that the Guild was not fundamentally opposed to all plays written by Americans. The romantic Belasco had long practiced realism as a matter of authentic scenic detail; now several authors offered candid naturalism in content: Lula Volmer in *Sun up* and the *The Dunce Boy* and Hatcher Hughes in *Hell Bent for Heaven*, all three depicting the hillbillies of the Carolina mountains without false-folksy vaudeville humor. The American theatre seemed on the verge of coming of age. Literary critics — Joseph

Wood Krutch in *The Nation* and Stark Young in *The New Republic* — deemed it worthy of aesthetic evaluations and Nathan was no longer its sole highbrow commentator.

The Theater Guild board had exceptionally sagacious judgment in its salad days. Among its early productions were Molnár's lovely fantasy, *Liliom*; Andreyev's mystic tragedy in a circus setting, *He Who Gets Slapped*; Strindberg's *Dance of Death*; Tolstoy's *Tower of Darkness*; Georg Kaiser's expressionistic *From Morn to Midnight*; Wilhelm von Scholz's strange play of premonition, *The Race With the Shadow*; and the world premiere of Shaw's *Heartbreak House*. The only American play it sponsored in its first years was Arthur Richman's bitter account of middle-class futility, *Ambush*. It was accused of neglecting American playwrights, but its announced function then was the introduction of modern world drama.

Commercial managers, impressed by its success, took note and to some degree followed its example. Brock Pemberton introduced Pirandello with a season of *Six Characters in Search of an Author* and *Henry IV*. William Brady imported the Capeks' *The World We Live In*, a Czech allegory in which the actors impersonated insects; Gilbert Miller produced *The Czarina* from the Hungarian of Lajos Biro and Melchoir Lengyel; and Arthur Hopkins staged Hauptmann's *Rose Bernd* with Ethel Barrymore.

Scenically, too, the American theatre was being transformed by European influences. The visit of the Diaghilev ballet during the war had been a revelation, dazzling Americans with Bakst's exotic décor and costuming. Joseph Urban, an Austrian theatre architect, ornamented Metropolitan Opera productions and designed gorgeous tableaux for the Ziegfeld Follies. Gordon Craig's theories of scenic reform were assiduously imitated by the younger set designers: Robert Edmond Jones, Norman Bel Geddes, Lee Simonson, Jo Mielziner, Aline Bernstein, and Cleon Throckmorton. The Russian artist, Erté, living in Paris, did designs for smashing production numbers of George White's *Scandal* revues, and the Mexican painter and cartoonist Miguel Covarrubias enlivened the Guild staging of Shaw's *Androcles and the Lion* with cubist riots of jungle flair.

Morris Gest, financed by Otto Kahn, threw more light on European theatrical innovations by engaging Nikita Balieff's Moscovite cabaret entertainment, *Chauve-Souris*, for an American tour. This novel show with its folk music and dance, its *March of the Wooden Soldiers* and Balieff's comic mangling of English as its master of ceremonies was an instant success and encouraged Gest to sponsor the Moscow Art Theater's visit to the United States.

The famous company arrived with all its leading players — Stanislavsky, Ivan Moskvin, Vassili Katchalov, and Olga Knipper-Chekhova (Chekhov's widow) — in a repertoire of Ostrovski, Tolstoy, Turgenev, Chekhov, and Gorki. The Stanislavsky system of mood staging and in-depth interpretation was, at the time, already judged passé in Russia and on the continent, but it was a revelation to Americans and its impact on American actors and directors was lasting, the inspiration for the method acting taught by Lee Strasberg at the Actors' Studio forty years later.

Nathan joined his colleagues in according the Moscow Art Theater welcome. He had studied its technique on its home-ground before the war and issued a considered verdict, citing its perfection of organization. "There is an almost exact coordination of manuscript, acting and staging; the play, whatever it is, moves almost inevitably. It is all clock-like, yet without a trace of clock-like monotony," he wrote in *The Smart Set*. "From the colorful *Tsar Fyodor* to the drab *Lower Depths* and on through the drama of Chekhov, the precision of the Anglo-Saxon theatre at its best and much of the dazzling sweep of Central Europe meet in crashing dramatic chord. It is no more necessary to know the Russian language to understand such a live theatre and its plays than it is necessary to be deaf and dumb to understand the pantomime, *L'Infant Prodigue*."

This last statement was disproved at a supper party Nathan attended a few weeks later. Theodore Komisarjevsky, the emigré Russian director, had been invited to produce *Peer Gynt* in New York for the Guild. After listening to the rhapsodies of some guests fresh from a Moscow Art performance, he gravely inquired whether they had not been particularly impressed by the scene in which the gardener's wife laments her tribulations alone in a spotlight. When it was agreed by all that this was without doubt the evening's high moment, Komisarjevsky smiled sardonically and informed the pretenders that there was no such scene.

Broadway revivals of pre-war Broadway favorites failed to repeat their original success, an indisputable indication of changed tastes — or younger audiences. Laurette Taylor found that the gushy *Peg O' My Heart* had lost its box-office pull and hurried off to Hollywood. There she made a second discovery. The old hokum blossomed anew on celluloid and she had a movie hit, demonstrating Nathan's theory that the theatre's peanut gallery spectators had become cinema-addicts. Eugene Walter's once scandalous portrait of a kept woman, *The Easiest Way*, had but a brief run when revived, as did Doris Keane's comeback in Edward Sheldon's old-fashioned lace valentine in four acts, *Romance* (though it was to have eager audiences ten years later when Greta Garbo played it in the talkies). Stanley Houghton's British drama of a woman's sexual independence, *Hindle Wakes*, had been a sensation in 1911 but was box office poison in 1921. So were George Broadhurst's 1911 boob-shaker, *Bought and Paid For*, and the 1900 musical *Florodora* when they reappeared.

The profitable theatrical clichés of yesterday were being consigned to the flames and Nathan added some explosive fuel to the bonfire with a new book, *The Critic and the Drama*. In this slim volume he more or less formally declared his aesthetic creed and diagnosed the ills of the contemporary stage. "This, at least, is a book that I am not fully ashamed of," he scribbled in a copy he gave the Irish critic, Ernest Boyd.

"Art is a reaching out into the ugliness of the world for vagrant beauty and the imprisoning of it in a tangible dream. Criticism is the dream book," he stated in the initial essay, bearing the title "Aesthetic Jurisprudence."

> All art is a kind of subsconscious madness expressed in terms of sanity; criticism is essential to the interpretation of its mysteries, for about everything truly beautiful there is ever something mysterious and disconcerting. Beauty is not always immediately recognizable as beauty; what passes for beauty is mere infatuation; living beauty is like a love that has outlasted

the middle-years of life, and has met triumphantly the test of time, and faith and cynical meditation. For beauty is a sleep-walker in the endless corridors of the wakeful world, uncertain, groping, and not a little strange. And the critic is its tender guide.

After this florid, symbolic introduction he becomes more specific.

> To the Goethe-Carlyle doctrine that the critic's duty lies alone in discerning the artist's aim, his point of view, and, finally, his execution of the task before him, it is easy enough to subscribe, but, he finds, this is not a 'theory' of criticism so much as a foundation of a theory. The Goethe-Carlyle hypothesis is a little too liberal. It calls for qualification. It gives the artist too much ground, and the critic too little. It fits criticism of drama much better than it fits criticism of acting, just as it fits criticism of painting and sculpture much more snugly than criticism of music. The means whereby the emotions are directly affected, may at times be critically ridiculous, yet the accomplishment may be, paradoxically, artistic.

Then he offers in evidence some examples.

> Perhaps the finest acting performance of our generation is Bernhardt's Camille: its final effect is tremendous; yet the means by which it is contrived are obviously inartistic. Again, *King Lear*, searched into with critical chill, is artistically a poor instance of play-making, yet its effect is precisely the effect strived for. Surely, in cases like these, criticism founded strictly upon an infallible theory is futile criticism, and not only futile but eminently unfair.

Admitting that he is here exhibiting contradictions, he claims that through contradictions one conceivably gains more secure ground and suggests a combining of theories.

> "When his book is once opened, the author's mouth is shut," (Wilde [once] said . . .) But when a dramatist's play or a composer's symphony is opened, the author has only begun to open his mouth. To this composite end, I offer a suggestion: blend the Goethe-Carlyle theory with that of the aforementioned Wilde, to wit, that beauty is uncriticizable, since it has

as many meanings as man has moods, since it is the symbol of symbols, and since it reveals everything because it expresses nothing....

Without criticism, art would still be art, and so with all its windows walled in and its lights extinguished would the Louvre still be the Louvre? Criticism is the windows and chandeliers of art; it illuminates the enveloping darkness in which art might otherwise rest only vaguely discernible and perhaps altogether unseen.

The best definition in Nathan's opinion was Carlyle's "Criticism stands like an interpreter between the inspired and the uninspired, between the prophet and those who hear the melody of his words, and catch some glimpse of their material meaning, but understand not their deeper import."

In another essay he turns to drama as an art:

Drama is, in essence, a democratic art in constant brave conflict with aristocracy of intelligence, soul and emotion. When drama triumphs, a masterpiece like *Hamlet* comes to life. When the conflict ends in a draw, a drama half-way between greatness and littleness is the result — a drama, say, such as *El Gran Galeoto*. When the struggle ends in defeat, the result is a *Way Down East* or a *Lightnin*.

Nathan estimates drama as inferior to the higher art:

With a direct appeal to the emotions as its first and encompassing aim, it has never, even at its finest, been able to exercise the measure of direct emotional appeal that is exercised, say, by Chopin's *C Sharp Minor Nosturn, Op. 27, No. 1*, or by the soft romance of the canvases of Palma Vecchio, or by Rodin's superb *Eternal Spring*, or by Zola's *La Terre*.

The splendid music of *Romeo and Juliet* is not so eloquent and moving as that of *Tristan* or *Lohengrin;* no situation in the whole of Hauptmann can strike the heart so thrilling and profound a chord of pit as a single line in Allegri's obvious *Miserere*. The greatest note of comedy in drama falls short of the note of comedy in the *Coffee-Cantata* of Bach.

He questions most of the prescriptions for the writing of drama. Drama is struggle, a conflict of wills? Then what of *Ghosts?*

Nathan never apologized for changing his mind. He distrusted consistent critics. "A critic who sets himself a critical creed and abides by that creed with never a sidestep is generally wrong," he declared in his first book. "The theatre and its drama are as inconsistent institutions as the surface of the earthly sphere reveals." He cherished Walt Whitman's "Do I contradict myself? Very well, I contradict myself." At the end of his life he paraphrased the sentiment proudly. "It is said of me that now and then I contradict myself" — the last lines in his last book, published in 1954. "Yes, I improve wonderfully as time goes by."

The Critic and the Drama, supposedly his *magnum opus*, was respectfully reviewed and its epigrams borrowed. *Vanity Fair* placed Nathan on its "Hall of Fame" page. The caption under his photograph mentioned that he was the most exclusive member of the Manhattan literati. "That just means that I don't lunch with the Algonquin set," he laughed.

PART SIX

"I want to keep in right with Nathan and Mencken for they are the most powerful critics in the country," F. Scott Fitzgerald reminded his literary agent, Harold Ober, advising him to submit his stories to *The Smart Set* despite their low payment rates.

The average American learned about them not from what they wrote but when they were denounced by indignant university deans, in newspaper editorials, and from the pulpit, and thought of them as dangerous troublemakers, enemies of the status quo and the ideals of the republic.

The Saturday Evening Post was the popular periodical of the day. Designed for middle-class family audiences, it was the constant target of *The Smart Set* jibes. Its editor, George Horace Lorimer, was a shrewd diagnostician of the public pulse and, holding to Victorian precepts, built up a readership of millions. His editorials echoed all the suppositions and superstitions then in circulation, and advertising of tobacco and alcoholic beverages were sanctimoniously refused to preserve the image of Methodist purity.

Expression of radical political opinion met as speedy suppression as did realistic candor in fiction. Max Eastman's magazine of the extreme left, *The Masses*, was outlawed as subversive, while Margaret Sanger's lecture on birth control in the Town Hall was raided by the New York police on the orders of Cardinal Hayes.

The Smart Set now had new rivals. The little literary reviews were publishing the writers of the European avant-garde — Pirandello, Paul Morand, Cocteau — and Condé Nast's posh monthly *Vanity Fair* was becoming the bible of the would-be sophisticate. In its pages Cubism, Futurism, Dadaism, and surrealism were discussed and illustrated, together with the fiction of Colette, Schnitzler, and Aldous Huxley and stunning photographic portraits by Steichen and Man Ray of prominent figures of public life, letters, the theatre, and cinema.

Frank Crownenshield, the gentlemanly managing director of *Vanity Fair*, kept abreast of all the new movements in the arts and had them reported on with an attractive flair. Edmund Wilson, serving as its editor, introduced a "Hall of Fame" page in which each month tribute was paid to authors and artists of distinction. Occasionally Nathan contributed an essay to *Vanity Fair* and later was appointed its drama critic. In that capacity he delighted in defying the cautious Crownenshield's notions of good taste.

Though of broad and open mind, Crownenshield, with his impeccable sense of refinement, dreaded any breach of etiquette. The word "whore" must never be used, he ruled. So Nathan subversively worked in a reference to John Ford's Jacobian tragedy of incest, *'Tis a Pity She's a Whore*, bowdlerizing the title into "'Tis a Pity She's a Word Forbidden in 'Vanity Fair'." Mention of sexual "deviations" was absolutely banned by Crownenshield. To bypass this restriction Nathan, in discussing Bourdet's play on Lesbianism, *The Captive*, explained that its heroine was a member of "that Parisian acrobatic troupe, 'Les Bians'."

♦ ♦ ♦

As early as 1918 Mencken had begun to weary of *The Smart Set*. Its demands on his time and patience irritated him more and more, he complained to his partner. Noodle customers had to be coddled which meant that serious writing had to be sandwiched between trivia and such fiction as was available.

The Baltimore Sun — as soon as the blackout of wartime was lifted — invited Mencken to contribute his fireworks again at an augmented salary and with a promise of complete liberty. Each week on the evening edition's editorial page he spread his views, lashing with pent-up fervor at the imbecilities at large in the nation. Some *Sun* readers were aghast at his brazen irreverence — "He might speak of mental deficiencies in a more restrained tone," objected an outraged lady in the letter column. But to more readers his candor was a refreshing spring breeze after the gloom and muzzling that prevailed during the war.

1920 saw Mencken as political reporter again, covering the Democratic National Convention in San Francisco. Soon he was informing his newspaper readers of the West Coast spectacle. The Democrats, trying to mend their damaged fences for the campaign, were clearing their platform of Wilsonian idealism. Franklin D. Roosevelt, nominated for Vice-President on the ticket, attacked the United States' participation in the League of Nations, Wilson's pet project, in his acceptance speech. Women were to have the vote for the first time in the coming election and Mencken predicted that, as women were far more instinctively intelligent than men, they would reject the party that had taken the country into a futile war. They did.

Escaping from the racket and smoke of the convention hall, Mencken roamed San Francisco with the California poet, George Sterling, an incomparable companion and guide, especially for Mencken, who preferred saloons to salons. They tramped the hills and made pilgrimages to all the spots mentioned by Frank Norris in *Blix*, a fictionized account of his days as a cub reporter in the 1890s, long before the earthquake, and ended their explorations with nightlong sessions in waterfront dives where Prohibition had never been heard of. The poet was a stimulating talker and an eloquent raconteur with a limitless fund of fascinating information about the city and its personalities, but the critic was alarmed by his compulsive drinking and his resolute detachment from the present. His talk was only of the past — of wonderful, long-ago happenings and of dead friends. He still wrote prolifically, but he had lost faith in himself and in any future. On his return to New York Mencken told Nathan that he felt instinctively that Sterling, a fine poet and a unique character, was possessed by a death-wish.

A few years later, in 1926, when Mencken's reputation was at high tide, a much-publicized cross-country tour brought him again to California. He visited Hollywood for a week or two, seeing such old friends as Anita Loos, Joseph Hergesheimer, Jim Tully, and Upton Sinclair, being entertained by the intellectual film folk as though he were a new movie "find" and attending services in Aimée Semple McPherson's temple. Then he decided to see San Francisco once more and have a reunion with Sterling.

A banquet at the Bohemian club in his honor was sponsored by Charles Norris, the novelist, and Idwal Jones, the drama and film critic of the local *Examiner* who had been a *Smart Set* discovery, but Sterling, impatiently awaited, failed to appear. Mencken had even been to his lodging, but his loud knocking had brought no response and he supposed that Sterling had gone out. Next morning came the news that Sterling had committed suicide during the night by taking poison. Sterling, wrecked in health, had not the courage to face his now-famous admirer. "He was a true poet," Mencken told inquiring reporters. "He knew intuitively that his hour had come and, like the wise Greeks of antiquity, he responded to the call of his destiny by taking his own life."

On election night, 1920, Eugene O'Neill's *Emperor Jones* had its premiere at the Provincetown Playhouse in Greenwich Village. O'Neill had submitted the play for publication in *The Smart Set*, but Mencken had vetoed its inclusion on the grounds that it would fill too much of the magazine, a dangerous precedent, he explained. Nathan was upset by this unexpected rejection, but their dual editorship was based on no disputes so he refrained from objecting. Such an arbitrary move and such a weak excuse disturbed him nonetheless and he pondered on his partner's shocking shortsightedness.

Mencken was casting his eyes on new fields to conquer. He had attained an important position as a literary critic, but now he wanted to comment on broader matters. For this purpose he took the entire national scene and its relation to the international scene. He had just written a book on the American language and felt ready to pontificate on the American people. His application to this subject widened his audience. In the years ahead he was to become such a well-known public figure that in Walter Lippman's 1927 estimate he was "the most powerful personal influence on a whole generation of educated people."

In his monthly pages in *The Smart Set* he selected for review books on politics, economics, sociology, and religion as springboards for his views. Only now and then did he give fiction substantial space. Certain authors who were gaining popular readership—Hergesheimer, Willa Cather, Dos Passos, Fitzgerald, and Sherwood Anderson—received notice, advice, and encouragement. He extolled the last novels of Conrad and the new ones of

James Branch Cabell. He continued to beat the drums for the titan of realism, Theodore Dreiser, but this was in retrospect. Dreiser, deep in writing *An American Tragedy*, had published no novel since 1915.

For some of his former idols he had harsh words. H. G. Wells was accused of having been transformed from first-rate novelist into a popinjay world-saver by war hysteria. Arnold Bennett's fiction showed a decided decline. George Bernard Shaw, about whose work Mencken had written the first serious study in book form, received the cruelest rebuff, being described for his improvement manias an "'Ulster Polonius,' an orthodox Scotch-Presbyterian of the most cocksure and bilious sort, the archtype of the blue nose."

In 1922 Mencken made his first post-war trip to Europe, but his reports of his travels suggest the political observer rather than the critic of the arts. News of his growing importance had reached literary England. Robert Bridges, the poet laureate, said Mencken was the only American he wanted to meet. Conrad compared his prose style to a powerful dynamo and T. S. Eliot, Arnold Bennett, A. G. Orage, Ezra Pound, and Hugh Walpole were among the growing army of his admirers. To the disappointment of the British literati, the younger set of English authors — E. M. Forster and Aldous Huxley aside — seemed to him grossly overrated and inferior to their American contemporaries. Katherine Mansfield, then being hailed as a genius, he classed below Ruth Suckow, an Iowa housewife whose stories of farm life he had recently discovered.

After the London stay and reunions with his journalistic colleagues he hurried to Holland to interview the exiled German Crown Prince. The exiled Kaiser, another admirer, wanted to meet him too and wrote to express his regret that Mencken had not called upon him. But Mencken was more eager to see the new Germany than its retired emperor. In Berlin war-profiteers wallowed in their wealth while misery stalked ominously around the corner. Inflation was its zenith. The mark was worthless paper and Mencken noted that he paid the equivalent of $1.50 a day for his quarters in the smart Hotel Eden. Old friends told him that they had been in danger of starving to death. A Communist rising had broken out after the armistice and, though it had been promptly crushed, the general disorder caused economic ruin. Outwardly the city had a serene air and everything was spick-and-span, but he felt that the tranquil surface was deceptive. Social unrest was brewing and Mencken predicted that if the catastrophe that he sensed came, there would be a colossal massacre of the Jews. His prophecy was made a year before Hitler's abortive putsch in Munich.

As usual his estimate of the political situation was accurate and far-seeing, but he apparently had little curiosity about the important cultural endeavors taking place in these hectic metropolises. He, who had spilt oceans of ink over his enthusiasm for pre-war German composers and authors—Richard Strauss, Hauptmann, Wedekind, Otto Julius Bierbaum, and the early Thomas Mann— failed to report on the amazing new developments in the arts: on Scheonberg's and Alban Berg's innovations in music, on the spread of Expressionism, on the impact of Freudian theories, on the psychological novel, on the modernistic stagecraft of Jessner and Piscator, or on the new trend in the German films with the bizarre style and amazing photography that was to alter cinematic technique everywhere. Nor did he tackle in any depth a review of the book of the moment, Oswald Spengler's *Decline of the West*, which philosophized on the march of history, comparing the seasons of civilizations.

Beer seems to have taken precedence over books on this semi-holiday jaunt. There were *Bierabenden* with Berlin acquaintances and a sortie to Prague with a side-trip to sample the brews at Pilsen, now in a land that Woodrow Wilson had been instrumental in creating: Czechoslovakia. From there he hurried on to Munich, his favorite city, to attend the Oktoberfest.

The return ocean journey allowed him time to meditate on what he had seen and on his future. Nathan and he—in unison— had made names for themselves, but he felt that it was the moment to change trains. *The Smart Set* had been their national forum for more than a decade and had drawn the crowds. The vehicle in which they had travelled on the high road to fame was worn-out, tawdry, and detrimental to their present ambitions. The hour for greater things had arrived and they must seize it or lose a once-in-a-lifetime opportunity.

True, the American scene showed the results of their efforts. Many of the authors he had sponsored, in opposition to the narrow traditional standards which set English authors above Americans, were enjoying success. Sinclair Lewis's *Babbitt* was a best-seller and its title gave a new word to the American language. Willa Cather was awarded the 1922 Pulitzer Prize for her war novel, *One of Ours*. Dos Passos' *Three Soldiers*, which Mencken had also championed, presented a more accurate record of the Great War. It appeared at the same time, but was too brutally truthful for the Pulitzer judges.

F. Scott Fitzgerald's *The Beautiful and the Damned* came out that year. It was evident that the clever college boy of *This Side of Paradise* had matured into a novelist of serious purpose, and it was sold to the movies, making him temporarily rich. Ben Hecht, a *Smart Set* alumnus, published his novel *Gargoyles*, which had the honor of being banned in Boston, a restriction that increased its sales everywhere else; Cabell's *Jurgen*, freed from censorship's claws, was being widely read.

All this was a tribute to his pioneering as a critic, but it echoed a victory won in a war fought in the past. Mencken was in no mood to rest on fading laurels. He was eager for fresh frays and larger campaigns.

Nathan found him restless and impatient on his return from Europe. On his semimonthly visits to New York they would forgather with their intimates — Tom Smith, now editor-in-chief at Horace Liveright's publishing house; John D. Williams, the producer who had just directed the sensational *Rain*; and Ernest Boyd, the Irish essayist — to make the rounds of the town. Luchow's was the most usual meeting place and occasionally they went to nightclubs or theatrical suppers, but Mencken ducked as many of these as he politely could. More often he preferred to adjourn to Nathan's dimly lit quarters at the Royalton and talk until the early hours about ways to improve their magazine.

Alfred A. Knopf had thrown out a hint to Mencken that he was contemplating the launching of a magazine. Scribners and Harpers brought out monthlies, and such an organ would boost the reputation of his rising firm. Knopf invited the two critics to luncheon in the autumn of 1922 and discussed with them the negotiations for his magazine. It had been Knopf's plan to engage Mencken alone as the editor of his proposed review, but Mencken, remembering Nathan's refusal to accept *The Smart Set* editorship without his collaboration, felt morally obligated to continue their fruitful association. He believed that Nathan would tire of his infatuation with the theatre and broaden his interests, and that together they would assail the vast territory of the contemporary American scene.

Meanwhile, Warner, *The Smart Set* publisher, was calling emergency meetings. He was disturbed about the magazine. It operated on a small budget out of a low-rent office and with a single secretary, the loyal, over-worked Sara Golde, to cope with the voluminous correspondence, take the telephone calls, and drive away bores and cranks. Yet other publications were robbing it of readers. Condé Nast's *Vanity Fair*, a slick magazine with a chic tone, Continental flavor, handsome photography, and alluring image, rivaled *The Smart Set* in cultural sophistication. A new comic magazine, *Judge*, sprang up in 1922 to compete with the venerable humorous weekly, *Life*, with a similar diet of cartoons, wisecracks, and light fooling. Nathan had accepted the post of drama critic on the newcomer and before long it was outselling the monthly he co-edited.

At a meeting with the worried Warner, Nathan proposed that experimental measures be risked to augment *The Smart Set* circulation but the publisher feared that any radical change might drive away faithful fans. Nor was it the moment for Mencken to suggest that he finance a nonfiction review that he and Nathan would edit as they had the moneymaking *Black Mask*.

The American literary scene at that time was divided into three parts: the older generation of novelists, playwrights, and critics; the middle category that was slowly replacing the elders; and the avant-garde young who were clamoring to set up new standards. In the first category were prewar favorites—the likes of Booth Tarkington and Robert W. Chambers—who continued to appear regularly on the bestseller lists. In the theatre, Augustus Thomas and David Belasco still had loyal audiences. Conservative spokesmen deplored the new trend in fiction and objected to Cabell, Sherwood Anderson, and Hergesheimer as "sex-obsessed," "morbid," "neurotic," and "unpleasantly disturbing," while Nathan and Mencken were held responsible for championing such literature and leading callow innocents astray. The two critics were accustomed to abuse from indignant fogies. It brought them extra attention and they would quote excerpts from the attacks upon them to illustrate the quaintly old-fashioned literary views.

However, their juniors, too, were displeased. The expatriate set in Paris — and its copycats in Greenwich Village — declared war on *The Smart Set*. The magazine, they fumed, was a tottering relic and its editors were philistines indifferent to the latest European movements.

Gertrude Stein had been enshrined as a goddess by these youngsters. At receptions in her Paris flat, its walls lined with modern art canvases, she installed herself as an oracle uttering deeper than deep pronouncements on style, composition and values. She was doubtless an impressive personality — and more comprehensible when she spoke than when she wrote — and the 24-year-old Hemingway was dazzled, as were such occasional callers as Sherwood Anderson, Fitzgerald and Thornton Wilder. Another guest as these soirées, Virgil Thompson, remembers that it was lesemajesty to mention James Joyce. You might, not knowing that article of decorum, refer to him once and be excused for your ignorance of the rule. If you repeated the offense you were not invited again.

Under fire from old and young, from the right and from the left, Nathan and Mencken introduced a contingent of writers with prodigious futures.

Dashiell Hammet, afterwards world-famous as a crime novelist with *The Thin Man* and *The Maltese Falcon*, then employed as a private detective in Nevada, supplied accounts of his experiences as a sleuth in 1922 and 1923 issues. Jim Tully, an ex-hobo who was to describe his vagabond days in his books, *Beggars of Life* and *Circus Parade*, emerged from oblivion with a staccato statement of his philosophy in a 1923 issue.

Walter Seabrook, whose subsequent accounts of voodoo rites elevated him to national popularity, was among the latest recruits as was Alister Crowley, a self-professed wizard, who tried to evoke the devil with black masses in a Greenwich Village flat with the credulous Dreiser as an onlooker. Charles MacArthur, to collaborate with his reporter colleague, Ben Hecht, on the uproarious newspaper comedy, *The Front Page*, wrote ghoulish accounts of murders and executions, and Nunnally Johnson, a beginner from the deep South, showed a similar penchant for the macabre. Dorothy Parker, the esoteric Djuna Barnes (yet to write *Nightwood*), and the future dramatist, S. N. Behrman, provided diverting fiction.

In the poet's corner were Maxwell Anderson (before any play of his had been exposed to the Broadway footlights), and Thorne Smith, the fantastic humorist of *Night Life of the Gods* and *Topper*, with a fragment of his lyric work, *Autumn in the Subway*.

John Gunther, yet to become a noted foreign correspondent with *Inside Europe*, reported inside of the University of Chicago, and Henrik Wilhelm Van Loon, who had written *The Story of Mankind*, told the story of Cornell. John Macy, the critic, turned the spotlight on the American suppression mania with an article still remembered, entitled, "Rum, Reading and Rebellion."

Several earlier "discoveries" who could now demand higher payment than *The Smart Set* could afford made return engagements out of loyalty. F. Scott Fitzgerald gave the editors one of his most characteristic stories, "The Diamond as Big as the Ritz," and Cabell, Hergesheimer, Sinclair Lewis, and Carl Van Vechten occasionally reappeared.

"The Yellow Peril," by Edward E. Paramore, predicted the Japanese conquest of the United States and prophesied the improvements that it would bring to American culture. It appeared as a leading feature in 1922, nineteen years before the attack on Pearl Harbor.

Topical cartoons mocking popular delusions were inserted, and the policy of running a one-act play each month continued. George Sterling in playlet form pessimistically pictured the human experience in *The Rabbit Hutch*, and George M. Cohan spoofed the

Broadway mystery melodrama with a short play in which all the characters were detectives.

Nor did *The Smart Set* go all-American. Aldous Huxley and James Stephens wrote for it. Walter Hasenkelver, the German dramatist, was represented by an expressionistic movie scenario and the Hungarian, Fernic Molnár, by a sketch or two. Readers were still getting their money's worth in quality, originality and variety.

Alfred Knopf was growing restless as his project for a magazine hung fire. Nathan had advised him to buy *The Smart Set* and rejuvenate it. Knopf made a bid of $30,000 for ownership, but it was rudely declined by Warner who declared the offer an insult. Later Hearst was to purchase it for twice that sum.

When Knopf next met with its editors he told them about his attempt and confessed that he was relieved to have been turned down. It would have been a gigantic job to transform *The Smart Set* into the high-toned review he envisioned. Better to make a clean start than to inherit a magazine in trouble. He urged the editors to captain his new venture, promising them a free hand.

Knopf maintained a country estate in Westchester County where he entertained his authors. There, in the spring of 1923, Nathan and Mencken discussed ideas for the forthcoming review with Knopf's wife and partner, Blanche, and his father, Samuel Knopf, who would be its business manager. The question of the new magazine's name had not been settled. Mencken clamoured for *The Blue Review*, but the title was judged as vague, arty, and misleading. It was Nathan's suggestion — *The American Mercury* — that finally won unanimous approval.

The imminent departure of the editors from *The Smart Set* was kept secret from the press, but during the summer, while Nathan was on his annual European tour, Mencken wrote to various authors, breaking the news and soliciting contributions to the forthcoming magazine.

"I am leaving *The Smart Set* for something grander and gaudier than anything ever seen in the Republic," he informed Carl Van Doren. "Contents: any damned thing that seems amusing, including especially politics. Knopf will spread himself on the format and printing. Can't you do something for us? We grey-haired veterans must set the pace."

"In politics it will be, in the main, Tory, but civilized Tory," he explained to Upton Sinclair. "You know me well enough to know there will be no quarter for the degraded cads who now run the country. I am against you and against the Liberals because I believe you chase butterflies, but I am even more against your enemies."

Meanwhile, clandestine preparations for the January 1924 inaugural issue of *The American Mercury*, which had to be out in late December, went forward. When Nathan returned from Europe, he and Mencken were called to do double duty, co-editing two magazines simultaneously. The Nathan-Mencken abdication from the editorial chairs of *The Smart Set* was set in motion. All shares in the company were signed over to an escrow account which was to be divided proportionately among the shareholders if and when a sale took place. The departing editors chose Morris Gilbert, a young reporter on *The New York Tribune* who occasionally contributed to *The Smart Set*, to take over. He remained in charge until August 1924, when Hearst bought the magazine and altered its policy to "all-fiction." Nathan and Mencken each received $15,000 from this deal and their former battleship heaved and rolled along, a pathetic wreck of its quondam self, until it sank, a victim of the Depression, in 1930.

Knopf issued a press release which appeared in *The New York Times* on August 3, 1923, beside a eulogy for President Harding, who had died suddenly the previous day:

> The aim of *The American Mercury* will be to offer a comprehensive picture, critically presented, of the entire American scene. It will not confine itself to the fine arts; in addition, there will be a constant consideration of American politics, American industrial and social relations, and American science. The point of view will be that of the civilized minority.
>
> It will strive at all times to avoid succumbing to the current platitudes, and one of its fundamental purposes will be to develop writers in all fields.
>
> The names of the editors offer assurance that, whatever its deficiencies otherwise, it will never be obvious or dull.

A subscription drive was begun. The first subscriber was Nichols Murray Butler, president of Columbia University and often a target of Mencken's jibes.

Though their time was divided, Nathan and Mencken provided lively copy for *The Smart Set* as their terms of office drew to a close. They were more mischievous than ever and their irreverent remarks about President Harding's funeral train crossing the continent from San Francisco (where he had died under rumored mysterious circumstances) to Washington incensed Warner. For the first and the last time he interfered, forbidding the printing of their mocking remarks.

Another of their farewell pranks, conceived by Mencken and elaborately embroidered by Nathan, received worldwide if fleeting attention and was believed to be authentic and terrifying news by several London newspapers.

In June 1923, *The Smart Set* duo announced that, urged on by friends and customers, they were announcing their candidacy for the offices of President and Vice-President of the United States. Neither had any active preference for either office, they admitted, and after the 1924 election, or before, if legally necessary, the matter might be determined satisfactorily by shooting dice. The planks of the platform which they were assured would install them in the White House were outlined in the "Répétition Générale" department for the next few months.

They agreed to suggest and advocate the hanging of all the members in good standing of the New York Stock Exchange.

They would abolish the present custom of opening Congress with a prayer and would substitute a jazz selection by Paul Whiteman's band.

They agreed to invite the Kaiser to America and to make him Governor-General of West Virginia.

To these astonishing resolutions readers responded joyfully and asked for more. When the presidential election rolled around in November 1924, faithful converts to the proposed political program wrote the names of Nathan and Mencken on their ballots.

The December 1923 issue of *The Smart Set*, which carried the announcement of their retirement, was characteristic of the formula they had long practiced in a decade of rising and falling circulation. It contained a complete short novel by F. Hugh Herbert, soon off to the Hollywood gold fields; feuilletons by Roda Roda, John Forbes, the dramatist, Charles G. Shaw, Jim Tully, and John Mosher.

"Major Owen Hatteras," the editors' invention and mouthpiece, made his curtain call as the reputed compiler of the "Americana" pages, which reprinted idiotic items from small-town papers. The selections were prefaced by ironic comment in mock respect for the newspapers and communities from which they were culled. "Americana" was a success at once and became a regular feature of the *The American Mercury*, though Hatteras was no longer credited with its research, being unsuited to a periodical devoted to more serious appraisal of the national situation. The spirit of his articles, however, went marching on. A volume culled from the "Americana" findings appeared annually during the late 1920s.

Mencken contributed an essay titled "15 Years" in which he took a backward glance at his decade and a half as a book reviewer, giving the opinion that there had been a great change and improvement for the imaginative American author during the period.

> In 1908, strange as it may seem to the literary radicals who roar so safely in Greenwich Village today, the old tradition was still powerful, the young man or woman who came to New York with a manuscript which violated in any ways the pruderies and prejudices of the professors had a very hard time getting it printed. It was the day of complacency and conformity.
>
> If Hergesheimer had come to New York in 1908 with 'Cytherea' under his arm, he would have worn out his pantaloons on publishers' shelves without so much as a polite kick. If Eugene O'Neill had come to Broadway with *The Emperor Jones* or *The Hairy Ape* he would have been sent to Edward E. Rose to learn his trade. The devilish and advance thing in those days was for a fat lady star to give a couple of matinées of Ibsen's *A Doll House*.

He felt that the American fiction writer, whether he be novelist, poet, or dramatist, was in 1923 quite as free to depict life as he deserved to be. Publishers were hospitable to novelty and the Broadway stage was the freest in the world — not only to sensations but also to ideas.

> Its members are liberated from two great delusions which from the beginning, have always cursed American letters: the delusion that a work of art is primarily a moral document, that its purpose is to make men better Christians and more docile cannon-fodder, and the delusion that it is an exercise in logic, that its purpose is to prove something. These delusions, lingering beyond their time, are responsible for most of the disasters visible in the national literature today — the disaster of the radicals as well as those of the 100 per cent dunderheads. The writers of the future, I hope and believe, will carefully avoid both of them.

Until the coming of the Depression the better ones followed his advice.

Nathan, in his farewell address, wrote neither of the past nor of the likely future, concentrating on the affairs of the Broadway moment. A local production of Pirandello's *Come Prima Meglio di Prima* — as *Floriani's Wife* — afforded him an opportunity to discuss the Italian's gifts and shortcomings. "His psychological philosophy is unquestionably well-grounded and sound, but it steps continually on the toes of his measure of theatrical talent," he complained. "And the impression that one consequently gets from his plays is of an able psychological novelist carrying on a rather difficult and baffled conversation with a Broadway theatrical manager."

He concluded his *Smart Set* days with a typical paragraph of short notices:

> *The Shame Woman,* by Lula Vollmer, is considerably beneath her *Sun Up. For All of Us,* by William Hodge, is sentimental claptrap. *The Dancers,* by Gerald du Maurier and Viola Tree is an amusing example of British boob melodrama. By playing its second act first, the New York presentation has been made more effective than the London one. *White Desert,* by Maxwell Anderson, is a thoroughly interesting play, finely acted, that has been marred by an undue cutting of the text.

His curtain line — "and now, with monthly critique No. 181, to pastures new" — showed no regrets at abandoning his old home. Warner's censorship of the bit of fooling over President Harding's funeral train was a broad hint that it was high time to change trains.

The year 1924 was a decisive one for Nathan. It opened with the inauguration of *The American Mercury*. Within twelve months he and Mencken had had disputes about the magazine's policies. Their long collaboration, which had influenced a generation of writers and readers, was ended and by the end of the year preparations were in progress for Nathan's resignation as its co-editor.

On February 14, 1924, Nathan turned forty-two. He still could be mistaken for a college boy. Sometimes he was. At a soirée in Zoë Akins' Hispanic apartment he seated himself on the floor at the feet of Ethel Barrymore who — "queen of the American stage" — was appropriately ensconced in a replica of the Spanish throne. As they chatted Muriel Draper, the beturbaned hostess of Manhattan's bohemia, approached and stood listening to Nathan's authoritative discourse.

"Who is this erudite undergraduate, Ethel?" she inquired.

"This erudite undergraduate is George Jean Nathan," declared the critic, springing gallantly to his feet and beaming at Mrs. Draper.

It is true that he had changed little since his campus days. He took pride in being a fashion plate in attire and his bachelorhood fitted him as snugly as his smart matter of dress. Anton Kuh, the Viennese wit, once said that a well-dressed literary man was just a gigolo who didn't know how to dance. Nathan could dance and tangoed with aplomb.

The first issue of *The American Mercury* was on the New York news-stands on Christmas Eve, 1923. Before midnight it had sold out to become a collector's item. A readership of 12,000 had been its most optimistic goal, but its potential public had been underestimated and the initial issue had to be repeatedly reprinted to meet the demand. Thereafter, its circulation mounted monthly, climbing to 77,000 in the late twenties.

An early ad ran:

Are you tired of politicians? Tired of the uplifters and Good People? Tired of the Ku Klux Klan, the Anti-Saloon League, the Y.M.C.A.? Tired of liberals and Radicals? Tired of drives and Crusades? Tired of 100% Americanism?

Then there is consolation for you in *The American Mercury*. It costs 5 dollars a year, less than the price of a bottle of very doubtful Scotch. It is worth a whole case of the very best Scotch. It is the only American magazine that makes a direct appeal to the civilized minority exclusively.

No Greenwich Village 'art'. No translations from the Finnish and Bulgarian. Nothing about politics in Russia, Iraq and Czechoslovakia. No sure cures for all the sorrows of the world. Simply highly civilized entertainment for highly civilized readers.

Its first issue gave a foretaste of what could be expected and of its intended scope. There was free verse by Dreiser and Carl Van Doren's estimation of Stephan Crane, the pioneering realistic novelist of *The Red Badge of Courage*. Samuel C. Chew, an American professor, reported on his interview with George Moore in his Ebury Street residence in London, the Irish stylist passing on his own opinions of Henry James, Conrad, and Hardy. John McClure, whose ballads had graced *The Smart Set* and who was now editing *The Double Dealer* review in New Orleans (which published the early writing of William Faulkner and Thorton Wilder), supplied a short fantasy.

Nathan opened operations at his new post with an evaluation of Eleonora Duse's farewell performances in New York and the press reception she was accorded. He had always had high admiration for her art and the previous summer in London he had again fallen under the spell of her histrionic mastery. On her American tour — after a gala premiere at the Metropolitan Opera — he refuted the native critics who dismissed her superlative technique in a line or two and gushed about her "soul."

"Her tremendous competence was denied analysis, and columns were given to her 'aloof mystery', her 'lonely brooding nature', and her 'immortal spirit,'" he scoffed at the notices that proclaimed her return. "Thus a great artiste, the greatest artiste, of the theatre of her time, was sacrificed to sentimental bosh."

That Duse had deliberately "loafed on the job" because of the contempt she felt for American audiences, as Nathan charged, must be questioned, though he may be correct that she was less impressive on certain occasions than she had been in her prime. She was ill and old and exhausted. Shortly after the Nathan critique appeared she died suddenly, after a coast-to-coast tour, in Pittsburgh, where she performed for the last time a day before her death. Mussolini sent a battleship to carry her remains back to Italy.

Mencken's book reviews appeared in "The Library," which occupied the periodical's last pages, while several departments were established. One was "The Arts and the Sciences." In its space in the inaugural issue authorities on such diverse subjects as skyscraper architecture, gland surgery, and philology gave their opinions on their specialities. In "Clinical Notes" the editors aired their fancies on random topics in waggish paragraphs as they had in the "Répétition Générale" of *The Smart Set*.

Knopf had promised them complete editorial freedom so they unveiled "Americana," the feature Warner had killed at *The Smart Set*, in the first *Mercury*. It was a hit at once. Excerpts from it were republished in anthologies of national humour and its device was imitated in undergraduate reviews, in the radical press, and even in English magazines and newspapers.

Thousands of readers chortled every month over the news of their countrymen's imbecilities and, as planned, "it stirred up the animals," in Mencken's phrase. The implication of the feature was that the United States was a comically barbaric land. George Horace Lorimer of *The Saturday Evening Post* was outraged at this caricature of American boobs and, seeking to present "the other side," printed a page on the good works being accomplished by the Y.M.C.A., the Boy Scouts, Babbitt lodges, and church groups. Many of his selections reappeared verbatim in the *Mercury* "Americana," much to his chagrin.

The "Americana" method of burlesque may be illustrated with a few samples:

California:

How carnivals are made gay in the paradise of New Thought reported by the eminent *Daily News* of Los Angeles.

"Downtown cafés, hotels, clubs and other gathering places will be frequented by special investigators in the roles of waiters, check girls entertainers, doormen, waitresses and guests. Policemen patrolling the streets will be on the lookout for . . . confetti throwers. The anti-cigarette legion will aid in preventing women from smoking. The police will censor signs on automobiles."

Montana:

Contribution to journalistic English by the distinguished *Helena Independent:*

"An orchestra dispelled music . . . "

California:

From a Long Beach dispatch to the esteemed San Francisco *Examiner*:

"Claudius Martinez, who says he is 115 years of age, and looks it, is a prisoner at the city jail. Martinez, willingly confided to interviewers the secret of his longevity, which, in three words, is 'Plenty of liquor'."

Kentucky:

The Hon. Noël Faines of Frankfort, as reported by the Associated Press:

"Professors who teach that the human race has monkeys with tails for ancestors should be hanged."

Tennessee:

Sententious headline from the great Christian organ, the News of Chattanooga:

NEGRO RESISTS ARREST,
FUNERAL TOMORROW

"Americana" sniped ceaselessly at all the ugly stupidities and ignorant prejudices at loose in the land to achieve a startling caricature of the forces that opposed national enlightenment.

While the feature was indisputably the favoured novelty of the new magazine, in the inaugural number it was an article—"Aesthete: 1924" by Ernest Boyd, a Dublin-born author and a picturesque personality in jazz-age Manhattan—that stole the thunder. In his contribution to the first *American Mercury* he disposed with one majestic sweep of the pretenders of the American literary avant-garde. One of his victims, Malcolm Cowley, admitted that Boyd's caricature was inspired by the early careers of Gilbert Soldes, Kenneth Burke, Edmund Wilson, and Matthew Josephson with touches borrowed from John Dos Passos, Cowley, and John Farrar.

According to Boyd, the 1924 aesthete was the product of superficial American university education, someone who had served in Wilson's crusade and then lingered in Paris to pick up the fads of the French literary left wing. On returning home, this pundit began laying down the law on literature and liberal politics in *The New Republic*.

The insulted intelligentsia of Greenwich Village marched on Boyd's residence on East 19th Street. When Boyd came out of his house he was met with a fusillade of ripe tomatoes, eggs, sticks, and stones. He retreated into his quarters and the siege continued for three days. The neo-Dadaists jammed his doorbell, kept his phone ringing, and set up a loudspeaker in the street so that their derogatory broadcast could be heard for blocks. Cowley, on getting through on the phone to Boyd, delivered an abusive, profane harangue. Boyd pretended to take this for one of Cowley's literary works, whereupon Cowley vowed to beat him up. Within a week the demonstration had run its course.

The launching of *The American Mercury* was one of the major events of the season. Simeon Strunsky wrote in his *New York Times* column: "The dead hand of yokelry on the instinct for beauty cannot be so heavy if the hand green and black cover of *The American Mercury* exists." The liberal *Nation* approved and *The New Republic*—whose staff Mencken had characterized as "keep idealists"—predictably disapproved, while T. S. Eliot's lofty London review, *The Criterion*, suggested that English editors imitate the zestful approach of the American publication.

To celebrate its debut Knopf invited the press to birthday cele-brations in his offices, soon to be moved to luxurious quarters on Fifth Avenue. Although the authors and reviewers mingling at the gathering noted that the dual editors, pleased with their triumph, were in happy harmony, behind the scene were serious disagree-ments.

Nathan had assured Eugene O'Neill that he would be proud to print O'Neill's new play, *All God's Chillun Got Wings*, in *The Mer-cury*. The script did not arrive in time for the first issue, but he had scheduled it for the second, that of February 1924. But after read-ing it, Mencken shook his head. He thought it did not fit into the magazine's proposed scheme and voted to reject it. Knopf, who was to intervene if the editors differed, was called upon to arbitrate. The publisher, aware of O'Neill's growing importance and hoping to have the dramatist on his list in the future, sided with Nathan. It was a profitable decision, for the February *Mercury*, with O'Neill as a contributor, surpassed the sales of the inaugural issue and added enormously to the magazine's literary prestige.

The play — in which a black man marries a white woman — stirred nation-wide controversy. Although its detractors had not read the play, its subject caused violent protests, and race prejudice flared at its mention both in the South and the North. The play made the front pages when it was announced that a black actor, Paul Robeson, would be cast opposite a white actress, Mary Blair (then Edmund Wilson's wife) in a production being prepared by the Provincetown Players in Greenwich Village. The Hearst daily, *The New York American*, waged a campaign against the project, warning that race riots would occur and urging Mayor Hylan to forbid its performance in the name of public safety. O'Neill re-ceived letters from the Ku Klux Klan threatening to kill his son and bomb the theatre if he allowed the presentation of the play. Mem-bers of the company and the production staff were similarly ha-rassed, and a false report was spread that Otto Kahn, the philanthropist and patron of the arts, was withdrawing his financial support of the enterprise.

When the audience gathered for the premiere in the MacDougal Alley Playhouse, security police were patrolling the doors under orders to arrest the company if any city ordinance was defied. The house was electric with anticipation of some disaster. A hush fell over the first-nighters when James Light, the director, came before the curtain. He explained that to prevent the performance city officials had refused permits for child actors to take part in the prologue. Therefore, he would read the first scene, and the rest of the play, in which no children appeared, would be acted. The performance took place without incident and, after such advance notoriety, the play was described by the majority of reviewers as anticlimatic. Nathan, Stark Young, and Joseph Wood Krutch analyzed it in greater depth as did Robert Benchley, who took a swipe at the WASP measures to suppress it and reported that white women were as safe after its performance as before. The lurid publicity augmented its ticket sales, assuring it a lengthy and prosperous engagement.

Mencken had missed not only the merits of the O'Neill play, but the grotesque humor of the white Protestant editorializing that sought to halt its showing. Excerpts from the latter would have fitted neatly into the "Americana" column. It is significant that he declared that the best thing to appear in *The Mercury* during its first year was Frank Kent's derogatory sketch of Coolidge's career.

The sweltering summer of 1924 took Mencken away to cover the presidential conventions for *The Baltimore Sun*. The Democratic convention, one of the longest in history, was held in New York at Madison Square Garden, but its day and night sessions kept the editor-turned-reporter from his *Mercury* desk. The show it provided was exactly to his taste.

The convention was deadlocked by the rival candidacies of William G. McAdoo, Wilson's son-in-law, and Al Smith, the Catholic governor of New York. After a bitter battle between the McAdoo and Smith forces, a genial nobody, John W. Davis, former ambassador to Great Britain and a native of West Virginia, emerged as compromise candidate to unsuccessfully oppose Coolidge. Mencken wrote of the spectacle with satirical flair.

Mencken was a hero of all young newspapermen. Privately, he was troubled with doubts about the future of his magazine. It provided him with an unprecedented opinion to mold public opinion, but he dreaded faltering. The initial success of the *Mercury* did not reassure him in the least. He felt its high sales were due to its appeal to a superficial and unstable class of readers on whose support it would be fatal to depend. He wanted, he told Nathan, a magazine in which a coherent body of doctrine could be vigorously maintained. He had in mind an organ of superior journalism, reviewing the American scene (with occasional glances at the country's past) with the skeptical, good-natured irony that was his speciality. Literature would be granted only a secondary place in this scheme. Even the fiction he favored was chiefly that with a documentary-like flavor.

Nathan approved of the outspoken opinions and startling exposés, as these would emphasize the iconoclastic and courageous independence of the magazine. What he opposed was excessive coverage of ephemera; the interminable studies of matters more suited to daily newspapers. The arts, he insisted, must not be slighted, and he sought to balance the sociological contents with literary material. It seemed to him that his genially cynical comrade had been stricken with a messiah complex and was bent on trying to reform American noodles. Did any cultivated person really care whether Coolidge opened his mouth or remained mum, or long to learn what backwoods Baptists preached about hell?

By October 1924, Mencken was ready to challenge his partner's amused indifference to the state of the nation and of the world. In a memorandum to Nathan he listed his grievances, complaining that he was being overburdened with routine chores. When he was absent from the office for a few days he came back to find his desk in chaos, which prevented him from performing his true functions: tracking down ideas, manuscripts, and authors. He could work smoothly if he had a competent slave, he groaned, but not if he had to be that slave himself:

> I believe that either of us, with a simple and vigorous policy, could make *The American Mercury* something much better than it is. But I doubt that the job is one for two men. Divided council makes for too much irresolution and compromise. In particular, I doubt that you and I could carry it off

together. Our interests are too far apart. We see the world in wholly different colors. When we agreed it is mainly on trivialities. This fundamental difference was of relatively small importance on *The Smart Set*, for neither of us took the magazine very seriously. It is different with *The Mercury*. I see no chance of our coming closer together. On the contrary, I believe we are drifting further and further apart. I cite an obvious proof of this: we no longer play together. Another: when we sit down to discuss the magazine we are off it in ten minutes.

This communication was an announcement that an irrevocable parting of the ways had come. It could not have been entirely unexpected. After losing the battle over *All God's Chillun*, Mencken had grown increasingly irritable. Nathan, reluctant to deal with articles on politics and other subjects alien to his interest, left them entirely for Mencken's decision. The system of smooth cooperation under which they had co-edited *The Smart Set* had collapsed. The two were in frequent disagreement.

Nathan tried to negotiate a reconciliation, putting his friend's discontent down to nervous strain. In conversation and letters he beseeched Mencken not to act rashly, to remember the happy years when they had worked in harmony. It would be tragic if their long association were to be shattered in the very moment of their greatest success. But Mencken, unsettled by his spectre of possible failure, would not listen. The magazine, he had decided, must be a one-man show. Mencken gave Knopf an ultimatum: either he or Nathan must resign. He added that if Nathan was chosen as a sole editor he would feel only relief, and that the publisher would probably have a more popular magazine. Knopf had originally wanted Mencken alone as editor and in the crises that now arose Knopf sided with Mencken.

"The Nathan divorce proceedings" — Mencken's flip phrase for his severing relations with his long-time associate — were conducted with the utmost secrecy. There was no leakage to the press. It was agreed that Nathan would retire as co-editor and remain on the masthead as "contributing editor." Christmastime 1924, Mencken, in a friendly letter from his Baltimore home, briefly summarized the situation to Nathan and asked him what he would accept in cash for his financial holdings in the magazine. Nathan, who held a one-sixth interest in the firm— decided to retain his stock.

♦ ♦ ♦

While the editorial rumpus was in progress, Nathan's personal life was undergoing some changes. Adele Astaire, sister and in a long series of musicals dancing partner of Fred, had been a girl-friend of Nathan's. They had done Europe together and his book, *The House of Satan*, is dedicated to her with an odd inscription that many readers mistook for Greek. Once when they were in the Swiss mountains she had written with a stick in the snow the words "I love you." A sudden beam of sunshine had caused the snow to melt and Nathan made a design of the letters run together and had the printer insert it as his book's dedication. Adele had been with him in Paris and London and gave an interview in which she placed him among the great living Americans. Adele had hoped to marry Nathan and with her characteristic, uninhibited manner told him so, but shortly after that she noticed a change in his attitude. When she telephoned him he would beg off meeting her using various ex-cuses. Once he told her that the French ambassador, Paul Claudel, a famous poet-dramatist, was in town and that he must confer with him. "I found out that the French ambassador was Lillian Gish," she declared later.

Nathan had been denouncing the movies as a menace to the arts for many years, but the screen appearance of Miss Gish be-witched him. A year earlier he had published a rapturous essay about her in *Vanity Fair*, attempting to explain the spell her cellu-loid image cast.

> That she is one of the few real actresses that the films have brought forth, either here or abroad, is pretty well agreed upon by the majority of critics. But it seems to me that, though the fact is taken for granted, the reasons for her emi-nence have in but small and misty part been set down in print. The girl is superior to her medium, pathetically so. Her genius lies in making the definite charmingly indefinite. Her technique consists in thinking out a characterization di-

rectly and concretely and then executing it in terms of semi-vague suggestion. The smile of the Gish girl is a bit of happiness trembling on a bed of death; the tears of the Gish girl are the tears that old Johann Strauss wrote into the rosemary of his waltzes. The whole secret of the young woman's remarkably effective acting rests as I have observed, in her carefully devised and skilfully negotiated technique of playing always, as it were, behind a veil of silver chiffon. She always dominates the scene, yet one feels somehow that she is ever just out of sight. There is ever something pleasantly, alluringly, missing, as there always is in the case of women who are truly 'acting artists.'

Nathan proposed that Hergesheimer profile Lillian Gish and the novelist complied with an essay that ran in the August 1924 *Mercury* and is considered one of the memorable contributions to the magazine. The critic also told Hergesheimer that he would very much like to meet Miss Gish, but just then she was away filming in Italy.

In November 1924, back from Italy, Miss Gish was on her way to spend a weekend at Joe Hergeshiemer's home in Pennsylvania when, on the train to Philadelphia, a man introduced himself to her. She remembered him as being handsome and charming. She was suprised to find that he was George Jean Nathan, as she had imagined him to be a much older and ruder fellow, in keeping with his destructive humor. He, too, probably by pre-arrangement, was to be a guest at the Hergesheimers, and they chatted away the two hours of railroad journey. He was immediately and utterly enchanted.

Miss Gish, however, was not entirely at ease with her new admirer. Once back in her New York apartment she was reluctant to accept Nathan's frequent telephone calls. When he caught her on the line she would disguise her voice and, pretending to be her maid, would say that her mistress was out. Eventually, though, she began to accept Nathan's phone calls and his invitations to first-nights and dinners.

She met his literary friends: Dreiser, Sinclair Lewis, O'Neill, and, of course, Mencken. Despite their differences over the management of *The Mercury* their social relationship remained close.

Miss Gish described in her memoirs the first time the three had lunch together:

> I sat between and thanked them for printing an article Hergesheimer had written about me in *The Mercury*. Then, to my surprise, they both started talking at once, neither listening to the other, each keeping up a barrage of conversations and witticisms. I found out at subsequent lunches that it was their customary way of communicating with each other.

After Miss Gish departed for Hollywood to fulfill her film obligations there, Nathan, deeply in love, wrote her daily — sometimes twice daily:

> Ever and ever my love:
>
> Again pen and ink must take the place of my arms, my words and my kisses. But not, I hope and Pray, for long. . . .
>
> I adore and love you more than ever. And I'll prove and reprove it to you with each passing future year. . . . [I]n imagination, put my arms around you.
>
> George

♦ ♦ ♦

In February 1925, following further conferences with Knopf, the public was informed of Nathan's partial withdrawal from *The American Mercury*, with Nathan himself making a statement in praise of Mencken. He continued to contribute his monthly theatre article and — now without Mencken's collaboration — wrote the "Clinical Notes" department.

"The divorce proceedings" had been negotiated with such discretion and diplomacy that it was generally assumed that the famous Mencken-Nathan union had undergone a minor readjustment rather than been dissolved. This legend persisted, but the fact is that, though the two remained on amicable social terms, their professional association was permanently terminated. Never again did they collaborate on any project. Neither was anxious to discuss the break. Mencken always minimized it and Nathan pretended that no schism existed.

♦ ♦ ♦

As Lillian moved from film to film, Nathan continued to state his obsession with her absence:

> Blessed Girl:
>
> With each passing day, I love you more, need you more in my life, wait your home-coming more impatiently. I want your love and companionship. Please give them to me.
>
> George.

♦ ♦ ♦

In the spring of 1926 it was the turn of *The American Mercury* to come under censorship fire. J. Frank Chase, secretary of the Boston Watch and Ward Society, informed the press that the April issue of the magazine contained an obscene story and that he would prosecute anyone who dared sell a copy of it in the Massachusetts capital. Chase's action was motivated by articles in *The Mercury* that exposed and ridiculed his holier-than-thou activities that had made Boston, once the center of American culture, a byword for prudery and bigotry.

The story that he claimed a danger to public morals was "Hat-rack," a sketch, about a wretched, half-starved small-town prostitute who plied her trade in the local cemetery of a sanctimonius community. Its author was Herbert Asbury, a reporter on *The New York Herald Tribune*, who intended to include it in the autobiography he was writing, *Up From Methodism*. He submitted it to Mencken who accepted and printed it.

When Mencken learned that Chase was trying to ban his magazine he conferred with his publisher, Knopf, and they decided to challenge in court Chase's right to decide what New Englanders be allowed to read. It was a brave action on Mencken's part for if convicted of trading in pornography — and everything from the *Arabian Nights* to a cookbook had been banned in Boston — he risked being sentenced to a two-year prison term.

Accompanied by his lawyers Mencken went to Boston to hear the dictatorial Chase. Chase was summoned to buy a copy of the April *Mercury* from its editor. The site selected for this transaction was where in the 17th century women found guilty of witchcraft by the puritan fathers had been burned at the stake. Chase hesitated, dreading a public encounter, but he was informed that if he failed to appear the magazine would immediately go on sale in the square and his reign as censor would be ended.

At the stipulated hour Chase arrived to elbow through a jeering mob. Report of the showdown had spread and Bostonians had gathered in Brimstone Square together with elated Harvard students to enjoy the sport. Trying to ignore his hostile reception, Chase identified Mencken, handed him a silver half-dollar (which the editor put between his teeth and bit to certify its validity), snatched a copy of *The Mercury*, and ordered the offender's arrest.

Press cameras clicked as Mencken was marched by two officers of the law to police headquarters and booked for the sale of obscene literature. Bail was arranged and the trial was set to be heard on the morrow.

Judge James P. Parmenter listened to the charges. When those against "Hatrack" weakened at the hearing, a prosecuting attorney jumped up to call the judge's attention to another "immoral" item in the magazine. This was a flip remark by Nathan in his "Clinical Notes" pages. "A civilized man knows little difference between his bottle of vintage champagne, his Corona-Corona, his seat at the Follies, and the gratification of his sex impulse," the critic had commented.

Judge Parmenter declared that he would read the allegedly obscene articles and give his verdict the next morning. Twenty-four hours later the judge announced that he found nothing in "Hatrack" that would make vice attractive and that Nathan's comment was a mere statement that sex plays a far less important place in life than is often believed.

The verdict on the hearing spelled Chase's doom. The Watch and Word Society rejected him as their representative because of his clumsy strategy and his defeat in court, and he died the same year.

♦ ♦ ♦

A calamity brought Lillian Gish from Hollywood on a lightening visit in the summer of 1926. Her mother, who had gone to

London where her daughter Dorothy was filming *Nell Gwynn* had suddenly suffered a severe stroke. Lillian was in the last week of shooting *The Scarlet Letter*. She learned that by leaving Los Angeles in three days she could catch the liner, *Majestic*, leaving New York for England. The last week of filming was compressed into the three days available and she was rushed to the Los Angeles depot with a police escort. Nathan saw her off on the *Majestic* and continued to write to her:

> Darling, I hope for all time:
> I tell you again what I have told you daily for the last solid year; that you are the only girl who can ever figure in my life, that you are the only one I can ever really and deeply love, and that I wish you would feel the same way about me as I do about you.
> G.

The Gish girls nursed their mother in London and in a few weeks she was sufficiently improved to be transported to New York. There they broke the journey, preparing for the five-day train trip back to California. Nathan was most attentive during their New York stay. He gave Lillian a wirehaired terrier which she named Georgie, a playful puppy who cut his teeth on all the best chairs of the hotel drawingroom. Nathan also presented the actress with a ring on which his profile was engraved. She wore it often and it attracted the attention of interviewers who asked whether it represented her engagement. To this she would evasively reply, "Mr. Nathan is a very brilliant man and my friend."

After Lillian went back to California, Nathan sailed for an inspection of the London theatres. While there, he visited A. B. Walkley, the British drama critic. During a day spent with Walkley at his seaside home, Nathan asked his host—who showed little partiality to Americans in general—how he explained the affinity that made his host and he friends.

"You are the only American I have ever met who when you speak does not make me fear that all the dishes on the table will crash to the floor," replied the advocate of Artistotelian reasoning.

The summer theatre season — with one towering exception — did not meet with Nathan's approval.

"Omitting a consideration of American plays, as plentiful as sour notes in the Paris Opéra company, and disregarding Sacha Guitry's *Mozart*, there is nothing of native or colonial confection that shows the slightest quality," he reported in a round-up in *The American Mercury*, in which he rapidly dismissed Clemence Dane's *Granite*, Benn W. Levy's first play, *This Woman Business*, Kate O'Brien's *Distinguished Villa*, Edgar Wallace's *The Ringer* — "cheap and obvious crook stuff" — Ivor Novello's *Down Hill* — "Trashy melodrama" — and Arnold Ridley's *Ghost Train* — "the conventional mystery dingus with a mysterious train substituted for the burglar."

The magnificent exception was Sean O'Casey's *The Plough and the Stars*, admirably acted by Sara Allgood, Maire O'Neill, and Arthur Sinclair. Nathan's initial introduction to O'Casey's work occurred when *Juno and the Paycock* had its American premiere in a miniature hall on Forty-fourth Street, converted into a theatre a few months earlier. *The Plough*, with its savage portrait of the defeat of 1916 rising of Easter Week, had caused riots in Dublin at its first performance in March 1926. James B. Fagan had decided to risk its presentation with an ensemble of ex-Abbey Theater players at the tiny Fortune Playhouse in the shadow of the mighty Drury Lane Theater. James Agate and other English critics hailed it as a masterpiece, the best play to have been written in English since the war, not excepting Shaw's *Saint Joan*. Nathan, who was later to be O'Casey's most enthusiastic endorser, was more critical, spotting the flaws in its technique, but declaring it "a dream of excellent characterizations, rich in an irony that reaches the heights of cruelty, and remarkably powerful in its lasting impression."

Back in New York in the autumn of 1926, with another long Broadway season stretching before him, he was desolate. The publication of his latest book, *The House of Satan*, and that of Isaac Goldberg's biography about him occupied him as did the theatre openings, some 250 productions being presented during the 1926–27 season. But he ached to see his beloved, chained three thousand miles away with movie commitments and the nursing of her mother.

> Darling of mine:
>
> My spirit is low as Christmas Eve approaches without you. We two should be together when this night comes. Can I tell you with the pen what I would tell you? It no longer seems possible since my lips must be against your own when they speak that is in my heart. Our love has so many things in it that love usually lacks. I have known the surface of love for many years, but never the depths until you came to me. Under heaven and on earth you are my all.
>
> George.

In January 1927 Nathan could wait no longer and went to visit Lillian in California. "No one seems to have heard of your secret trip to California — that is no one save the Associated Press, the Department of Justice and the various radio announcers," Mencken wrote teasingly to his friend.

Nathan, who had been waging a vehement campaign against the movies and movie folk, found himself a welcome guest in the film capital. Apparently a self-protective diplomacy was exercised there. Those who had read his diatribes forgot or forgave his insults, while those who had never read a word of his knew of him as a national personality and wanted to meet him.

Lillian introduced him to her "discoverer," D. W. Griffith. The critic found chatting with the pioneer movie-maker instructive, but Griffith, probably remembering the sneers at his art, was uneasy and distrustful and cautioned Lillian against her sarcastic guest.

Well-known authors were everywhere. F. Scott Fitzgerald had come to write a campus comedy for Constance Talmadge, something about a co-ed who used kiss-proof lipstick. Fitzgerald delivered his script, but it was rejected and he was dismissed. Embittered by the rude treatment — he had hoped to repair his financial state with easy movie money — he and his wife, Zelda, threw a drunken brawl in their Hotel Ambassador quarters to draw attention to their departure. It certainly drew the attention of the fire department, for the Fitzgeralds set about burning everything in sight, including the furniture. John Barrymore, their next-door neighbor, attended the conflagration, but Nathan, though invited, wisely refrained from putting in an appearance.

Many other friends were on the studio payrolls. Robert Benchley, a fellow Broadway reviewer, was earning a handsome salary composing wise-cracking subtitles for the features of Raymond Griffith, a movie comic who sported top hat and tails in imitation of the French funny-man, Max Linder. Joseph Hergesheimer, whose novels had been profitably reproduced on the screen, was on temporary duty as a scenarist at Paramount, and Anita Loos, who began her literary career by concocting plots and situations for the stars, was back on the lots to supervise the filming of her bestseller, *Gentlemen Prefer Blondes*.

Douglas Fairbanks and Mary Pickford were the king and queen of the movies and, with Charlie Chaplin, constituted the trinity of the cinema's superstars. The couple had just returned from a world tour, having been mobbed by their fans in London, Paris, Berlin, Moscow, and Tokyo. Nathan knew Fairbanks from his Broadway days and liked him. He knew Mary Pickford, too, but their relations were slightly strained by some comments he had made on her work. The regal couple were Lillian's close friends and when Mary Pickford heard that Nathan was in town and would be a frequent guest at Pickfair she voiced her criticism of him.

"Why, George wrote that I was back with my bag of tricks in my last picture," she complained to her husband. "Why doesn't he get a bag of tricks?"

The genial Fairbanks, a fellow of even temper, laughed.

"Oh, George is all right," he allowed. "He'll be full of news and have some amusing things to say. I call him George Jean Nothing. He poses and criticizes everything and everyone. We slave and he makes a living laughing at us."

During Nathan's California sojourn Lillian consulted him on her professional future. Her two-year contract with MGM was soon to expire and she was reluctant to sign with that studio again. The material she was being offered, she felt, was of poor quality. Fairbanks and Mary Pickford wanted Lillian to join them at United

Artists, and Max Reinhardt, who was in Los Angeles with the tour of his cathedral spectacle, *The Miracle*, was trying to persuade her to be Marguerite in a *Faust* film he hoped to make in Berlin. Nathan wanted her to quit motion pictures to act on the New York stage.

♦ ♦ ♦

In 1930 Nathan, withdrawing completely from *The American Mercury*, sold back his one-sixth interest in the magazine. In 1932 he launched *The American Spectator* with Ernest Boyd, Theodore Dreiser, James Branch Cabell, Eugene O'Neill and Sherwood Anderson. In policy it was much like *The Smart Set*. Also in 1932 he wrote *The Intimate Notebooks of George Jean Nathan*, which consists of the lives of Sinclair Lewis, Eugene O'Neill, Theodore Dreiser, Ernest Boyd, Jim Tully, Clarence Darrow and H.L. Mencken. In all he wrote forty-five books; the last being *The Theatre in the Fifties*, written in 1953. The Royalton Hotel in Manhatten was his place of work, and his residence for over fifty years.

Because of the Depression *The American Spectator* ceased publication and in 1935 Nathan left it to join *Vanity Fair, Liberty, Esquire* and magazines in Europe.

Nathan kept encouraging Lillian Gish to pursue the theatre in her career. She eventually did decide to enact mature drama as well as motion pictures. She gave her initial Broadway performance as Helena in Chekov's *Uncle Vanya* on April 15, 1930. Jed Harris, a flamboyant producer, led the moving measure of the company and the excited public.

Her next three plays were *Camille* by Alexandre Dumas fils, Sean O'Casey's tragedy about a prostitute, *Within the Gates*, and John Gielgud's *Hamlet*, she playing Ophelia.

AFTERWORD

Sean O'Casey, the Irish dramatist, came to New York in 1934 to stage the play, *Within the Gates*, on Broadway. I was in Moscow at the time studying drama and cinema so was not to see O'Casey this time, but later.

In early 1944 I was stationed in London, a soldier in the U.S. Army awaiting the invasion of the Continent. I had letters of introduction from George Jean Nathan to his friends and colleagues in England. The one I prized most was to Sean O'Casey and I dispatched it at once to Devon where he and his family established residence.

The letter of introduction to O'Casey brought a prompt reply. He would like to meet me but was far away and very busy with the care of his young children.

A month later, I obtained a short leave and wrote to O'Casey that I would come down to Devon to meet him. "If you come," he wrote, "Mrs. O'Casey and I will try to be polite."

To me this was too irresistible — even if it were an impolite reception it would be an experience. So I arranged to stay at the soldiers' hostel and boarded for Totnes on a dark winter day in the blackout.

Eileen, his wife, opened the door and behind, beaming welcome, was O'Casey, tall, lank, 64, in neat gray flannels and turtleneck sweater and wearing a skullcap, his dark eyes blazing behind his spectacles. I told him of my plans to stay at the hostel but he waved them away. He seemed eager at this first meeting and our initial subject was of course Nathan.

"One of the great adventures of my life was when I visited America in 1934, " O'Casey exclaimed. "George Jean Nathan was a guest at my hotel when I staged my play *Within the Gates* on Broadway. It was the only time I had been outside the British Isles. When I came down the gangplank on landing in New York, Nathan was there to meet me. Frankly I was in awe. There were 2,000 years of drama standing before me," he laughed.

O'Casey went on with enthusiasm, "I felt that Whitman and Emerson were close friends when I read them here, but over there I shall never forget my personal meeting with Dreiser, O'Neill and Sherwood Anderson."

Shortly after the death of George Jean Nathan on April 8, 1958, after he was stricken with arteriosclerosis in 1956, Lillian Gish came to see me. She spoke of the letters she had owned since 1924. Most of her friends believed that he wanted to marry her. But in 1933 she wrote him that she had no more love for him. He replied that he was ready to commit suicide.

She persuaded him to survive and he swallowed the bitter experience.

Lillian Gish died on February 27, 1993.

In 1935 Nathan met a young, shy actress, Julie Haydon. She was in such plays as Paul Vincent Carroll's *Shadow and Substance*, William Saroyan's *The Time of Your Life*, and Tennessee Williams' *The Glass Menagerie*. Nathan married Julie Haydon in 1955 and they went on a wedding trip abroad to Curaçao in the West Indies.

Julie Haydon died on December 24, 1995.

In spite of what Walter Lippman once said about Mencken, that his was "the most powerful personal influence," somewhere in the 1930s he seemed to fall apart in many directions and his readers became less influenced, the reviews less favorable. He was often referred to (by himself as well) as "the late H. L. Mencken."

His wife's health was failing as well and she died in 1935. Sara was thirty-seven years old.

In 1940 I was to meet the hobo writer, Jim Tully, in New York as he had written from Hollywood to say he would like to see me, I came upon him in the breakfast room of the Algonquin Hotel and there was someone else with him. It was H.L. Mencken, and he seemed to be his old self again.

In fact, he returned to high summit in his later years, after the war in 1945-48. But on November 24, 1948, he was stricken with a cerebral thrombosis. He died on January 29, 1956.

Thomas Quinn Curtiss

Hepburn, Katharine, 199
Herald Square Theater, 69-70
Herbert, F. Hugh, 222
Herbert, Victor, 25, 68, 138
Hergesheimer, Joseph, 211-212, 218, 222, 234-235, 241
Herne, James A., 61
Hervieu, 11, 186
Heyse, Paul, 91
Heyward, William "Big Bill", 122
Hichens, Robert, 152
Hildebrandt's (music shop), 96
Hippodrome, The, 19, 183
Hirshberg, Dr. Leonard K., 47-48
Hitchcock, Alfred, 126
Hitler, 214
Hobart, George, 39
Hobohemia, 167
Hodge, William, 223
Hoffenstein, Samuel, 141
Hofmannsthal, Hugo von, 90
Hole in the Ground, A, 9
Holiday, 192
Hollaender, Victor, 91
Holland House, 49, 52
Holland, 118, 213
Höllenfahrt, 200
Holmes, Sherlock, 71
Hooligan at the Gates(article), The , 184
Hoover, President Herbert, 183
Hopkins, Arthur, 112, 150-151, 160, 197, 201
Hopper, De Wolf, 9
Hopwood, Avery, 72-73, 114
Horace, 115
Horner, Jack, 22
Horthy, Admiral, 183
Hotel Eden, 213
Hotel Knickerbocker, 18, 35, 77, 183
Hotel Royalton, 39, 68, 242
Hotel Universe, 76
Houghton, Stanley, 203
House Beautiful, The , 43
House of Satan,The , 233, 239
Houseman, Lawrence, 152
How He Lied To Her Husband, 61, 82

"How I Discovered Bernard Shaw"(essay), 112
How's Your Second Act?, 150
Howard, George Bronson, 98
Howard, Leslie, 188
Howard, Sidney, 155, 192-193
Howe, Ed, 115
Howells, William Dean, 46, 136
Hoyt, Charles T., 8-9, 73-74
Huck Finn, 42
Hudson Theater, 38
Hudson, W. H., 144
Huebsch, Ben, 111, 138, 143, 166
Hughes, Charles Evans, 36
Hughes, Hatcher, 200
Hughes, Rupert, 46
Huneker, James Gibbons, 12, 40, 62, 131, 166
Hungary, 183
Hunter, Glenn, 153
Hurst, Fannie, 110
Huxley, Aldous, 209, 213, 219
Huxley, Thomas Henry, 51-52, 149,
Huysmans, 41, 53
Ice Palace, The , 163
Iceman Cometh, The , 28
Iffland, 179
Ile, 157
Illustrated American, The , 9
Imperial Purple, 148
Improvement Society, The , 90
In Defense of Women, 143
In Gay New York, 21
In the Baggage Coach Ahead, 28
Independent Theater, The, 190
India, 4
Indiana, 3, 5
Ingram, Rex, 71
Intermezzo, 198
Interpretation of Dreams, 190
Intimate Notebooks of George Jean Nathan, The , 242
Intolerance, 186, 188
Invasion of America, 174
Irving, Henry, 12, 60, 190
Isle of Champagne, The , 8

THE WORLD OF
GEORGE JEAN NATHAN
SELECTED ESSAYS AND REVIEWS
edited by Charles Angoff

"Nathan's is THE MOST IMPORTANT DRAMA CRITICISM to be found today, the most important voice to be heard about a highly important medium of American expression in a vital world period."
—*New York Times*

"THE MOST REWARDING COMMENTATOR DEALING WITH THE STAGE."
—**Wolcott Gibbs**, *The New Yorker*

"The best of the regular theatre critics . . . he consistently puts all his critical colleagues to shame with his superior taste and brains."
—**Eric Bentley**

Discovered and championed by Eugene O'Neill, George Jean Nathan set the standards for the best in American criticism from 1918-1955, writing for the New York Herald, Harpers, Vanity Fair, Esquire, the Saturday Review, Newsweek, The Smart Set, and forty books published by Knopf.

ISBN:1-55783-313-3

THE COLLECTED WORKS OF HAROLD CLURMAN

Six Decades of Commentary on Theatre, Dance, Music, Film, Arts, Letters and Politics

edited by Marjorie Loggia and Glenn Young

"...RUSH OUT AND BUY *THE COLLECTED WORKS OF HAROLD CLURMAN*...Editors Marjorie Loggia and Glenn Young have assembled a monumental helping of his work... THIS IS A BOOK TO LIVE WITH; picking it up at random is like going to the theater with Clurman and then sitting down with him in a good bistro for some exhilarating talk. This is a very big book, but Clurman was a very big figure."

JACK KROLL, *Newsweek*

"THE BOOK SWEEPS ACROSS THE 20TH CENTURY, offering a panoply of theater in Clurman's time... IT RESONATES WITH PASSION."

MEL GUSSOW, *The New York Times*

CLOTH •ISBN 1-55783-132-7 PAPER • ISBN 1-55783-264-1